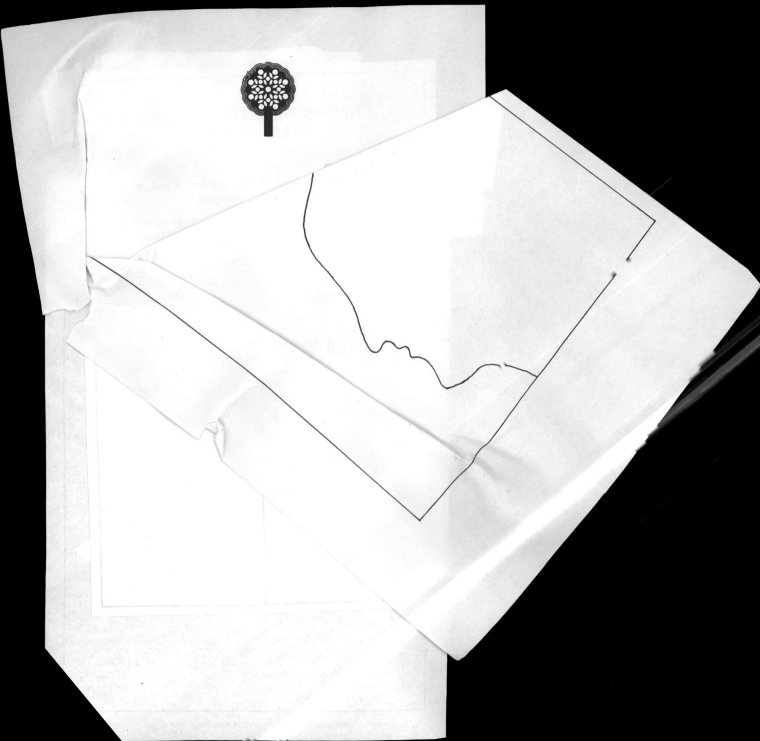

Gods and Men

A Survey of World Religions

Brian W. Sherratt, M.A., Ac.Dip.Ed.
Deputy Head
Sandown Court School
Tunbridge Wells

David J. Hawkin, B.D., M.A., Ph.D.
Memorial University of Newfoundland
Corner Brook
Newfoundland

Blackie

Glasgow and London

BLACKIE & SON LIMITED
Bishopbriggs
Glasgow G64 2NZ
Furnival House
14-18 High Holborn
London WCIV 6BX

Printed in Great Britain by
Thomson Litho Ltd, East Kilbride, Scotland

Foreword

This book is intended to be a general introduction to the study of world religions. While our aim was to present impartially a somewhat complex diversification of ideas and practices in as straightforward a manner as possible, in an attempt to foster an appreciation of the intrinsic importance of the study of religion, we were at pains to avoid oversimplification. It is hoped that this survey will be of value not only in schools and colleges of education but to the general reader also.

We live today in a culturally pluralistic society. This fact in itself is of profound significance for all those engaged in education. The educated person can no longer be ignorant of the various forces—ideological, philosophical, social, ethnic—at work in the community and yet it is sad to reflect that education often tends towards parochialism and that the majority of people who consider themselves to be educated have only the vaguest notions of what is involved in cultures other than their own. It is from this kind of situation that prejudicial ideas so often arise. Education for cultural pluralism must, therefore, at least in part include the study of world faiths.

Further, no one can be unaware of the intensity in east-west relationships. Yet the Westerner is unlikely to know very much, if anything at all, about the way in which people think on the other side of the world. The study of world religions will not solve the problem of estrangement but, given the right conditions, it may help to create the kind of situation from which understanding and mutual respect might come about.

We invited a number of representatives of the religions we have described each to contribute a 'profession' of their faith and these professions are placed at the end of the relevant chapter. The professions complement what we have written in that, since they are personal in nature, they indicate that religious faith is not merely a matter of intellectual acceptance of abstract philosophical notions. We are indebted to the contributors of the professions and their names appear below the statements, except in the case of a few who wished to remain anonymous. The Confucian 'profession' was kindly supplied by Mr Osman Durrani. Mr Michael Pye of the Department of Religious Studies, University of Lancaster, was kind enough to suggest the passage from Ono's book, *Shinto, the Kami Way*, as illustrative of the Shintoist position, and this passage is reprinted by kind permission of Charles E. Tuttle Co., Inc., Tokyo. The inclusion of a Taoist profession would have been pointless as it is doubtful whether one could find two Taoists who shared similar convictions. We also wish to acknowledge the help of Mr S. N. Bharadwaj, President of the Hindu Centre, London.

Foreign words have not been given diacritical marks for, since this is an introductory survey, it was considered of little value to make unfamiliar words even more unusual in appearance. By and large these words have been spelled as they are pronounced. Some words, mostly being foreign in origin and therefore capable of being anglicised in different ways, have a variety of spellings, e.g. Gautama/Gotama, Parsi/Parsee, etc. Usually the simplest form has been used.

B. W. S.
D. J. H.

Contents

Acknowledgments

The authors and publishers are grateful for the use of photographs as supplied by the following:

The Trustees of the British Museum: pages 6, 12
Archives Photographiques, Paris: page 9
Paul Popper Ltd.: pages 17, 25, 30, 49, 66, 68, 79, 82, 84-5, 90, 92, 107, 121, 133, 143, 166, 178, 180, 188, 195, 204, 207, 212, 226, 230, 231, 240.
Israel Government Tourist Office: pages 28, 31
Victoria and Albert Museum (Crown Copyright): pages 42, 128, 129, 135, 227
Church of Scotland: page 51
Associated Press Ltd.: pages 53, 217, 236
Camera Press Ltd.: pages 61, 125, 151, 229
Edinburgh University Library: page 77
Pix Inc., New York: page 140
Thailand Information Service: page 169

CHRONOLOGICAL CHART
SHOWING BEGINNINGS OF THE
WORLD'S RELIGIONS

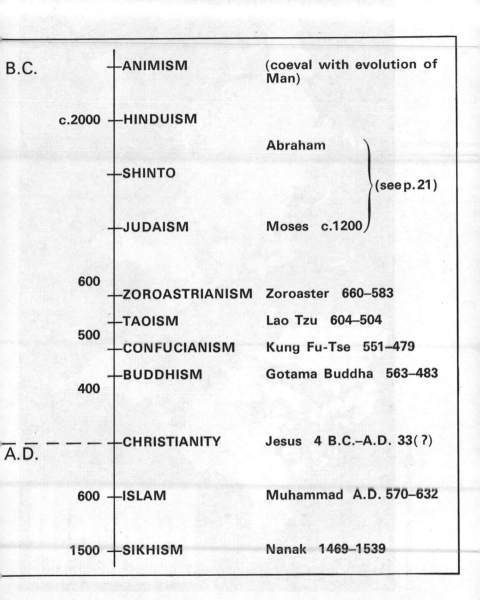

B.C.		ANIMISM	(coeval with evolution of Man)
	c.2000	HINDUISM	
		SHINTO	Abraham
			(see p. 21)
		JUDAISM	Moses c.1200
	600	ZOROASTRIANISM	Zoroaster 660–583
	500	TAOISM	Lao Tzu 604–504
		CONFUCIANISM	Kung Fu-Tse 551–479
	400	BUDDHISM	Gotama Buddha 563–483
A.D.		CHRISTIANITY	Jesus 4 B.C.–A.D. 33(?)
	600	ISLAM	Muhammad A.D. 570–632
	1500	SIKHISM	Nanak 1469–1539

Distribution of world religions

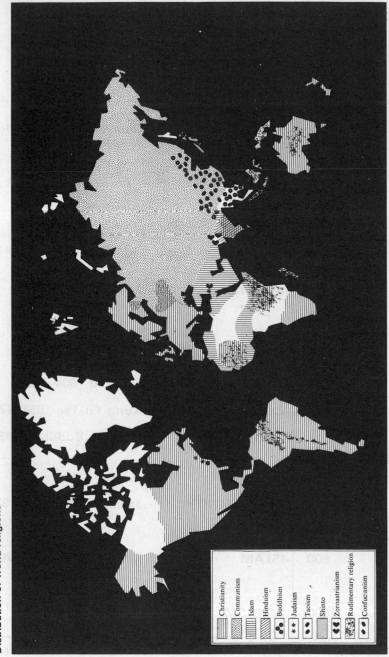

Christianity
Communism
Islam
Hinduism
Buddhism
Judaism
Taoism
Shinto
Zoroastrianism
Rudimentary religion
Confucianism

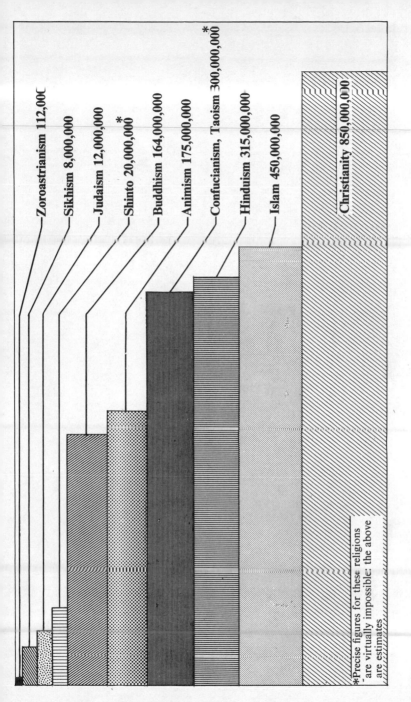

Zoroastrianism 112,000

Sikhism 8,000,000

Judaism 12,000,000

Shinto 20,000,000 *

Buddhism 164,000,000

Animism 175,000,000

Confucianism, Taoism 300,000,000 *

Hinduism 315,000,000

Islam 450,000,000

Christianity 850,000,000

*Precise figures for these religions are virtually impossible; the above are estimates

Numerical strength of the principal religions of the world

Rudimentary Religion

In an age when man is in the process of conquering the moon, when it is possible to have a new heart, when education is readily available, it is rather remarkable that on some parts of the globe man is to be found more or less as he was thousands of years ago in prehistoric times. It is natural that these 'primitive' peoples should fascinate us but apart from this they are of considerable interest in that in them we feel that we can see behind the sophistications of civilized society and, to some extent, catch a glimpse of what life was like when man first evolved from lower forms. In them we might well see how our ancestors would have been. They are important in the study of religion because in 'primitive' man we are most likely to see possible clues as to how religion began, what 'primitive' religion was like and how the more advanced religions have developed from it.

However, while all this is to some extent true, great caution must be exercised in the formulation of statements concerning the religion and culture of 'primitive' man. The word 'primitive' itself can be misleading: it can be *especially* misleading when it qualifies the word 'religion'. The attitude in the past has been to associate 'primitive' religion with underdeveloped areas and simple people, whereas an advanced religion, such as Christianity, is associated with advanced, capitalist countries. Such an assumption, however, simply does not fit the facts. No one would seriously maintain that Hinduism and Buddhism are 'primitive' or unsophisticated religions and yet poverty and a low standard of living is to be found in some areas where these religions predominate. On the other hand, the standard of living among some ostensibly Christian cultures (e.g. certain areas in South America and even some Mediterranean countries) can hardly be rated as particularly high. It does not follow that because men live out of touch with Western civilization or the standards which it inculcates, their religious beliefs will be naïve. The fact that they have not committed them to writing is no reason for assuming that they are less sensitive or less articulated than the religious notions of Western man. Lack of social and domestic amenities does not imply lack of thought. In fact 'primitive' man, unlike Western man, has time to sit down and think and is not influenced by the mass media which constantly presents Western man with pre-formulated concepts and vicarious experiences. Perhaps it is not an exaggeration to say that religious consciousness is far more highly developed among the so-called 'primitive' peoples than it is, generally speaking, among 'civilized' peoples. Professor E. E. Evans-Pritchard, in his book *Nuer Religion* (p. 322) has shown that the inner convictions of the Nuer people of the eastern Sudan are by no means simple:

> *The Nuer are undoubtedly a primitive people by the usual standards of reckoning, but their religious thought is remarkably sensitive, refined and intelligent. It is also highly complex.*

Religion in Africa has not, as it were, turned down an evolutionary cul-de-sac and remained static. On the contrary, African religion is a vital, living force. Evolution does take place in religion but it is wrong to assume that all evolved religion ends up like Christianity or Islam. Judaism, of course, is unique in having a written sacred history but Africans too have their own history: it is retained in the traditions of the tribe.

A West African fetish into which nails are struck each time the spirits are implored

It is also wrong to assume that because an African has been influenced by Western culture he will, therefore, jettison the beliefs of his people:

> *not only do the majority of Africans still hold to the traditional religion of their fathers, but also behind the veneer of the new beliefs of most educated people lie older ideas that will not disappear for a long time yet. This is only to be expected, since Europe still retains ancient pagan notions, albeit somewhat baptized, despite the thousand years and more of Christianity. To Africans, the spiritual world is so real and near, its forces intertwining and inspiring the visible world that, whether pagan or Christian, man has to reckon with 'things invisible to mortal sight'.*[1]

[1] E. G. Parrinder, *African Traditional Religion* (S.P.C.K. 1962), p. 10.

'Primitive' man lives very close to nature and terrible disasters; the withholding of crops, disease and the death of relatives, are thought of in terms of the intrusion of some kind of supernatural force. Man is afraid of his environment on which he is totally dependent but with which he must come to terms. He feels that things do not happen by chance but through the action of some controlling force behind all individual events. Who has ever felt his or her flesh creep? Who has ever experienced the strange eeriness which people say comes over them when listening to a ghost story or when contemplating the possibility of 'spirit-communication'? It is a sense of fear plus fascination. The number of books about ghosts and hauntings and the attractiveness of 'spiritualism' are evidence of the fact that many of us still at times feel what we would probably call in others a primitive kind of awe or irrational superstition.

In a famous book[1] Dr Rudolf Otto argued that this combined sensation of attraction and awe—the *numinous* (Latin, *numen*, the divine)—is a basic constituent of all religious experience, not just primitive religious experience:

> *There is no religion in which it does not live as the real innermost core, and without it no religion would be worthy of the name. It is pre-eminently a living force in the Semitic religions (Judaism, Christianity, Islam), and of these again in none has it such vigour as in that of the Bible.*

In its origins the numinous is:

> *the feeling of 'something uncanny', 'eerie', or 'weird'. It is this feeling which, emerging in the mind of primeval man, forms the starting-point for the entire religious development in history.* (ibid. p. 15.)

Much could be said of the numinous in advanced religion but this is a study in itself and, as such, is not appropriate to an introductory book on world religions. However, the following brief examples from the Christian religion will give the reader some idea as to the extent of the numinous characteristic in an advanced religion. To begin with it would appear evident that Jesus must have had about him a numinous quality; otherwise the Church would not exist. Jesus did not proclaim himself but rather the 'Kingdom', the meaning of which he embodied in himself (see Chapter Two on Christianity). Nevertheless, his first disciples were prepared to leave their nets. They experienced him as 'the numen itself' (*ibid.* p. 162). In the gospels there are further indications of this experience: e.g. Peter's

[1] Rudolf Otto, *The Idea of the Holy*, trans. by J. W. Harvey (Oxford, 1926), p. 6.

reaction to the miraculous haul of fishes—'Go, Lord, leave me, sinner that I am' (Luke 5:8); the centurion at Capernaum—'Sir, who am I to have you under my roof? You need only say the word and the boy will be cured' (Matthew 8:8); or the sense of foreboding experienced by the disciples on the fateful journey to Jerusalem—'They were on the road, going up to Jerusalem, Jesus leading the way: and the disciples were filled with awe; while those who followed behind were afraid' (Mark 10:32).

> *This passage renders with supreme simplicity and force the immediate impression of the numinous that issued from the man Jesus, and no artistry of characterization could do it so powerfully as these few masterly and pregnant words.* (ibid. p. 163.)

This numinous element in Christian experience today is expressed by Dr Albert Schweitzer in the concluding paragraph to his important book *The Quest of the Historical Jesus* (*Von Reimarus Zu Wrede*, 1906)[1]:

> *He comes to us as One unknown, without a name, as of old, by the lake-side, He came to those men who knew Him not. He speaks to us the same word: 'Follow thou me!' and sets us to the tasks which He has to fulfil for our time. He commands. And to those who obey Him, whether they be wise or simple, He will reveal Himself in the toils, the conflicts, the sufferings which they shall pass through in His fellowship, and, as an ineffable mystery, they shall learn in their own experience who He is.*

The numinous element in Christianity is also powerfully demonstrated in worship and the sacraments, e.g. the Catholic who receives at Mass the body and blood of Christ himself.

This union of fear and fascination appears to be a basic constituent of religion, especially primitive religion, and is to be found in advanced religions where, far from being a preoccupation with the uncanny, it tends to produce in man a humility and reverence in the presence of something which he feels to be all-demanding and altogether holy, something which, although awe-inspiring, has an irresistible power of attraction. The focal point of religious experience may or may not be gods or God. Many primitive tribes have either no notion or a very naïve notion of deity. Theravada Buddhism, while being explicitly agnostic, is possibly implicitly atheistic; the spirits of Ceylon are no part of Buddhism proper but represent

[1] Albert Schweitzer, *The Quest of the Historical Jesus*, trans. by W. Montgomery (A. & C. Black, 1956), p. 401.

an animism on which Buddhism was superimposed. But behind all religious belief there appears to be a sense of mystery in the presence of something which cannot be fully comprehended; there is a sense of repulsion and attraction. Man dare not, yet at the same time must, draw near; he is, as it were, like a speck of iron dust equidistant between the north poles of two magnets of equal strength. In this repulsion and attraction he is spellbound.

RELIGION IN PRIMITIVE SOCIETY

There are numerous problems associated with the study of tribal life and not least among them is that of language. How can you be certain that you, as a member of Western civilization, understand the precise meaning of the words, and in particular religious words, used by 'primitive' man? Very detailed knowledge is required before one can begin to analyse and fully understand their way of life. A close look will reveal that 'primitive' religion, or

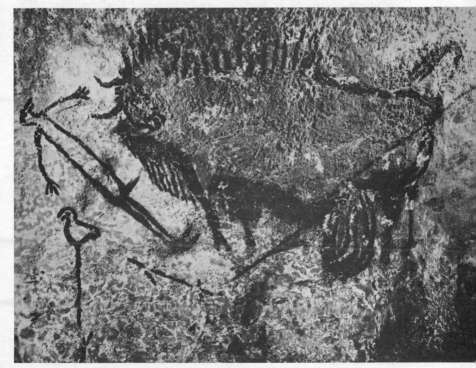

A stone-age rock painting from the Lascaux caves in France, showing a wounded bison, a wounded or dead man and a bird perched on a stick. Theories vary about its meaning, but it could depict an entranced priest before a bison about to be sacrificed, the bird being the priest's spirit keeping watch over the ritual event

animism as it is usually called, is so bound up with the general life of the people that it is as much a culture as a faith. Generally speaking, animism is the belief that all living things, including those things which 'primitive' man thinks of as being alive or exerting some kind of force, are animated by spirits which differ from living human beings in degree of power only. Animism is usually thought of as the root of religion from which all other religious faiths have, over many years, evolved. Although it is true to say that there is archaeological evidence to show that religion has existed from the beginning of human history it must be pointed out that there are few animistic peoples who have not been influenced to some extent by the missionary religions, not to mention the fact that all religious ideas are subject to evolution, and so some caution is required before one can say that any particular group practises religion precisely as it was practised in prehistory.

It has been estimated that there are about 175 million people living at the animistic level in the world today. Unlike the great religions, animism is without scriptures and oral tradition. The animist thinks of the universe as being peopled with numerous spirits which can be classified as follows:

1   Spirits of natural objects thought of as living, e.g. sea, fire, trees, rivers.
2   The spirits of the dead who tend to be dangerous unless treated with great respect. They maintain a close relationship with the tribe and are jealous to preserve ancient customs. These ancestors are frequently presented with gifts from the living.
3   Free spirits or those which are not the spirits of the dead or of natural objects but which are to be located in specific areas, such as in caves and among rocks. Some of these spirits tend to be mobile and may take up residence in any object, including a human being, as the mood takes them.

The attitude of primitive peoples to these unseen powers is one of fear and, in the case of ancestors, of trust also—a kind of ambivalence. Whereas there is the desire to escape from the power there is also the urge to draw near to it. If, in childhood, one has ever been scared by stories of the supernatural and felt sure that behind every door lurked some kind of apparition then one will have some inkling as to the mental state of the animist.

Alongside religion in primitive culture there runs a rudimentary kind of science or magic. Magic is a method of obtaining results by known means. For example, the aborigines of Central Australia believe that the pearl shell contains a concentrated form of water.

They suck at the shell and then spit into the air believing that the concentrated water will fall as rain. This kind of activity obviously belongs to the realm of magic rather than to that of religion but, of course, the two overlap to such an extent that at times no valid distinction can be made. Religion is more concerned with unseen forces but, like magic, it deals with an area which cannot be manipulated by ordinary methods. Magic and religion have become intermeshed.

MANA

In some 'primitive' societies there is belief in an impersonal kind of power which can be utilized to the advantage of the individual. For example, the Melanesians believe in a strong power which they call *mana*; it cannot be seen or touched yet it is all about. It is not the supreme being for the Melanesians have no notion of God or gods. It is nothing physical but it can be used to produce good or ill and consequently it is useful to have it under control. It manifests itself in human characteristics; for example, it gives a person great strength, special skills and various other qualities. Mana is not to be located in any particular place but the spirits have it and are able to dispense it so it is advisable to be well in with them. Melanesian religion consists of making mana work for yourself and this is the object of all petitions and sacrifices to the spirits. A similar kind of belief is held by the Bantu in Africa and by several Red Indian tribes.

ANCESTORS AND SOUL SURVIVAL

The idea that the human soul survives death is the common denominator of all animistic religion. In Western society, when a close friend or relative dies the normal emotions are those of sadness and affection but in primitive societies the overriding emotion is that of fear. Animists are most punctilious in their funeral rites so as to ensure that the spirit of the departed will not haunt them or bring calamity upon them. When the Bantu, for example, bury a corpse they kneel around the grave and place a variety of articles on the body so that the deceased will be well provided for in the spirit world. They wish him a happy journey and beg him not to forget that they have just given him milk, tobacco, food and other useful things. In other words, 'We have taken care of you: make sure that you treat us in the same way.'

The offering of food to the spirit of the corpse is a universal feature of animism. Often it is put on a fire to reduce it to a form more acceptable to a spirit. In some tribes animals are killed, especially when a dignitary dies, and in the past there were human sacrifices so that the dignitary did not go to the spirit world without servants. Many, however, can only afford simple offerings.

Unless the correct rituals are observed the spirit of the corpse might be extremely dangerous. The spirit world is said to be a happier place than this one but your position in it is dependent upon the circumstances of your death as well as of your earthly status. After death the soul is said to survive either for an indefinite period or for ever. Many Africans believe in transmigration and human souls are said to inhabit animals. The spirit tends to remain close to the grave and has difficulty in detaching itself from the dead body. Ghosts are said to appear to relations in dreams and they are frequently spoken to and listened to by means of a medium. Dreams are interpreted by clairvoyants. The appearance of spirit-relations indicates that they are still concerned with the tribe and their family, and men will go to great lengths to find out the requirements of the departed. They are said to become extremely annoyed when neglected by the living. A ghost will enter a living person and sap him of strength: it will produce insomnia and various allergies.

Animists are nowhere near as much afraid of their gods, if they have any, as they are of their ancestors: the departed are blamed for any number of irritating occurrences. Yet although the dead are obviously thought of as possessing more power than the living it is not quite true to say that the animist prays to them; in fact he often rebukes them: 'Stop being such a nuisance: we've given you what you want so now give us what we want.' Thus devotion offered to gods amongst animistic peoples appears to be of a different order to that offered to ancestors.

Life in the spirit world is nearly always thought of in terms of the present physical life. The Melanesians believe that the spirits of the dead make their way up to the

A shield-like figure in wood from New Guinea, representing an ancestor

top of an extinct volcano which is located in one of the Melanesian islands. The crater has become a lake and nearby is a volcanic vent which is the way down to the home of the dead. In this subterranean world beautiful countryside and comfortable lodgings are to be found where the spirits spend their days in peace.

So far we have only attempted to give a very general impression of what animism entails and have not mentioned animisms which have a place for a god in their religious systems. It will now be beneficial to study a particular group in some detail.

THE KIKUYU OF KENYA

The Kikuyu (a Bantu-speaking tribe) believe in *Ngai* (also named Marunga) who is their supreme, all-pervading, invisible and all-powerful deity having his residence in four mountains simultaneously. He is also to be found in all places: he is not limited in space.

During acts of family worship connected with important events such as birth, harvest, marriage and sickness, petitions are made to the ancestral spirits but only after brief prayers to Ngai who is worshipped with the rising of the sun. He is worshipped in groves where fig trees are grown and sacrifices are offered. At the centre of the grove is the main fig tree and the other trees are subsidiary only. The trees must not be damaged in any way; animals, women and children may not approach the grove and anyone who spoils it is punished, but fugitives from justice may hide there.

When sacrifice is to take place the elders summon the people and a ram without defect is killed, part of the blood being offered to Ngai at the foot of the fig tree while the rest is eaten by the people. The bones are burnt as an offering when the meal is over. Ngai is then thanked for his goodness in various aspects of life.

Like all animists, the Kikuyu are very much concerned with the spirits of their ancestors. They believe a person has two kinds of spirit. At death one spirit joins the ancestors in the realm of the dead whereas the other is a sort of family spirit which while being one is also divisible and is, as it were, shared out among all members of the family of the deceased and dwells in them. At the same time the family spirit is in the air round about the family and will go into each newly-born member at a special ceremony called 'second birth'.

Veneration of ancestral spirits is mostly a family affair and whenever Ngai is worshipped the Kikuyu are constantly aware of the fact that the ancestors are near by, so prayers to Ngai are always accompanied by petitions to the spirits of the families concerned. The ancestors are thought of as joining their living relations in the worship of Ngai.

The ancestral spirits are said to live in the hearth stones of the Kikuyu huts as well as in the courtyards of the homesteads. Like Ngai they have special homes as well as being everywhere. Whenever a Kikuyu takes anything to eat he will always drop small pieces of the food on the ground (near the hearth if he is at home) for his ancestors and whenever he drinks beer, blood or milk he will always pour some out for them. At marriage ceremonies the spirit-relatives of the two families are said to be present to give their consent. Various ailments and natural disasters are thought of as the direct action of discontented ancestors and this is specially believed to be the case when someone has broken one of the conventions of the tribe.

Regarding the Kikuyu belief in God, Mr Jomo Kenyatta wrote as follows[1]:

> First we have Gothaithaya Ngai, which means 'to beseech Ngai,' or 'to worship Ngai.' Ngai is a name of the High God. The difference between deity worship and ancestor worship is demonstrated by the fact that Gothaithaya is never used in connection with ancestral spirits. . . .
>
> The Conception of a Deity. The Kikuyu believes in one God, Ngai, the Creator and giver of all things. He has no father, mother, or companion of any kind. He loves or hates people according to their behaviour. The Creator lives in the sky, but has temporary homes on earth, situated on mountains, where he may rest during his visits. The visits are made with a view to his carrying out a kind of 'general inspection,' Koroora thi, and to bring blessings and punishments to the people . . .
>
> Ngai cannot be seen by mortal eyes. He is a distant being and takes but little interest in individuals in their daily walks of life. Yet at the crises of their lives he is called upon. At the birth, initiation, marriage and death of every Kikuyu, communication is established on his behalf with Ngai. The ceremonies for these four events leave no doubt as to the importance of the spiritual assistance which is essential to them. . . .
>
> In the ordinary way of everyday life, there are no prayers or religious ceremonies, such as 'morning and evening prayers'. So long as people and things go well and prosper, it is taken for

[1] Jomo Kenyatta, 'Kikuyu Religion, Ancestor-Worship, and Sacrificial Practices,' Africa, X (1937), pp. 308-11.

granted that God is pleased with the general behaviour of the people and the welfare of the country. In this happy state there is no need for prayers. Indeed they are inadvisable, for Ngai must not needlessly be bothered. It is only when humans are in real need that they must approach him without fear of disturbing him and incurring his wrath. But when people meet to discuss public affairs or decide a case, or at public dances, they offer prayers for protection and guidance. When a man is stricken by lightning it is said: 'He has been smashed to smithereens for seeing Ngai in the act of cracking his joints in readiness to go to smash and chase away his enemies.'

It is said that lightning is a visible representation of some of God's weapons which he uses against his enemies. Ngai has no messengers whom he may send on ahead to warn people of his coming and to prepare and clear the way. His approach is foretold only by the sounds of his own preparations. Thunder is the cracking of his joints, as a warrior limbering up for action.

The Kikuyu also share the usual animistic belief in spirits which are not ancestral and have nothing to do with the idea of Ngai but are thought of in relation to such things as trees, rocks, waterfalls and epidemic diseases. Whereas these spirits are not given as much attention as the ancestors or Ngai there are, nevertheless, numerous ceremonies devised to pacify them. For example, when the Kikuyu fell trees in a wooded area they always leave some large trees unfelled so that the tree-spirits from the felled trees are not left homeless. A tree (or trees) is selected for the new spirit-home and felling begins some distance away and continues in the direction of the new home so that the spirits can move from tree to tree. As the tree falls the spirit is asked to move on towards the selected tree. When all the trees have been felled it is believed that all the tree-spirits in the area are packed into the tree which has been left standing. A sacrifice is offered at the foot of this tree with requests and apologies.

If removal of the special tree proves imperative then complicated precautions must be taken. Elders will gather round the tree in the evening and offer sacrifice. Then a branch or pole is placed against it and when they have apologized for what they are about to do, the elders ask the tree spirits to enter the pole so that they may be transported to another tree. A large tree is selected and the pole is carried with due solemnity and placed against it so that the spirits may take up residence.

In family quarrels spirits or supernatural powers are invoked to settle the dispute. If both parties believe that they are in the right the ceremony of the *Githathi Oath* is resorted to. For this ceremony a stone with seven holes is required, the holes representing the seven apertures of the human body and the number seven which is said to have an evil force. Each party inserts one of seven sticks, seven times, in each hole and declares that if he is in the wrong the oath-stone can justly exert a force and kill one of his relatives or himself. Those who take part in the ceremony, together with their relatives, must abstain from sexual intercourse for the duration of seven planting seasons (about $3\frac{1}{2}$ years) while all their male animals are castrated. The Kikuyu are convinced that within the $3\frac{1}{2}$ years the stone will have exerted its special killing power, and the first death in either family indicates on which side the guilt lies. The stone always works, of course, because the families are large and death by natural causes is not infrequent.

As is the case with most African tribes the Kikuyu have been subjected to Christian influence in the form of missionary activity. Many have embraced the Christian teaching. But it is the opinion of a number of educated Africans that, generally speaking, this missionary activity has done more harm than good. With a few exceptions the missionaries of the past have understood little of African society and have been most unsympathetic in their attitude towards beliefs and practices which do not conform to their own religious persuasion. It is sad to reflect that some missionary societies have evidently considered Africa as of little consequence in that they have sent out to that continent persons ill-fitted to the task.

An example of the intolerance of the Christian missionaries is to be seen over the question of polygamy. Kikuyu society, like many other African societies, has long been based on polygamy. The Kikuyu does not understand why Christians object to this ancient traditional practice, when some of the most prominent biblical figures organized their family life in much the same way. The Kikuyu is naturally suspicious of the missionary for he sees him as attempting to undermine the essential nature of the Kikuyu family unit.

A further essential Kikuyu custom is the initiatory circumcision (*irua*) of both boys and girls at the attainment of puberty. The Christian missionaries have not complained too much over the circumcision of boys but have objected violently to clitoridectomy, which they regard as a savage, cruel practice, and some have tried to abolish the irua of girls by law. However, a Kikuyu man would

A Kikuyu girl, dressed in her finery, on her way to be circumcised. After circumcision she becomes a full member of the tribe, eligible for marriage

think twice before marrying a girl on whom the irua operation had not been performed, and vice versa. Without clitoridectomy there is no true initiation. The ramifications—social, moral, religious— of irua reach far beyond the mere surgical act.

> The real anthropological study, therefore, is to show that clitoridectomy, like Jewish circumcision, is a mere bodily mutilation which, however, is regarded as the conditio sine qua non of the whole teaching of tribal law, religion and morality.[1]

However, with the availability of education there appears to be less emphasis on tribal initiation among the Kikuyu than used to be the case.

[1] Jomo Kenyatta, *Facing Mount Kenya* (Mercury Books, 1961), p. 133.

The presence of Christian teachers among the Kikuyu has led to the growth of a variety of curious sects which are Christian in outline while retaining the Kikuyu social and moral customs and most of their religious assumptions. They usually succeed in adding something quite new to both religions. Many of them exhibit enthusiastic traits such as possession by the Holy Spirit which manifests itself in convulsions and the imitation of wild animals. Some sects forbid their members to own property. Some are intensely nationalistic but on the whole are far too involved in religious practices to take any active part in politics.

PART ONE

The Near East and the West

CHAPTER ONE

Judaism

The word 'Jew' comes from the adjective 'Yehudi' which is to be found in the later parts of the Old Testament only and refers to a descendant of Yehudah (Judah), Jacob's fourth son, whose tribe, together with that of his half-brother Benjamin made up the kingdom of Judah as distinct from the remaining tribes (Israel). Today the word has both cultural and religious meaning. Judaism goes back to the Hebrew scriptures but extends far beyond that time: it does not end with the close of the Old Testament books but still thrives today. In 1970 it was reckoned that there were some 12 million Jews in the world: 2 million in Israel, 6 million in the U.S.A. and the remainder in Russia and Europe. As many as 6 million were slaughtered by the Nazis in purges between 1939 and 1945 in their attempts to 'purify' their race.

Although it is recognized that the putative sources of Judaism go back to Abraham,[1] the organiser of Judaism and its decisive and pivotal point was Moses (1200 B.C.). It will be convenient for us to examine his life under four headings: stories associated with his birth and early life; divine revelation; the exodus from Egypt; and the giving of the Torah.

MOSES THE FOUNDER AND TRANSMITTER OF JUDAISM

1 STORIES ASSOCIATED WITH HIS BIRTH AND EARLY LIFE

Most readers will know that Moses, the Hebrew, was born in Egypt. The Hebrews had entered Egypt during the time when it was dominated by a Semitic warlike race called the Hyksos. The Hyksos would have controlled Egypt from c. 1730 to 1580 B.C. The fact that they were Semites explains why Joseph, the Hebrew, rose to such prominence during their occupation—they shared Semitic origin. It was during Joseph's time that a band of seventy Hebrews

[1] The revelation given to Moses at the burning bush includes the statement 'I am the God of your forefathers, the God of Abraham, the God of Isaac, the God of Jacob' (Exodus 3: 6).

entered Egypt at the invitation of the Hyksos pharaoh but by the time Moses was born the Hyksos had been driven out and an Egyptian pharaoh was back on the throne (probably Rameses II). The Hebrews constituted a substantial proportion of the population and therefore became a threat to political stability. Rameses II planned to use the Hebrews to the best economic advantage while at the same time restricting the population explosion. They were treated like prisoners-of-war and their morale was broken by forced labour. With this newly-found labour force Rameses II erected many public buildings.

We read of a somewhat naïve attempt of the pharaoh to deal with the Hebrew population: all the male children at their birth are to be thrown into the Nile. It is obvious from the text, however, that this 'king of Egypt' is only a leader in a village inhabited by both Egyptians and Hebrews. It is at this point that the Moses story is introduced. His mother keeps him hidden for three months, after which he is set adrift on the Nile. Pharaoh's daughter discovers the child and, no doubt contrary to the instructions of her father, adopts him as her own. Thus it came about that the future deliverer of Israel was reared as the adopted son of an Egyptian princess. The fact that he was suckled by a Hebrew woman makes him, according to ancient custom, fully Hebrew but, in order to be the deliverer of his enslaved people, he could not himself be a slave: he had to be one to whom the pharaoh would listen.

The name 'Moses' appears to be Egyptian (*mosis* = child of). It may, on the other hand, be based on the Hebrew verb *mashah*, to draw forth: i.e. 'one who is drawn forth' from the water, or 'one who draws forth' his people from Egypt. *Sheh*, however, is an Egyptian word for 'pond' and so Musheh might simply mean 'the child of the Nile'.

When he was adult Moses, on seeing an Egyptian maltreating a Hebrew, killed the Egyptian and hid the body in the sand supposing that no one knew of it. Next day he tried to stop two Hebrews from fighting whereupon the Hebrew who was wronging his brother taunted Moses with the murder of the Egyptian. Fearing punishment from the pharaoh, Moses made his escape to the Sinaitic Peninsula and settled with Hobab, or Jethro, priest of Midian, whose daughter he eventually married. He spent forty years in Midian as a sheep farmer and his son Gershom was born there.

2 DIVINE REVELATION

Readers will no doubt be familiar with the story of the burning bush which Moses came across while looking after Jethro's sheep. In the Old Testament fire is often associated with the appearance or presence of deity. Moses immediately responds to the call of God from the bush and removes his sandals as a sign of respect just as Muslims do before entering a mosque. The God who reveals himself to Moses is not a new God but the one who made himself known to the earlier Hebrew leaders. He has come down to commission Moses to lead his chosen people out of Egypt to a place they can call their own.

In ancient cultures it was considered important to know the name of the deity you worshipped for the name told you what kind of character the god was. So in order to assure his fellow Hebrews that God has in fact contacted him he must be able to give them the divine name. God reveals his name as *Yahweh*. This is the name which is never uttered by Jews for it is the name of God and therefore too holy to mention: instead the Jew will say 'Lord' (*Adonai*) to avoid taking God's name in vain. The word 'Yahweh' is most probably based on the Hebrew verb *hayah*, 'to be'. Yahweh is the living God: he is he who is, he who causes to be (the creator God), he who will be what he will be. He is revealed as *'ehyeh 'asher 'ehyeh* —*I am who I am*: he is the God who never came into being, is, and always will be what he is. He is the God who directs the course of history and reveals himself within historical events. As he promises to be with Moses, so he promises to be with his people, the Hebrews, and to manifest his power in the great saving act in history—the exodus.

3 THE EXODUS FROM EGYPT

The historical problems associated with the actual coming out of Egypt (13th century B.C.) are far too complex to be dealt with here. What is important is to grasp its significance for Jews throughout the ages. What the crucifixion and resurrection of Jesus is to Christians the exodus from Egypt is to Jews. The story of the exodus is fundamental to their creed. They remember it yearly at Passover, weekly in the synagogue, and daily in their private devotions. Since Moses was the human means by which the event was achieved he naturally commands a place of great esteem within Judaism.

It used to be thought that the Hebrews actually passed dry-shod through the Red Sea but recent research has shown conclusively that the Hebrew *Yam Suph* means 'the sea of reeds', 'the papyrus sea'. This was most probably situated in the area of the Bitter Lakes (incidentally, there are no reeds by the Red Sea) not far from Rameses. Archaeological evidence indicates that at the time of the exodus the Bitter Lakes were linked to the Gulf of Suez. If this were the case then there would have been shallow water or marshland covered with reeds through which the Hebrews could pass with their leader, Moses, but which would provide difficulties for heavy chariots.

Thus Moses is the central character in the all-determining event in the history of the Jews. He is the sheep farmer who became prophet and liberator.

4 THE GIVING OF THE TORAH

The word *Torah*, usually translated 'law', 'teaching', may possibly come from a Hebrew root which means 'to point out', 'to signpost'. It is God's signposting of the way for Israel and is part and parcel of the pact which Yahweh has made with Israel: Yahweh has chosen Israel and Israel must be obedient to him: what he requires is found in the Torah. The essence of the Torah is to be found in the Ten Commandments which, according to the scriptures, were delivered to Moses on Mt. Sinai on stone tablets. But the first five books of the Hebrew Bible (Pentateuch = five books) are usually referred to as the Torah, as is the Talmud, a vast body of Jewish writing which interprets the biblical books.

The Ten Commandments teach that religion and morality are related: the one depends upon the other. Nature worship and idols are strictly forbidden for Yahweh is one and not to be found in material objects. A day of rest must be set aside and observed; parents must be honoured; property, life and a woman's honour must be respected. Any deed or thought which might in any way harm any person is to be avoided.

Gradually laws were introduced to deal with every aspect of life, with every action you perform, so that Jewish life is lived out according to a pattern. Yahweh is holy (*kadosh*), therefore the Jew must be holy: he must keep himself separate from the contaminating influences around him and be dedicated to the service of God by whom he has been chosen. The Torah is the means to morality which is centred in the character of Yahweh himself. *Kadosh*, therefore, expresses itself in terms of justice and righteousness.

Six fundamental human rights are to be found in the Torah teaching: the right to live, the right to possession, the right to work, the right to clothing, the right to shelter, the right to liberty (e.g.

leisure—the Sabbath). Concern for others, especially the poverty-stricken and all unfortunate persons, is stressed in the Torah. All possessions are given by God and since all men are the children of God the Jew must show pity and generosity to all unfortunates whether they be Jew or Gentile. 'Thou shalt love thy fellow as thyself' (Leviticus 19:18)—and that includes strangers (Leviticus 19:34). Jews think of Moses as the transmitter of this Torah. The follower of the religion of Moses must keep himself pure from the world and yet must be very much in the world where it is his duty to establish goodness which is the very nature of God.

Moses, then, is the central character in the history of Judaism: he is the one to whom God revealed his name and he is the one through whom God manifested his saving power in history. Jews call him *Moshe Rabbenu*, 'Moses our Teacher'. Indeed, not only does he occupy a unique position in the history of Judaism but he is also of considerable consequence to her daughter religions—Christianity and Islam.

To the Jew Moses is a great *prophet*. He is described as 'the master of the prophets' and the book Deuteronomy states that 'there has not arisen a prophet since in Israel like unto Moses whom Yahweh knew face to face'. His teaching that was not written down in the

Young Jewish people gathered round a scroll

Pentateuch is believed to be contained in the Talmud. He is said to have spoken what all subsequent prophets have spoken: he is the final means of God's self-revelation. This notion of Moses as the prophet was expressed in the 'Thirteen Principles of the Faith' of Moses Maimonides (A.D. 1135-1204), the famous medieval rabbi:

> *I believe with perfect faith that the prophecy of Moses our teacher . . . was true, and that he was the chief of the prophets. . . .*

Moses is also thought of as the *saviour* and *redeemer* of Israel. The Talmud refers to him as the *first redeemer* whereas the messiah-to-come is the *last redeemer*. As Moses brought redemption to Israel in the past, so would the messiah in the future.

He is also spoken of as *rabbi for all generations*. In his morning prayers the Jew repeats, 'Moses commanded us a law, an inheritance in the congregation of Jacob'. When he goes into the synagogue he sees above the Ark the Ten Commandments which Moses transmitted to the Jews for ever. Every Jew learns the beautiful *Shema* (Hebrew for 'hear'):

> *Hear, O Israel: the Lord our God, the Lord is one . . . and thou shalt love the Lord thy God with all thine heart, and with all thy soul and with all thy might, and these words which I command thee this day shall be upon thine heart; and thou shalt teach them diligently unto thy children and shalt talk of them when thou sittest in thine house and when thou walkest by the way. . . .*

The *Shema* is one of Judaism's oldest prayers. It was one of the daily prayers in the temple and was adopted by the synagogue. It is the first prayer to be said by Jewish children and the last to be uttered by the dying. The Jew must carry out God's will through love, not fear. Yahweh is the loving God and therefore the Jew must love his neighbour. Hillel, one of the most famous of all Jewish rabbis (apart from Moses) was once asked to teach the whole Torah while balancing on one foot. Hillel replied, 'What is hateful to thee do not to thy fellow man. This is the whole Torah, the rest is the explanation thereof. Go and learn it.'

Moses, the man who spoke with God, died, according to tradition, by the 'kiss of God' and God himself was regarded as the digger of his servant's grave so that 'no man knoweth of his grave unto this day' (Deuteronomy 34:5-6).

JEWISH LIFE AND RELIGIOUS OBSERVANCES

THE SABBATH

The Sabbath is observed from Friday sunset to nightfall on Saturday. When the parents arrive home from the synagogue service on Friday evening it is the custom for them to pronounce the blessing upon their children: 'The Lord bless thee and keep thee; the Lord make his face to shine upon thee and be gracious unto thee; the Lord turn his face upon thee and give thee peace.' Before it becomes dark the housewife will light the 'Sabbath Lights' or candles and say, 'Blessed art thou, O Lord our God, king of the universe, who has sanctified us by thy commandments and commanded us to kindle the Sabbath Light.' The word *Sabbath* means 'rest': it is a time when all unnecessary work is set aside so that the Jew can be free to relax and also to think about God. Jews are particularly family-conscious and the Sabbath observance helps to strengthen the bonds of family life and affection. The whole family sits down to a special family meal on the Friday night. Bread and wine are blessed and the husband reads aloud the last twenty-two verses of Proverbs (Proverbs 31:10-31), the theme of which is 'the perfect housewife'. The bread and wine is then passed to the wife and children and the father blesses the children as Jacob, the patriach, blessed his. Then the meal follows.

Unlike Indian religion, Judaism takes stock of the material world: the Jew believes that God created the world for the benefit of man who should therefore enjoy it. Worldly comforts are the gift of God.

Most Jewish festivals are in fact family ones and this is no doubt partly due to the fact that since Jews have been compelled to live in minority groups they have felt a greater need for family fellowship. It is the Sabbath which keeps Judaism intact and even those Jews who are not interested in religion will maintain Sabbath traditions in their homes.

THE SYNAGOGUE

It is their religion which has held the Jews together throughout their long history, though today Jews tend to share the lack of interest in organized religion that has been characteristic of the Christian churches. Since the destruction of the temple at Jerusalem in A.D. 70 Judaism has ceased to be a sacrificial religion and has become instead a way of life based upon prayer and regulated by the Torah (including the Talmud). Jews do meet for corporate Torah study and worship in the synagogue but for the Jew religion is first and foremost a matter for the home. Because of this it is not fair to judge whether a Jew is a good or a bad Jew on the basis of synagogue attendance only.

In the synagogue the scrolls of the Law are kept in the Ark which is a large cubicle draped with curtains over which an ever-burning lamp is suspended. The minister (i.e. the *chazan* or *cantor*) leads the prayers from the reading desk or *bima* which faces the Ark and the *rabbi* (teacher) expounds the Torah in sermons from the pulpit (although a pulpit is not an essential item of synagogue furniture). There is no organ accompaniment in an Orthodox synagogue. Round three sides of the building is a gallery for the women who sit apart from the men, although in Reform synagogues both may sit together. Synagogues may be square, oblong or round but the Ark is always at the east end and the seats are arranged so that the whole congregation can see it.

On Friday night there is usually a service which is attended mostly by men but the main service is on Saturday morning. The word 'synagogue' comes from the Greek, meaning 'assembling', 'gathering'. Synagogue worship was introduced into Judaism from the fourth to the second century B.C. when the Jews were ruled by the Greeks. In 620 B.C. King Josiah had decreed that sacrificial worship should be centralized at the temple in Jerusalem and that all local sacrificial shrines should be demolished: this was to avoid idolatrous worship but it also meant that Jews outside the capital city were without a place of worship. From 586 to 538 B.C. many Jews were exiled in Babylon and because they had no hope of journeying to Jerusalem they had to devise a new form of worship along non-sacrificial lines. Many synagogues were built and by the time of Jesus synagogue attendance was the accepted thing in Palestine itself and the temple was only visited on special occasions.

Synagogue officials wearing talliths and blowing sophars (horns) to usher in the year of Jewish pilgrimage on Mount Zion

During the service each man will wear a skull cap (*yarmelke*) and a *tallith* which is a shawl worn by Orthodox Jews at prayer. The Jew will kiss the ends of the tallith and cover his eyes with it while he says a short prayer before he uses it to cover his head. At the two ends of the tallith are tassels, each made up of eight strands tied in five knots at uniform intervals. The numerical value of the Hebrew letters for the word 'tallith' is 600. When the number of strands in each tassel (8) and the number of knots (5) are added to this the total is 613, the number of regulations in the Torah. The tallith thus reminds the Jew that he must keep the Torah regulations constantly in mind. Jews cover their heads when entering a synagogue or when praying as a sign of respect.

If you visit a synagogue you will notice that there are no statues or replicas of any kind. Jewish art tends to be symbolic, for 'images' are forbidden in the Ten Commandments. The scrolls are often covered with beautiful Torah mantles.

The most important synagogue official is the rabbi. It should be noted, however, that the rabbi is a teacher, a student of the Torah and not a priest or leader of worship. It is the *chazan*, the synagogue cantor or reader, who leads the service. Since much of the service has to be sung it is necessary for the chazan to have a good voice.

Before any service can start at least ten male Jews above the age of thirteen must be present: this quorum is called a *minyan*. In Orthodox synagogues the service lasts for about three hours whereas Reform synagogues reduce the length by about half. The chazan, wearing a black gown, hat and white scarf, enters and mounts the bima. Prayers are said by way of introduction and then the Eighteen Benedictions (*Amidah*) are recited, blessing God for his kindness towards his chosen people. Prayers and psalms are intoned in Hebrew, although in Reform synagogues they are sung in the language of the land. The congregation sits for most of the time but everyone rises for the Shema.

The central event is the opening of the Ark and the removal of the Torah. One of the scrolls is carried processionally round the synagogue and, as the bearer passes by, members of the congregation bow towards the scroll—they must never turn their backs upon the Torah. When it has been divested of its ornaments the scroll, which is hand-written on parchment, is placed on the reading desk of the bima, unrolled, and the appropriate passage is read. During the course of the service three or four men (women also in Reform synagogues) ascend the bima to read short passages in Hebrew. (Very few, however, are capable of reading the Hebrew correctly so

Open ark with Torah mantle and menorah (as used at the Feast of Chanucah) in the foreground

the chazan does it for them while they stand by on the bima.) Sometimes this is followed by a translation, unless, of course, the synagogue happens to be in Israel. When the reading is over the scroll is held aloft for all to see, is re-adorned with its finery and returned with due ceremony to the Ark.

Sometimes the service will end with a short sermon delivered by the rabbi and in some synagogues this is followed by a *Kiddush* (sanctification) in which the congregation eat bread and drink a small quantity of wine—a kind of communion service. No collections are taken at the Saturday morning service for the Torah forbids the exchange of money on the Sabbath. However, each member gives a fixed amount at regular intervals towards the upkeep of the synagogue.

FESTIVALS

Judaism is rich in its provision for teaching spiritual truths through religious festivals and the Jewish calendar is a perpetual reminder to the Jews of God's activity throughout their history, revealing his nature and purpose.

Pesach or *Passover* is the festival which commemorates the exodus of Israel from Egypt. It lasts for eight days, the four middle days being half holy-days. Pesach is also called 'the Feast of Unleavened Bread' because the Egyptians told the Israelite slaves to leave Egypt immediately and consequently they did not have enough time to allow the dough of the bread they were kneeding to become 'leavened' through yeast fermentation. They therefore had to bake unleavened cakes (*matzos*) which are flat and thin (something like a cream cracker). These matzos are known as the 'bread of affliction'. This is why only unleavened bread may be eaten during Pesach and no leavened bread should be present in the house at all.

On the Passover eve the Jewish father will go round the house with the children, who hold lighted candles, to see if they can find any leavened bread or yeast. If they do find any it is ceremonially burnt. The mother will have made sure that the house is spick and span and that no leaven is present on any of the eating utensils. It is customary, however, for her to hide some leaven especially for the young children to find.

On the first two nights of Pesach a special home service called a *seder* (order) is held. These are particularly important family occasions. The object of the seder is described in the *Hagadah* which is a recital of the exodus events 'that in every generation each person is bound to think of himself as if he personally had gone forth from Egypt'. The seder abounds in historic ceremonial.

The family sit around the Pesach table which is lit with candles. Each person has a wineglass and some matzos. The following are also on the Pesach table:

shankbone of mutton as a reminder of the Pesach lamb which was eaten in haste before the exodus from Egypt. It also reminds the Jew of the lambs which were sacrificed at Jerusalem before Pesach when the temple was still standing.

bitter herbs which are eaten to recall the unpleasantness of existence under the Egyptian yoke of slavery.

paste made from apples, almonds, cinnamon and other spices mixed with wine in which are dipped the bitter herbs: this reminds the Jew that his ancestors worked with mortar and bricks in Egypt.

salt water reminds the Jew of the passage of his ancestors through the 'Red Sea'.

Jewish children participating in a seder ceremony

The child plays an important rôle in the Pesach ceremonies, in fact the whole thing is designed to enable him to realize the great heritage in which he shares. The youngest child present at the meal asks the question, 'Why is this night different from all other nights?' The answer is given by the father and read by all at the Pesach table. 'Because we were Pharaoh's slaves in Egypt, the Lord our God brought us out from there with a mighty hand and an outstretched arm and if the Most Holy, blessed be he, had not brought out our ancestors from Egypt, we and our children and our children's children would still be in bondage to the pharaohs in Egypt.' The whole service is geared to enable the participants to go back in imagination and relive what their ancestors actually experienced.

Gentiles are invited to some Pesach ceremonies. A special goblet of wine is always reserved for the prophet Elijah (who never died) and the children leave the door ajar in case he arrives during the course of the meal to announce the day of the Lord.

Seven weeks after Pesach comes *Pentecost*, or the *Feast of Weeks* which celebrates the end of the corn harvest. A kind of harvest festival is held at the synagogue.

The *Jewish New Year* is celebrated in the autumn and the first ten days are spent in making things right with your neighbour and with God. The Jew will try to patch up quarrels, pay outstanding debts and right any wrong he has done. The tenth day is the *Day of Atonement* when devout Jews will abstain from food and drink for twenty-four hours as an act of penitence before God. It is a time when a Jew examines his conscience and the fast should result in positive good. Notice the social implications of these festivals.

Succoth, or the *Feast of Tabernacles*, occurs soon after the Day of Atonement and commemorates the time when the Israelites had to live in tents in the desert after they had left Egypt.

Chanucah, or the *Feast of the Dedication of the Temple*, occurs near Christmas and lasts for eight days. It is often called the Feast of Light when the nine-branched candlestick (*menorah*) is used to recall the legend that one day's supply of oil lasted eight days and nights in the temple candelabra above the Ark. This was meant to have occurred when Judas Maccabaeus cleansed the temple in 165 B.C. after it had been defiled by Antiochus Epiphanes: the temple was rededicated to God. One light is kindled on each of the eight days of Chanucah from the ninth, or 'servant' light.

Purim occurs in springtime and in Israel carnivals are held. The book of Esther is read and Jews are reminded how a Jewish queen saved her people in ancient Persia.

OTHER OBSERVANCES

Circumcision. All Jewish boys are circumcised eight days after birth. This consists of an operation, performed by the rabbi either in the home or in the synagogue, in which the loose skin is excised from the male sexual organ. It is the sign of the pact God made with Abraham when he promised that he was to be the parent of the great nation—Israel. It is God's signature in the flesh which acts as a constant reminder to the Jew of his great religious heritage.

Bar-Mitzvah. When he is thirteen years of age the Jewish boy becomes bar-mitzvah—a son of the commandment. During the synagogue service he is called up to the bima to read a passage from the Torah. He now has all the religious responsibilities and privileges of an adult Jew.

Dietary laws. Observant Orthodox Jews are particular about keeping the food laws as prescribed in the Torah. Perhaps originally the laws were introduced for reasons of hygiene. The meat of the pig and of other unclean animals (e.g. shellfish, because they eat refuse) is forbidden and on no account should the blood of any meat be consumed. In ancient Hebrew custom it was considered that the life-force of any living thing was in the blood: since all life is given by God the least one can do when slaughtering an animal is to give back to God the life he gave. This is why the Jew does not buy meat from a Gentile butcher. The animal must be killed by a ritually trained official called a *Shochet* (the actual method of slaughter is called *Shechita*) and pronounced *Kosher*, or clean. The Shochet ensures that the animal dies with as little pain as possible and at the same time loses as much blood as possible. It should be pointed out that the Shochet is a skilled religious official and that Shechita conforms to the high standards of humane slaughter required by law.

The Messiah. The Jews have always hoped for the 'anointed one' of God, the messiah, who will bring all men into closer relationship with God. Nowadays, however, more liberal Jews think of the advent of the messiah not as a person but rather as a community of peace and trust in God and, quite naturally, many look to the State of Israel as the messiah, the future perfect society on earth. This idea is reflected in the beliefs of the Zionist Movement with its emphasis on the national rebirth of Judaism and the restoration to popular use of the Hebrew language. Indeed the State of Israel is a visible sign of the fact that Judaism is a most vital religious and national movement striving towards a future of peace and security in the spirit of the great Jewish prophet and deliverer, Moses.

Why I am a Jew

My consciousness of being Jewish is an amalgam of different events and experiences, personal, historical and religious, which began with my earliest memories of life and continues unabated till the present day. When I was eight days old my parents saw that I was received into the 'Covenant of Abraham' in the manner described in Genesis 17. In my childhood I was made aware of the positive nature of my Jewishness by a code of Jewish practice and custom which gave my home and my early life their scriptural stamp.

Intermingled with the ordinary life of a British schoolboy, 'conkering', buying 'gob-stoppers' and writing out 'lines', as well as the more normal activities of the classroom, my wakeful hours were accompanied by the voice of Jewish prayer, before breakfast, at table, even as my eyes closed for sleep, expressing not only the expected praises of God and mankind's thanksgiving, but the yearning for God's return to Zion; the hope of deliverance for suffering and persecuted kinsfolk; the restoration of the dignity of Israel. Sabbaths and Biblical Festivals, the latter even when they coincided with weekday school, were days of peace and renewal with their emphasis upon the spirit of man, righteousness and the love of truth and justice. Even the food I ate was in accordance with Leviticus 11, avoiding the 'unclean' in flesh and fowl, shedding, as was intended, an aura of holiness upon the normal and the casual.

As a youth and as a young adult, the revolt of the young seized me, as it does every independent searcher for what is right. I questioned, I doubted, I attacked, but the citadel held. Slowly there emerged the adult evaluation of those early impressions that had been so deeply assimilated with the years. Truth became a vital world foundation, not just the 'not telling of fibs'; justice was the rights of people in terms of freedom, surpassing the image of the court of law; mercy assumed a dimension which took in the poor and the hungry of the world and had nothing to do with 'not cutting off your enemy's head', which I felt unable to do even without the restraint of my religious doctrine. God no longer roared in the thunder and the tempestuous wind. He became part of the still, small voice of conscience; of the triumph of humility, however hard it was ground into the dust; of the vindication of righteousness, even though it was thrust aside by a generation here or there, which sought its pleasures in the extremes of abandon. 'Chosen' stood for duty, not for privilege. It told me why 6 million of my kinsfolk, men, women and children, had to die in the inhuman holocaust of Nazism, the '*suffering servants*' *of their day, imparting their message,* '*with all their heart and with all their soul and with all their might*'.

And then, at the height of man's greatest crime, the slaughter of the innocents, came the cry of—'*enough*'. *And the word of the prophet was no longer a word, for the word became a reality. And my people returned to their ancestral homeland;* '*they that had sown with tears*' *were* '*reaping with rejoicing*'. *All the darkness of the ghetto was rolled away. Forgiven, but not forgotten, was the storm and terror of the dark oppressors. The words of the prophets were once more a* '*light for my feet*'.

Today I am a Jew because the spirit of the Hebrew prophets stirs within me still, making me restless and sad for the great madness of the nations who whet their swords again, and with deceit and intrigue and lies avow that they do so for the defence of their precious heritage, which otherwise interpreted means, for the subjugation and oppression of defenceless nations and individuals. I know that even though I can only represent the tiniest of sparks in the great fire of mankind, I must not rest from declaring fearlessly to rich and to poor, to the powerful as well as to the weak, the need for social justice, the need for international justice, the principle of the equality of men in the sight of God no matter creed or colour. Today I feel myself a Jew not only for the cause of my people but for the cause of just men everywhere. For the vision of the lion and the lamb is a vision of tomorrow and I must be here today and now, to add my peg to the great tent, the tabernacle of universal good, that mankind can erect for itself. I am a Jew because my history, my background, my upbringing, my people's voice calling across the ages leaves me no choice. I am a Jew because I must be true to my destiny.

Rabbi S. Brown, B.A., Ph.D., H.C.F.
Senior Rabbi
United Hebrew Congregation
Leeds

CHAPTER TWO

Christianity

Christianity is a monotheistic religion which differs from other religions of that kind in that the regulative principle in all Christian thought and practice is the historical character, Jesus of Nazareth, by whom and in whom man's redemption has been once and for all accomplished. The 'good news' of the Christian proclamation is Jesus Christ and him crucified. Other prophets *taught* religion but the Christian belief is that ultimate truth was and is uniquely and decisively presented in the *person* of Jesus: Jesus is God's gracious gesture to man: Jesus *is* God.

Christianity is the largest of all world religions, having about 850 million followers. Unlike Judaism, from which it sprang, Christianity is not the faith of a particular cultural group but finds adherents in virtually all cultures. The Christian faith is conveniently summed up in the Apostles' Creed which is used in the worship of most Christian denominations (although it is not always thought of as being a true statement of belief in a literal sense). Roman Catholics, Anglicans, Presbyterians, Methodists, the Continental Protestant churches, all use the Creed and the Eastern Orthodox Church uses a lengthier version of it. Quakers, Baptists, Congregationalists, Plymouth Brethren, etc. prefer not to use it.

I believe in God the Father Almighty, maker of heaven and earth; and in Jesus Christ his only Son our Lord, who was conceived by the Holy Ghost, born of the Virgin Mary, suffered under Pontius Pilate, was crucified, dead, and buried; he descended into hell; the third day he rose again from the dead; he ascended into heaven, and sitteth on the right hand of God the Father Almighty; from thence he shall come to judge the quick and the dead.

I believe in the Holy Ghost; the Holy Catholic Church; the communion of Saints; the forgiveness of sins; the resurrection of the body; and the life everlasting.

Most Christians believe that the events recorded in the gospels and the Creed are historical. God, at a particular time in history, booamo onfloohod, or inoarnatod, ao man. Jooue woo rom of God but an authentic human being: this is the Christian paradox. Whereas, the Christian will say, in all other religions man has to seek out God or salvation, the Christian religion teaches that God has come to man as a man—the man Jesus. Once it was impossible to understand what was meant by the word 'God' but the Christian can now interpret the meaning of that word by means of the revelation of 'God' in the person of Jesus Christ. In him the Christian sees God. He is God. Gotama, Confucius, Muhammad are dead but Jesus, says the Christian, rose from the dead and lives for ever in the life of the Church of which he is the head. Obviously not all the Christian denominations interpret the gospel material in exactly the same way but space does not allow us to deal with the great variety of doctrines held among Christians: all Christians, however, believe that Jesus is the final and fullest revelation of what is meant by the word 'God'.

THE CHRISTIAN SCRIPTURES

The Christian canon of scripture, or those writings considered by the Church to be inspired and of equal merit to the books of the Jewish canon, took form between A.D. 170 and 220. These writings, however, were used by the Church long before this time but as they were numerous a good deal of sorting out was needed. The word *canon* is Greek for 'measuring rod' or 'rule' and the books of the Christian canon of scripture are those considered by the early Church to measure up to the standard required for the Christian proclamation in all ages. Christianity is thoroughly Hebraic in origin and the Christian bible consists of the Jewish scriptures (Old Testament), the Christian writings (New Testament) and the Apocrypha[1]. The New Testament comprises the four gospels, the Acts of the Apostles, the epistles (letters) of Paul and the 'Catholic' epistles and the Book of Revelation.

Although the gospels come first in the New Testament they were probably written after Paul's epistles. The earliest and shortest gospel is that of Mark which Matthew and Luke used as a source book. Luke wrote a gospel and the Acts of the Apostles. Matthew and Luke did not simply re-write Mark: they had their own special material and both used a sayings source (oral or written) which was unknown to Mark and which is usually referred to as Q, from *Quelle*, the German word for 'source'. Matthew, Mark and Luke are

[1] I.e. 'the hidden (things)'.—Jewish writings which formed part of the Greek bible (Septuagint) but which were excluded from the Hebrew canon. The Church of Rome accepts most of the Apocrypha as canonical.

known as the *synoptic gospels* since they present a relatively small number of recollections of what Jesus did and said. Most scholars would agree that it is impossible to write a 'life' of Jesus because the details at our disposal do not lend themselves to biographical presentation. The object of the gospel-writers was not biography for, from the point of view of faith, their central character, Jesus of Nazareth, was not a historical person only but God incarnate, the Lord Christ. The gospels, then, are the product of the Church's faith and not just reconstructions of the life of Jesus.

Concerning the person of the historical Jesus Professor T. W. Manson wrote as follows:

> *Not a single chronological point can be fixed with certainty. The life of Jesus lasted probably between thirty and forty years: concerning at least twenty-eight of them we know precisely nothing at all. What information we have is mostly concerned with the public career of Jesus, that is, with the last period of his life, a period whose length is uncertain, but probably not less than one year nor more than about three. But there is not even enough material for a full account of the Ministry.*[1]

Nevertheless, it is true to say that there is more written about the 'life' of Jesus than there is about Zoroaster, Confucius or the Buddha.

JESUS

Since the time of Jesus there has arisen an amazing variety of belief and practice among Christians and non-Christians often find it difficult to see how, for example, Roman Catholics and Plymouth Brethren can possibly belong to the same religion. But although there is much disagreement among Christians, there is one belief that they all share. They all believe in Jesus as the revealer of God.

We do not attempt here to give a 'life' of Jesus. The gospel story will be known in outline by most readers. Any reference to the gospel accounts involves also interpretation. As Professor T. W. Manson put it, 'By their lives of Jesus ye shall know them'[2]: books about Jesus tell us more about their authors than about the historical Jesus.

Jesus was born either at Nazareth or Bethlehem. Matthew and Luke name Bethlehem as the birthplace and Luke mentions that

[1] T. W. Manson, *The Bulletin of the John Ryland Library, Manchester* (vol. 27, no. 2, June 1943), p. 323.

[2] *The Interpretation of the Bible* (ed. C. W. Dugmore, 1944), p. 92.

Jesus' parents had travelled the seventy miles from Nazareth because Quirinius, the Governor of Syria, had ordered a census and for this purpose Joseph and Mary had to travel to the place where Joseph's ancestor, David, had lived many generations before.

His birth occurred during the reign of Herod the Great who died in 4 B.C. Quirinius, however, the Roman legate of Syria, carried out his census between A.D. 6 and 9. There may have been a census in which the parents of Jesus were registered but Luke appears to be in some confusion regarding the date. A prophecy in the Old Testament book of Micah (Micah 5:2) states that the messiah would be born in Bethlehem and this is probably why Matthew and Luke state that the birth of Jesus took place there. The precise year of his birth is uncertain and the traditional year which marks the beginning of the Christian calendar was not accepted until the sixth century A.D. It was calculated by Dionysius Exiguus, a Scythian monk and scholar who lived at Rome and his dating of the start of the Christian era and of Easter was accepted by the Synod of Whitby in Yorkshire in 664, and thereafter on the Continent.

Matthew and Luke write of a virginal conception of Jesus. He was born as the result of the influence of the Holy Spirit (Holy Ghost) upon Mary. However, there is no reference to this miraculous birth in Mark, John and the epistles of Paul, and from this it can be assumed that the doctrine of the virginal conception was not necessarily a part of early Christian belief. From the beginning of the second century, however, it would appear that Christians believed that Jesus was conceived without a human father. This notion may have been due to the fact that man's fallenness (see Genesis 3) was considered the outcome of the sexual union of Adam and Eve. Since this was commonly held to be the case it was thought that sexual intercourse was the means whereby this state of fallenness was transmitted to all men and women. Therefore, if God is to be incarnated as a man it would be quite impossible for him to be born as a result of sexual union between two fallen creatures. The idea of the virginal conception, then, may have evolved from the Christian belief in the sinlessness of Jesus. Many Christians today, however, would want to say that unless Jesus was born as we were born then he does not in any sense share our human nature: he is somehow less than human and the whole point of the Christian religion is that God becomes a genuine, authentic man and experiences the human situation in the fullest possible sense. Since this is the case it is possible for us to know God because he has become one of us.

We are told little about the early life of Jesus. The birth stories are of course known by all Christians. Luke mentions a visit to Jerusalem at the age of twelve when Jesus shows an awareness of his unique relationship with God, his Father.

John the Baptist appears on the scene to prepare the way for the coming messiah, God's anointed servant and the saviour of his people. In late popular Jewish belief it was held that the prophet Elijah (who never died—II Kings 2:11) would one day return to call Israel to repentance (Malachi 4:5) and announce the messiah's coming: in the gospels the Baptist plays the rôle of Elijah. The proclamation of this Elijah-figure marks the beginning of the public ministry of Jesus. At the time of Jesus the Jews were a conquered people, with all the humiliation which that involved, and longed for deliverance from Roman rule. The messiah-to-come would surely be a great military leader, a king, who would drive out the oppressors and establish peace and prosperity among God's chosen people. However, Jesus is not accepted as messiah by his fellow Jews for his conception of messiahship bears nothing in common with theirs. At his baptism, however, Jesus hears the words 'Thou art my Son, my Beloved: on thee my favour rests' (Matthew 3:17; Luke 3:22). In this mystical experience Jesus is again represented as being conscious of his unique relationship with God. In the Old Testament both Israel and the king were addressed as 'son of God'. The son's task is to be obedient to the Father, to follow the way the Father has pointed out. Israel and her kings had frequently not shown obedience to Yahweh. Jesus, then, here receives the call to follow the way which Israel and her rulers should have followed: perfect obedience, perfect sonship is required of him. The words of the voice at Jesus' baptism also recall the beginning of the first 'servant song' (Isaiah 42:1) where Yahweh calls his servant, Israel, to follow the way of self-abasement and suffering, a way which would lead ultimately to triumph. For Jesus, therefore, to be messiah is to follow the way prescribed by Yahweh, the way of obedient sonship, a way which will involve humiliation and death. Jesus is the suffering messiah, the servant-messiah.

'Messiah' is most probably a word which Jesus would not have wished to use of himself: it could be so misleading and the Roman authorities had dealings with numerous would-be political-messiahs. Instead Jesus uses of himself the title 'son of man'. As students of the New Testament will know, this phrase can have a variety of meanings and perhaps it was the intention of Jesus that the meaning of the term as applied to himself should not be subject to a cut-and-dried definition. According to Jesus the 'son of man' is one who has to undergo great sufferings: this is his mission to which the Father has called him and in following the call he will be living out the *servant's* (*Israel's*) call to suffering. Triumph will be the reward: the defeat of death will come with resurrection. The following incident shows clearly Jesus' reticence over the use of the misleading title 'messiah'. It also shows how he rejected entirely the popular conception of the messiah. ('Messiah' comes from Hebrew and the word 'Christ' comes from the Greek translation of 'messiah': both words mean the same—'anointed'.)

> *Jesus and his disciples set out for the villages of Caesarea Philippi. On the way he asked his disciples, 'Who do men say I am?' They answered, 'Some say John the Baptist, others Elijah, others one of the prophets'. 'And you,' he asked, 'who do you say I am?' Peter replied: 'You are the Messiah.' Then he gave them strict orders not to tell anyone about him; and he began to teach them that the Son of Man had to undergo great sufferings, and to be rejected by the elders, chief priests, and doctors of the law; to be put to death, and to rise again three days afterwards. He spoke about it plainly. At this Peter took him by the arm and began to rebuke him. But Jesus turned round, and, looking at his disciples, rebuked Peter. 'Away with you, Satan,' he said, 'you think as men think, not as God thinks.'* (Mark 8:27-33.)

Throughout his life Jesus was constantly beset with the temptation to prove himself to be the popular messiah and to attract followers by performing 'miracles'. The temptation remains until the very end: '"Let the Messiah, the king of Israel, come down from the cross. If we see that, we shall believe." Even those who were crucified with him taunted him.' (Mark 15:32.)

This leads us to the difficult subject of the miracles of Jesus. Many feel that the miracles ascribed to Jesus by the gospel writers are far-fetched and a stumbling-block to belief. It should be pointed out, however, that the early Christians regarded these unusual events as *signs*: they point to the identity of he who performs them. Take, for example, the stilling of the storm on the lake where the concluding question of the disciples is that of the reader also. The 'works' of Jesus are of such a kind that they demand decision as to who he is.

That day, in the evening, he said to them, 'Let us cross over to the other side of the lake.' So they left the crowd and took him with them in the boat where he had been sitting; and there were other boats accompanying him. A heavy squall came on and the waves broke over the boat until it was all but swamped. Now he was in the stern asleep on a cushion; they roused him and said, 'Master, we are sinking! Do you not care?' He stood up, rebuked the wind, and said to the sea, 'Hush! Be still!' The wind dropped and there was a dead calm. He said to them 'Why are you such cowards? Have you no faith even now?' They were awestruck and said to one another, 'Who can this be whom even the wind and the sea obey?' (Mark 4:35-41.)

The New Testament writers certainly do not present Jesus as a wonder worker who is out to 'prove' something about himself. In Mark's gospel, for example, Jesus tells those who observe the miracles not to publish the fact. He silences the 'evil spirits' because

Christ healing the sick, from a Rembrandt etching

they must recognize God's messiah for his advent means that their reign is coming to an end.

Jesus is presented as refusing to perform miracles to order just to convince the religious orthodoxy of his day (the Pharisees) that he had authority from God. Messiahship was to be intuited, not proved; and miracles proved nothing. The real issue was not whether Jesus could perform miracles but rather by what authority he performed them—'Who gave you authority to act in this way?' (Mark 11:28). As Alan Richardson points out:

> Miracles were everyday events in an age which knew nothing about the fixity of natural law, and every village had its wonder worker. To cast out a demon or to work some other kind of miracle was no proof of divinity: one might be in league with Beelzebub or some other spirit (Mark 3:22).[1]

To miss the point of Jesus' 'signs' was like missing the point of his parables. The 'signs' do not prove that Jesus was God or that he had supernatural powers; they do not mean that faith healing was central (or even peripheral) to Jesus' teaching; they do not indicate that Jesus utilized techniques now practised by psychologists and hypnotherapists. The 'signs' are the 'signs' of the Christ, the messiah, the works performed by *him* and no other; they indicate that the kingdom of God has arrived in the person of God's messiah. To those with eyes to see the meaning is unmistakable. The supreme sign is the resurrection of Jesus.

Jesus proclaimed the apocalyptic inbreaking of the kingdom of God. The kingdom of God, or the reign of God, the time when God's will would be realized among men, had been present among God's chosen people, the Jews, from of old: now, in the person of Jesus, it had arrived in a much fuller sense but, until the work of God in Christ was accomplished, it remained a future event. The kingdom had always been present, was present with the coming of Jesus and was to come in the future. This teaching was presented in parabolic form.

> The kingdom of God is like this. A man scatters seed on the land; he goes to bed at night and gets up in the morning, and the seed sprouts and grows—how, he does not know. The ground produces a crop by itself, first the blade, then the ear, then the full-grown corn in the ear; but as soon as the crop is ripe, he sets to work with the sickle, because harvest-time has come. (Mark 4:26-9.)

[1] A. Richardson, *An Introduction to the Theology of the New Testament.* (S.C.M.P., 1961), p. 95.

The kingdom had long been among the Jews but now, in the person of Jesus, it has arrived in a fuller sense: he is the kingdom. In the very near future, he believed, God's work would be wound up and the kingdom would come in the complete sense (the *parousia*).

Since Jesus swept aside much of traditional Jewish teaching and practice and taught that even the Torah took second place when it stood in the way of genuine human sympathy and compassion he naturally aroused the hostility of official Judaism. The Pharisees applied Torah to every aspect of life and in order to do this they developed a *tradition* of interpretation whereby every action one performed could be regulated. The Pharisees are presented as not giving an inch: they are slaves to their own ideal. Jesus often came into conflict with them for they were quick to point out that he neglected both Torah and tradition. In the collections of teaching material found in the gospels there are words of Jesus which indicate that he was at variance with Judaism as it was practised in his day.

You have learned that our forefathers were told, 'Do not commit murder; anyone who commits murder must be brought to judgement.' But I tell you this: Anyone who nurses anger against his brother must be brought to judgement. If he abuses his brother he must answer for it to the court; if he sneers at him he will have to answer for it in the fires of hell. (Matthew 5:21-2.)

You have learned that they were told, 'Do not commit adultery.' But what I tell you is this: If a man looks on a woman with a lustful eye, he has already committed adultery with her in his heart. (Matthew 5:27-8.)

You have heard that they were told, 'An eye for an eye, and a tooth for a tooth.' But what I tell you is this: Do not set yourself against the man who wrongs you. If someone slaps you on the right cheek, turn and offer him your left. (Matthew 5:38-9.)

You have learned that they were told, 'Love your neighbour, hate your enemy.' But what I tell you is this: Love your enemies and pray for your persecutors; only so can you be children of your heavenly Father, who makes his sun rise on good and bad alike and sends the rain on the honest and dishonest. (Matthew 5:43-5.)

His teaching was direct and uneducated fishermen were among his most loyal followers. Jesus had twelve specially close followers. Judas Iscariot, the disciple who aided the Jews in the capture of Jesus, may have been a revolutionary who thought of Jesus in terms of the popular messiah who would liberate the Jews from Roman domination. However, Jesus did not call upon God to send down angelic armies to destroy the enemy. Jesus' messianic mission was that of the obedient servant and his messianic destiny was now to be fulfilled.

It is possible that he thought that his death would usher in the kingdom in the complete and final sense. He was put to death by crucifixion in Jerusalem and three days later rose from the dead having, according to Paul, defeated the powers of evil which for so long had held men and women in bondage. During the following forty days he appeared to many of his disciples and then was taken up into the sky (heaven). Ten days later (Pentecost) 120 of his followers in Jerusalem received the Holy Spirit which manifested itself by *glossolalia* (speaking in tongues) and gave the Christians courage to proclaim the good news of Jesus Christ, the looked-for messiah. The message was that Jesus, the long-expected messiah, was not recognized by his people but had been put to death by them according to the plan of God. God had vindicated his messiah by raising him from the dead and it is now through him that all men may be saved. Those who believe in the Christ have a change of heart, are freed from the bondage of evil which he, in his death and resurrection, conquered once and for all.

The early Christians certainly believed that the *parousia* (i.e. the end of the present status quo and the final inauguration of the kingdom through the return of the son of man) would occur in their own lifetimes.[1] However, as time went on they began to realize that it might be a far-off event: nevertheless, they must live as if they were expecting it at any moment.

For the believing Christian the crucifixion is not merely an event in the past, a paying-off of the debt of human sin by one who was sinless, but a present and lasting reality having its origin in history but made real in the day-to-day life of the believer, confirming his belief in the love of God and calling him to be crucified with the Christ, and to be resurrected with the Christ to a new, authentic, real existence. The resurrection is not meant to prove that Jesus was divine: it does say, however, that his death was a victorious death for in it he conquered the powers of evil which bind men and women and which prevent them from being themselves and

---

[1] Jesus appears to have held this view. 'I tell you this: there are some of those standing here who will not taste death before they have seen the kingdom of God already come in power.' (Mark 9:1.)

distorts their personalities. For the Christian it is the Christ who makes possible real, meaningful existence as against just living. So the Christian feels that he shares in the risen life of the Christ in a very real way: he experiences the Christ in his new meaningful existence and in the continuing life of the Christian community— the Church.

THE TRINITY

Christian faith has never doubted the supremacy of the Christ. He is the man Jesus, the son of man but also the pre-existent *logos* or *word* of God who became 'enmanned' and 'historicized', was crucified, rose from the dead and lives for ever, the risen Lord. A product of this New Testament teaching was the development of the doctrine of the trinity which conceives of God as Father, Son and Holy Spirit. The orthodox doctrine of the trinity was formulated by Tertullian, a theologian of the second century, but there are trinitarian references in the New Testament.

This doctrine is widely held among Christians although in popular belief the Holy Spirit tends to be regarded as rather less significant than the Father and the Son. The belief that the deity exists in three natures is not peculiar to Christianity. In Hinduism Brahma, Vishnu and Shiva were regarded as three aspects of deity (as Brahma became less important the trinity became Vishnu, Shiva and Shakti). But apart from this 'trinity' Hindus believe that deity may take many forms.

The Christian conception of the threefold expression of deity is abhorrent to the Muslim who regards the doctrine as a sophisticated form of polytheism. The Hindu, however, finds it difficult to appreciate the Christian insistence that deity must be restricted to three modes of expression only.

The *Arian* controversy of the fourth century raised the problem as to the nature of the relationship of the Son to the Father. Arius contended that the Son was *homoiousion* (of like substance) with the Father, whereas Athanasius insisted that the Son was *homoousion* (of one substance) with the Father. The letter *i* made all the world of difference to the Christian estimate of the Christ. Arius used the term *homoiousion* because he maintained that the Son did not exist for all time with the Father but was created by the Father and that a clear distinction could therefore be made between the nature of the Father and that of the Son. Athanasius, on the other hand, affirmed that the Son was co-eternal and co-equal with the Father and the term *homoousion* expressed the oneness of their nature.

The Roman emperor, Constantine, considered this dispute to be a danger to his Christian Empire so the matter was settled at Nicaea in 325 in a statement known as the Nicene Creed which is said at the Mass and Communion services of most Christian churches today. At Nicaea Arianism was condemned and the nature of the Son was described as 'very God of very God'. Christians, therefore, worship God the Father, through the Son, in the Spirit.

THE SPREAD OF CHRISTIANITY

It was Paul who was to become the great organizer of Christianity. Paul was a dispersed Jew who was born at Tarsus (now in S. Turkey). As a thorough-going Pharisee he naturally found the new Jewish sect (Christianity) quite obnoxious and participated actively in its destruction. In A.D. 35 he was travelling to Damascus in order to capture some Christians who had fled from persecution at Jerusalem, when he had a vision of the risen Christ which was to change his whole life. Paul, the fanatical Pharisee, became the greatest missionary to the gentile world that the Church has ever known. Before his time Christianity had been for Jews only (Jesus was a Jew) but now it was for the whole world.

After the time of Paul Christianity suffered much at the hands of the Romans who felt that members of the new religion were anti-social and therefore a threat to the Empire; this was because Christians refused to take part in the cruel sports and licentious activities which were so popular.

However, when Constantine became emperor in 312 Christianity became the official religion of the Roman Empire. Constantine is said to have seen a cross in the sky and the words *In hoc signo vinces* ('In this sign conquer') before fighting the battle of the Milvian Bridge outside Rome which was to determine whether or not he should be emperor. From now on Christianity was a respectable and legal religion.

The effects of this legitimization of Christianity by Rome were far reaching. There is no doubt that the moral tenor of Roman society was improved. But the effect of Rome upon Christianity was greater than that of Christianity upon Rome. Western Christianity adopted not only much of Roman state ceremonial and the use of Roman vestments by officials at liturgical events but was also, in matters of administration and organizational procedure, indebted to the Roman form of government with its hierarchical framework and its proliferation of juridical technicalities and principles. One important result was that the Christian religion spread rapidly throughout the Roman Empire. The Church, with the example of the Empire before her, became conscious of her power and was not averse to using force in restraining those of her number who voiced heretical doctrines. A symbol of this power was the priest who became more and more distant from the layman he was ordained to serve. Christianity became a state church, Christian ministers received their income from the state, bishops were powerful state officials and the bishop of Rome (the Pope) was regarded as the most important religious official of all. Whereas the Empire regarded itself as Christian there were certainly elements in its composition which can hardly be described as such and this dichotomy has obviously persisted so that what goes for 'Christianity' in a secular context has often little or no specifically 'Christian' connotation. What the non-Christian tends to criticize is the external form and internal organization which the Christian religion has adopted rather than the example of the founder of that religion which, to the onlooker, appears to be insignificant in comparison with what he sees.

A split of great significance in the Christian Church occurred in 1054. In 330 Constantine had inaugurated the city of Constantinople (Istanbul) as the new capital of the Empire. Gradually, as Constantinople assumed more importance, its bishops began to differ with the Pope at Rome who had been regarded as having the final word in all matters ecclesiastical. The result was that the Eastern Church claimed independence of Rome, an independence which persists. The Eastern Church is known as the Orthodox Church and has about 150 million members. The senior bishop of the Orthodox Church is the Patriarch of Constantinople but the greatest number of Orthodox Christians is to be found in Russia.

However, the differences between Orthodoxy (Greek, *orthos* = true, *doxa* = belief) and Roman Catholicism are not so radical as those between the latter and some of the Protestant churches.

The Protestant Reformation began in 1517 when the German monk, Martin Luther, questioned the authority of the Pope, the head of the Roman Catholic Church and the representative of Christ on earth. There were, however, protestants before this time on the Continent and in England, e.g. John Huss in Bohemia who founded the Moravian Church and John Wycliffe in England who translated the bible into the vernacular.

Luther thought that essential Christianity had nothing to do with the great edifice of authority and doctrinal infallibility represented by Rome and the Pope but lay rather in the relationship of the individual believer to God in Christ. It was not participation in the beliefs and practices of Rome which made one a Christian but rather *faith*, which is the gracious gift of God through which he justifies the believer. One cannot justify oneself before God on the basis of one's good works. The Lutheran Church has about 70 million followers.

The other great Reformation figure is John Calvin who stressed the sovereignty of God and predestination (i.e. the idea that a man's life is predetermined by God who therefore wills whether he is to be saved or damned). Calvin also taught that the Roman Mass was a misrepresentation of the Lord's Supper.

The Church of Rome holds the belief that every object has both substance (i.e. that which it truly is) and accidence (i.e. that which

Martin Luther burning Papal Bulls

it appears to be). At the Mass, before the priest pronounces the words of institution over the bread and wine, the substance of the bread is bread and the accidence is bread also (this reasoning applies similarly to the wine). After he has pronounced the words of institution, however, the substance of the bread is no longer bread but the body of Christ whereas the accidence remains that of bread. This doctrine of the Mass is known as *transubstantiation*—change of substance. Calvin, however, taught that no such change takes place and that the Lord's Supper is a remembering of the events of the passion of Jesus. Presbyterianism and many of the reformed churches owe much to Calvin and the members of Calvinistic churches number about 41 million.

Scotland is the best example of how Presbyterianism works. In that country it has the official title 'Church of Scotland' and has far more communicant members than any other denomination in Scotland. Although it is the national Church it allows no state interference in its affairs for, as the following thoroughly Calvinistic statement indicates, Christ is sovereign over his Church:

> *This Church, as part of the Universal Church wherein the Lord Jesus Christ has appointed a government in the hands of the Church office-bearers, receives from Him, its Divine King and Head, and from Him alone, the right and power subject to no civil authority to legislate, and to adjudicate finally, in all matters of doctrine, worship, government, and discipline in the Church, including the right to determine all questions concerning membership and office in the Church, the constitution and membership of its Courts, and the mode of election of its office bearers, and to define the boundaries of the spheres of labour of its ministers and other office-bearers. Recognition by civil authority of the separate and independent government and jurisdiction of this Church in matters spiritual, in whatever manner such recognition be expressed, does not in any way affect the character of this government and jurisdiction as derived from the Divine Head of the Church alone, or give to the civil authority any right of interference with the proceedings or judgments of the Church within the sphere of its spiritual government and jurisdiction.[1]*

Presbyterianism is characterized by a particular form of government. As an episcopal church (e.g. the Church of England) is governed by bishops so the Presbyterian churches are governed by presbytery. The Church of Scotland follows the usual Presbyterian

[1] *Articles Declaratory* IV.

pattern. Each congregation has its own court, known as the Kirk Session, which consists of elders (both men and women) who are ordained to that office for life, presided over by the minister (man or woman). The Presbytery is the regional court which consists of the ministers of the parishes within a particular area together with one representative elder from each congregation. The Presbytery has the oversight of all the Presbyterian churches in its region, as an Anglican bishop has the oversight of all the Anglican churches in his diocese. Each congregation is free to elect its own minister but before he is inducted he must be approved by the Presbytery. Once the minister has been accepted he is subject to the discipline not of his congregation but of the Presbytery.

The Presbytery meets about once a month. Less frequently, a number of Presbyteries meet together in Synods. However, the supreme court of the Church of Scotland is the General Assembly which meets in Edinburgh each May. It consists of equal numbers of representative ministers and elders from the whole Church chosen at Presbytery level.

A Church of Scotland baptism service

The Church of Scotland is in the curious position of being the national Church of a nation which does not have a separate existence as a state. Because of this the meeting of the General Assembly is regarded as a national event of great significance (for there is no comparable secular national event). The notion outlined in Article IV is given cogent expression in the ceremonial of the Assembly. The Queen appoints her Lord High Commissioner to be present at the deliberations but although he is a person of some considerable consequence he has no authority at the Assembly whatsoever and must reach his gallery without actually entering the body of the hall where the representatives gather.

Traditionally the doctrine of Presbyterianism is essentially biblical and Calvinistic. The liturgy is simple (some avoiding a set form of worship altogether), the use of metrical psalms being a significant feature. Preaching is all important. The sacrament of the Lord's Supper is observed quarterly. Ministers of the Church of Scotland are noted as academics and they usually have two university degrees, one of which must be in theology. Today there are both conservatives and radicals within the Presbyterian churches.

The split between the Church in England and the Roman Catholic Church occurred during the reign of Henry VIII. However, the Reformation in England was by no means as thorough-going as that on the Continent and the Church of England (or Anglican Church) retains much pre-Reformation belief and liturgy. There are about 40 million Anglicans many of whom are to be found in the United States where they are called Episcopalians because, unlike some Continental churches, the Anglicans retained bishops (Greek, *episkopos* = bishop).

Since the Reformation in England did not go far enough for many people religious unrest tended to drag on for longer than it did on the Continent and many other branches of the Church were formed. John Bunyan (1628-88), the author of *Pilgrim's Progress* and of the hymn 'Who would true valour see', was an early Baptist who was often imprisoned for his beliefs. There are about 22 million Baptists. Another notable character was George Fox who founded the Society of Friends (Quakers) after being 'moved to sound the day of the Lord' on Pendle Hill in 1652. The Friends were called Quakers because it was thought that Fox 'quaked' before God.

The last important Non-conformist church to be founded in England was the Methodist Church which has about 18 million followers. The organizer of Methodism was John Wesley (1703-91) who never wanted to break with Anglicanism and urged his lay preachers and followers to 'be Church of England men still'. For fifty years Wesley travelled about England on horseback and preached to great crowds in the open air. He is said to have travelled some 250,000 miles and preached 40,000 sermons. His day's work began at the crack of dawn so that he could preach to factory workers on their way to work.

Disturbed by the Reformation, the Roman Catholic Church was moved to carry out her own internal reformation and this movement is usually referred to as the Counter Reformation. The Council of Trent (held at Trento in N. Italy, December 1545 to December 1563) cleared up points of doctrine and is still looked back to as authoritative. The Society of Jesus (Jesuits) was founded by Ignatius Loyola (1491-1556) who, after service as a soldier, became a student at Paris University where many were attracted by his religious teaching. His friends became known as the Society of Jesus. He organized his Society along military lines with stern discipline and wrote a manual of discipline called *Spiritual Exercises*. His movement won back many to the Catholic faith and did much to hinder the spread of Protestantism. The Jesuits became valiant missionaries and, as a result of their love of scholarship, they founded some excellent schools.

Today it is often claimed that the Christian religion plays no vital part in civilized society but this would appear not to be the case.

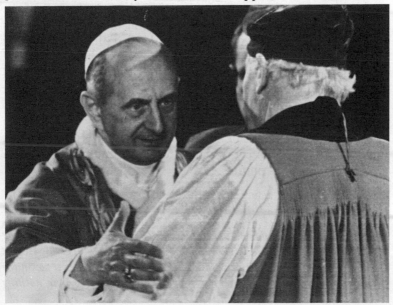

Pope Paul VI and the Archbishop of Canterbury embrace in a symbolic kiss of peace

There is in fact great activity among Christians in an attempt to reason out old differences and discuss together the possibility of unity. In the past the differences between the various branches of the Christian Church have often led to misunderstanding and even abuse. More recently, however, there has been a move towards greater understanding between the denominations. In 1948 the World Council of Churches was founded in Amsterdam. Pope John XXIII at his Vatican Council II showed that the Roman Catholic Church was prepared to welcome and talk on equal terms with Protestants. There is much greater friendship within orthodox Christianity than there was in the past. This does not mean that denominational barriers will be overlooked and one Church emerge: doctrinal and liturgical differences will persist but the tendency is towards constructive dialogue rather than, as previously, arguments which have only highlighted and widened the different points of view. This *ecumenical movement*, as it is called, is frowned upon by some denominations who see it as a move back to Rome and therefore a going back on the benefits derived from the Reformation.

Ecumenicalism is also perhaps part of the defence mechanism of the churches whose members are only too well aware of the intrinsic weakness of religious life in an age of growing secularity. Unity of some kind is essential, it is felt, if the witness of the churches is to be effective. In the face of Christian disunity what is needed is a new Reformation. Some of the most significant theologians of the twentieth century have, from the standpoint of theology, been as effective as Luther and Calvin, but what they have had to say has not really created a new religious situation, a new Reformation. The disunity of the Christian churches challenges Christianity to a radical re-shaping. Even the Roman Catholic Church recognizes that it must take to heart the criticisms levelled against it and that it must set its sights on what Pope John XXIII described as *aggiornamento* (renewal). But it is difficult to envisage that from ecumenical talk alone this renewal will come about. As one member of the World Council of Churches put it:

> *If somebody has sufficient courage to make a study of cynicism, he should buy the reports of all major ecumenical gatherings, read them, and see what the churches said together. Then he should go to the balcony of his house and look over his city at the churches that are standing there, from which steeples have risen to heaven since the Middle Ages, and see how nothing has happened to them.*[1]

[1] Albert van den Heuvel, *The Humiliation of the Church* (Philadelphia, 1966), p. 51.

Protestant theology has been uncompromising in the analysis of religious presuppositions. It has also developed the critical study of the bible. Since the tenets of the Christian religion are all important for the Christian estimate of man and of the meaning of life it is vital that the Christian assumptions should be constantly under review and that intellectual dishonesty be avoided at all cost.

The Evangelical wing of Christianity views 'modern' theology with great suspicion and sees in it an attempt to break away from biblical concepts: most Evangelicals believe that the bible is inspired by God and that truth is therefore to be found in it. Many theologians, on the other hand, insist that the same methods of critical scholarship should be applied to the bible as to any other ancient literature. Rudolf Bultmann, for example, regards the language of the New Testament as that of 'myth'. As used by theologians 'myth' is a technical word: a myth is a story which has no foundation in history but is used to communicate what the myth-teller believes to be the truth about man in his relationship with God.

Some radical theologians find it necessary to reject the concept of God (Bonhoeffer, van Buren, Altizer) and represent the movement which is commonly referred to as the 'death of God' theology. The tremendous advances in theology indicate that the Christian religion can still hold its own, albeit divorced from orthodoxy, at the intellectual level. On the other hand, some who call themselves Christians can find chapter and verse in the bible in favour of racial discrimination. Christianity has produced the good and the bad; and if it has been reactionary it has also produced social change and egalitarianism.

THE ROMAN CATHOLIC CHURCH

Since the majority of Christians are members of the Roman Catholic Church (about 400 million) we shall here examine briefly some of the basic beliefs of that communion. The term 'Roman Catholic' is really a post-Reformation title, for before that event Christians were either Catholic or Orthodox. Catholicism emphasizes the importance of tradition: Catholics believe that truth is to be found in the Christian beliefs and practices which have been handed down from the early days and that these beliefs are useful for the interpretation of scripture. The Pope, Christ's representative on earth and the successor of Peter, expounds and perpetuates the tradition. At times it is necessary for him to make a pronouncement which is considered to be authoritative and therefore to be accepted by all Catholics. When he speaks thus, on a subject regarding the faith and doctrine of the whole Church, he is infallible and the statement he makes is *ex cathedra* (from the chair—the seat of authority). The Pope is infallible only when he speaks *ex cathedra*. When an *ex cathedra* statement has been made it is binding on all Catholics and is irrevocable. Unless the Pope speaks *ex cathedra* he is merely expressing his own opinion. For example, it is not true to say that Catholics cannot practise birth control for no *ex cathedra* statement has ever been made on the subject. It is true to say, however, that conservative Catholicism certainly regards birth control as contrary to the natural law of God: i.e. contraceptive devices frustrate the purpose of God for the sex act is primarily the means of procreation and the purpose of Christian marriage is to raise a Christian family. In 1968 the encyclical *Humanae Vitae* made the Pope's position quite clear. The Popes have, in general, tended towards conservatism but many Catholics nowadays are quite prepared to question the personal decisions of the Pope.

> *The right of the Pope to make decisions such as that promulgated in* Humanae Vitae, *regardless of the advice of those better equipped by study and experience to form a judgment, has been firmly challenged. The question 'Who makes the decisions?' has become acute. The new emphasis on the collegiality of bishops cannot but alter the primacy of the Papacy, as the curial conservative sees only too clearly. The Holy Father, far from being a figure affording certitude in a changing world, has found his own role under question.*[1]

The three main divisions within the hierarchy of the Catholic Church are the Pope, the bishops and the priests. The claims of the ministry rely upon the authority which Jesus vested in his apostles, for example, 'If you forgive any man's sins, they stand forgiven; if you pronounce them unforgiven, unforgiven they remain' (John 20:23), and in particular upon his promise to Peter, the first Pope: 'You are Peter, the Rock; and on this rock I will build my church, and the forces of death shall never overpower it' (Matthew 16:18). Each Pope has been regarded as the successor of Peter and there is evidence for this belief from the fourth century. Priests are also the successors of the first apostles.

The life of Christ is conveyed to the believer by means of this hierarchical arrangement of Pope, bishops and priests and it is conveyed in particular by means of the *Seven Sacraments* which the clergy dispense. These are Baptism, Confirmation, Eucharist (the

[1] Kenneth Slack, *The British Churches Today* (S.C.M.P., 1970), p. 79.

Mass, Holy Communion), Absolution (forgiveness of sins), Extreme Unction (the anointing of the sick with oil), Ordination (to the priesthood) and Matrimony. (Generally speaking, the Protestant churches accept only two sacraments—baptism and the eucharist—whereas Quakers and the Salvation Army accept none.) By means of these Seven Sacraments sanctifying grace is imparted to the believer. Other religious rites and acts of devotion are referred to as *sacramentals*. Sacraments were instituted by Jesus (although there is no agreement as to when Confirmation, Extreme Unction and Matrimony were instituted) whereas sacramentals, while very worthwhile, were not so instituted and consequently are regarded as of less significance. For example, making the sign of the cross or reciting the rosary are considered to be sacramentals. Sacramentals are a great help in that they enable the believer to overcome sin and remove its consequences but sacraments are the means by which grace is given. The sacraments do not, however, convey grace to the recipient if he does not approach them in an appropriately devout state of mind. Sin or lack of faith will prevent him from receiving any benefit of grace and for him the sacrament is not efficacious. Acts which deprive the individual of sanctifying grace are known as *mortal sin* for if one dies in a state of mortal sin one will suffer eternal damnation. (*Venial sin* is less grave in that it does not entirely deprive the soul of sanctifying grace.) This is why the sacrament of Absolution (penance) is so important for, having confessed his sins to the priest, who has Christ's authority to forgive, and performed the prescribed penance (e.g. making good any harm he has done, saying certain prayers) and having resolved to avoid sin in the future, the believer is restored to a state of grace: he can now attend Mass and receive sanctifying grace. It is through the Eucharist that sanctifying grace is primarily conveyed and Catholics are encouraged to attend Mass as often as possible. The presence of Christ in the bread and wine on the altar recalls powerfully for the Catholic how God became flesh in Jesus and the Eucharist is regarded as a bloodless renewal of the sacrifice of Calvary.

THE VIRGIN AND THE SAINTS

When Mary, the mother of Jesus, visited Elizabeth, the mother of John the Baptist, Elizabeth was 'filled with the Holy Spirit and cried aloud, "God's blessing is on you above all women, and his blessing is on the fruit of your womb. Who am I, that the mother of my Lord should visit me?" ' (Luke 1:41-2). Mary remains the greatest saint of the Christian Church. Roman Catholics refer to her as 'Mother of God' (*theotokos*) and the *Ave Maria* (*Hail Mary*)—based on the salutations of Gabriel (Luke 1:28) and Elizabeth (Luke 1:42)— is said every day by both Orthodox and Catholic Christians. It has been used by Catholics in the following form since 1568 but a shorter form was popular from the eleventh century:

> *Hail Mary full of grace, the Lord is with thee:*
> *Blessed art thou among women and blessed is the fruit of thy womb, Jesus.*
> *Holy Mary, Mother of God; pray for us sinners now and in the hour of our death.*

Since Mary is 'Mother of God' she could not have been born prone to sin as are all other human beings: that is, she was born without *original sin*:

> *From the first moment of her conception the Blessed Virgin Mary was, by the singular grace and privilege of Almighty God, and in view of the merits of Jesus Christ, Saviour of mankind, kept free from all stain of original sin.*[1]

The Bull *Ineffabilis Deus* constitutes the doctrine of the Immaculate Conception of the Blessed Virgin Mary, belief in which is binding upon all Catholics. Although the *ex cathedra* statement was made in 1854 the doctrine of the Immaculate Conception was adhered to by the majority of Catholics from the sixteenth century and by individuals long before that. The Feast of the Immaculate Conception is celebrated on 8th December.

A further belief is that when her earthly life was over, the Blessed Virgin was assumed, body and soul, into the glory of heaven. Early formulations of this doctrine of the Corporeal Assumption date back to the sixth century but the *ex cathedra* pronouncement was not made until 1950 by Pope Pius XII in his *Munificentissimus Deus* (1st November, 1950).

In 1858 the Blessed Virgin appeared in visions to Bernadette Soubirous at Lourdes in the south of France. Lourdes has now become a famous pilgrimage centre for the sick and numerous healings have been authenticated.

Catholics also refer affectionately to the Virgin as 'our Lady'. Protestants reject the doctrines of the Immaculate Conception and the Assumption as quite unscriptural.

A further feature of the religious life of the Roman Catholic Church is devotion to saints. This practice arose during the second

[1] Bull *Ineffabilis Deus* of Pope Pius IX (8th December, 1854).

century when many Christians were martyred for the faith. It was customary for Christians to celebrate the death of martyrs and to collect their relics. Also, those who had withstood persecution for the sake of their religion were regarded as having special intercessory powers after death. The prayer of the saints was considered extremely valuable in that their virtuous lives made their petitions to God more effective than those of ordinary men. There should be no element of idolatry in the veneration of saints for the worship of God is qualitatively distinguishable from devotion to saints. The (aints receive *dulia* (homage); to the Blessed Virgin *hyperdulia* sspecial homage) is due; but God alone receives *latria* (worship).

During the Middle Ages the importance of the saints became somewhat exaggerated and their veneration a matter of superstition. This encouraged the Bogomiles, a Bulgarian sect, and the Waldensians, a movement founded by Peter Waldo of Lyons in the thirteenth century, to speak against prayer to the saints. At the Reformation the practice was fiercely condemned by the Zwinglians and Calvinists because it was not advocated in scripture. The Church of England also rejected many festivals of saints while retaining some of the more important ones. Generally, the Protestant churches do not advocate prayer to the saints.

WORSHIP

On entering a Roman Catholic church one sees at the east end the high altar which is the focal point of all activities (except baptisms). Six candles are arranged behind the altar—three on either side of a crucifix and often a statue of Christ. A small box, called a tabernacle, contains consecrated wafers (the body of Christ). The tabernacle is situated either on the high altar or to the side. In large churches there are also side chapels, each with its own altar. These are used when the congregation is small. Sometimes the 'reserved sacrament' is kept in a tabernacle in a side chapel rather than on the high altar. A red lamp indicates the presence of the reserved sacrament. When the sacrament is present Catholics genuflect (bow the knee) as an act of reverence: Christ himself is there. Sometimes a larger consecrated wafer (Host) is actually exposed for veneration in a *monstrance*, a special receptacle with a glass window. When this is the case the faithful must kneel.

Statues of various saints may be seen: these are not worshipped but aid men and women in focussing their attention upon the saint in prayer. Votive candles are often lit in honour of the Virgin and saints who will pray for the souls of the departed in purgatory, that place where the impure soul must be cleansed before it can stand before God; with this aid the departed may all the sooner be in God's presence. The impure soul cannot endure the divine presence.

Around the walls are fourteen pictures of the various stages in Jesus' journey to Calvary where he was crucified: they are called *stations of the cross*. Also there are one or two confessional booths where the priest listens to the confession of the Catholic from behind a screen and grants absolution.

The official language of the Roman Catholic Church is of course Latin but nowadays Mass is celebrated in the vernacular. The priest who performs the eucharistic rite (the Mass—usually called Holy Communion by Protestants) is called the *celebrant*. At Low Mass, which is usually said, the celebrant alone officiates, helped by a server; but at High Mass, which is usually sung, there are, in addition to servers, three ministers—the priest (celebrant), deacon and subdeacon. The Mass begins with an assertion of belief in the trinity: *In the name of the Father, and of the Son, and of the Holy Spirit*. In saying this everyone present makes the sign of the cross. The celebrant and his two assistants say a psalm after which comes the confession. Up to this point the congregation have been kneeling. They now stand for the *Kyrie eleison* which is a Greek prayer of great antiquity—'Lord have mercy'. At High Mass this is sung. The *thurible* (incense burner) is swung round the altar and then all sing the *Gloria in excelsis Deo* (Glory be to God on high); the congregation then sit while the subdeacon chants the epistle for the day, after which the deacon chants the appropriate gospel passage. After the gospel comes the singing of the Nicene Creed which is a lengthier and fuller statement of Christian orthodoxy than that of the Apostles' Creed cited on p. 36.

The celebrant now arranges the *paten* (plate for the wafers) and the *chalice* (cup for the wine). Everyone kneels. These utensils are blessed and the thurible is swung round them. Preparation is made for the consecration of the bread and wine by singing the *Sanctus* (Holy). The *tintinnabulum* (bell) is sounded three times so that everyone is aware of what is about to occur on the altar—Christ's very presence in the form of bread and wine. As the celebrant spreads his hands over the bread and wine the tintinnabulum is rung again. He reads aloud the gospel account of how Jesus instituted the Mass (the Last Supper). He kneels and lifts above his head a large wafer so that all the congregation can see and the tintinnabulum is rung three times. Everyone makes the sign of the cross. The celebrant

The Mass being celebrated in a Roman Catholic cathedral

breaks the large wafer over the chalice of wine into which he drops a small piece. He then consumes this wafer and the wine. Members of the congregation who wish to communicate stand up and go to the altar rail where they kneel and wait for the priest to give them one of the smaller wafers: he puts it on the tongue so that there is no chance of it falling to the floor. With the exception of the bride and groom at a Nuptial Mass the priest alone consumes the wine: the risk of spilling it would be too great were he to present the chalice to the faithful. It must be remembered that Roman Catholics believe in transubstantiation: the bread and wine are the body and blood of Christ. After all have communicated the priest and deacon cleanse the paten and chalice and the Mass ends with the reading of the prologue to John's gospel.

Catholics are bound to attend Mass every Sunday and on Holy Days of Obligation and should communicate at least once a year, at Easter or thereabouts.

The Sunday worship of the Protestant or Free Churches is generally far less colourful than the Roman Catholic Mass. The Roman Catholic priest wears eucharistic vestments (different colours for the various liturgical seasons) whereas the Free Church minister will usually wear a black gown. Also, the design of Nonconformist chapels makes for simplicity: the object of attention is the pulpit and bible and the communion table (not called an altar) is small and is clearly not of such importance as the high altar in a Roman Catholic church. The emphasis of Free Church theology is unmistakably indicated by the design of the chapel: it is preaching and the word of God.

Anglican churches differ appreciably among themselves as to how High (more like the Roman Catholic services) or how Low (more like the Non-conformist services) they are. The content of the services, however, is much the same.

Common to virtually all Christian denominations is the *Lord's Prayer* which was taught by Jesus to the apostles. In the New Testament it is given in two forms: Matthew 6:9-13 and Luke 11:2-4.

CHRISTIAN FESTIVALS

The Christian calendar begins with *Advent*, the preparation for the coming of Christ, which lasts for four Sundays prior to *Christmas*. This important festival commemorates the birth of Jesus and is celebrated on 25th December. On 6th January the feast of the *Epiphany* is celebrated: this marks the 'showing forth' of Christ to the Gentiles.

Lent, the period which recalls the forty days spent by Jesus in the wilderness, begins forty days before *Easter*: traditionally it is a time for penance, especially on *Shrove Tuesday* and *Ash Wednesday*. The Sunday before *Easter* is called *Palm Sunday* which commemorates the triumphal entry of Jesus into Jerusalem when the crowds carpeted his way with palm branches. Five days later comes *Good Friday*, the day of Jesus' crucifixion. This time of grief is followed two days later by *Easter*, the joyous festival of the resurrection. Forty days after Easter comes *Ascension Day* which is one of the major feasts of the Christian year. In his ascension the Christ reassumes the glory that was his before his incarnation. It is an affirmation of the belief that Jesus is God.

The next important event is *Whit Sunday* which recalls how the Holy Spirit came upon the 120 Christians in Jerusalem (Acts 2). Then comes *Trinity Sunday*, usually a time for ordination to the Christian ministry; the Sundays from Trinity Sunday to Advent are numbered according to the week; i.e. the second Sunday after Trinity, and so on.

CHRISTIANITY AND JUDAISM

The Christian Church has always thought of itself as the true Israel, the community which has inherited the promises of Yahweh to the old Israel. Christianity is descended from pre-Christian Judaism. Jesus was a Jew and, as might be expected, most of his sayings are thoroughly Jewish in character. Christianity also kept the Jewish scriptures (the Old Testament). The religion of the Christ became, and still is, the transmitter of Hebraic ideals to the world at large.

The Christian Church is indebted to Judaism for some of its festivals: Sabbath—Sunday; Passover—Easter; Pentecost—Whitsuntide. Christian liturgy has been greatly influenced by the synagogues which were the precursors of Christian churches.

SECTS

In recent times a number of new sects have grown up, mostly in the United States, and have attracted considerable attention. A study of the sects is most interesting both for the student of religion and for the sociologist. We here restrict ourselves to two sects, American in origin, with which the reader is likely to come into contact.

JEHOVAH'S WITNESSES

The founder of the Jehovah's Witness movement was Charles Taze Russell (1852-1916). His parents were Irish Calvinists and members of the Presbyterian Church. However, Russell was not happy about the doctrines of orthodox Protestantism. He was convinced that the bible was the inspired word of God in the fullest sense possible and that all the various denominations were untrue to the bible teaching. So Russell began to hold his own bible classes. These classes were the first gatherings of the Jehovah's Witnesses. Russell and his followers rejected so much of orthodoxy that he founded his own denomination. The movement spread rapidly in the United States, has flourished in Britain since 1880, and is now world-wide.

The doctrine of the Jehovah's Witnesses distinguishes them sharply from main-stream Christianity. First of all Jehovah (i.e. God—Yahweh) created his Son, Jesus, 'the faithful and true *witness*, the beginning of the creation by God' (Revelation 3:14). Before Jehovah's Son came to this earth he was called the *Word* or *Logos* (Greek) of God and was responsible for the whole creation. Jehovah created his Son but the Son created everything else (John 1:1-3). Jesus, because he was created by Jehovah, cannot be equal to his Father. This is where the Jehovah's Witnesses differ from orthodox Christianity. Whereas for orthodox Christians Jesus is God, for Jehovah's Witnesses Jesus is a god, but not sharing the nature of Jehovah God. Jesus never claimed to be equal to God: 'I cannot do a single thing of my own initiative' (John 5:30): 'The Father is greater than I am' (John 14:28). Jehovah is the only true God: his Son is to be followed. The Holy Spirit is the *active force* of God and is not in any sense personal. Jehovah's Witnesses reject as quite unscriptural the orthodox doctrine of the trinity.

The first man, Adam, was formed out of the dust of the ground and when God had breathed into him the breath of life he *became* a living soul. He did not receive an immortal soul: and the bible teaches that man will surely die. After death there is no continued existence: the popular idea of heaven and hell is unscriptural.

Adam and Eve disobeyed God but Jehovah has always had his faithful witnesses on earth who will one day receive eternal life even though at present they are dead. To bring about the state whereby eternal life might be obtained Jehovah sent his Son to earth to give his life in exchange for many lives and to point to the fact that God's kingdom is about to be established here. Because Jesus lived a perfect life and was obedient to his Father, Jehovah raised him from the dead and exalted him above all others.

Since the Day of Pentecost (see Acts 2) Jehovah has been selecting 144,000 witnesses: these will reign in heaven with Christ for a thousand years. They are referred to as the 'little flock'. Jehovah's Witnesses believe that 1975 marks the beginning of the thousand-year reign of Christ: Christ and the 'little flock' constitute the Kingdom Government. Every year on 14th Nisan (the Jewish Passover) Jehovah's Witnesses assemble in their respective meeting places (Kingdom Hall) for the *Memorial of Christ's Death*. The emblems of the body and blood of Christ are passed round but only those who feel sure that they are numbered among the 'little flock' of 144,000 may consume them. Christ is already reigning in heaven with the rest of the 'little flock'. When the time comes the remnant of the 144,000 left on earth will be raised to heaven and the thousand-year reign will begin. At the end of the thousand-year period Christ will hand back the reign to Jehovah.

The 'little flock' who go to heaven are not the only ones to receive salvation, however. Jesus spoke of his 'other sheep' (John 10:16) and the book of Revelation mentions a 'great crowd' (Revelation 7:9) who will be resurrected physically here on earth and over whom the Kingdom Government will reign. The 'great crowd' will reign upon the earth as subjects of Christ and his 'little flock'. Those who have been selected to be among the 144,000 are aware of the fact while still living here on earth. Men and women who died before Christ will not be among that number but they will, if they were faithful Witnesses of Jehovah, be among the 'great crowd' who will have eternal life on earth. They will, when the time comes, be resurrected on the earth for at present they are non-existent: the soul does not exist apart from the body.

The Witnesses believe that Christ returned in a spiritual sense in 1914. His presence is not to be detected in the sense that all things become perfect for he foretold that when the parousia occurred and the Kingdom Government began to reign there would be total war. 'Nation will rise up against nation and kingdom against kingdom, and there will be food shortages and earthquakes in one place after another' (Matthew 24:7). Since 1914, say the Witnesses, these things have happened. Another sign of the last days would be lawlessness (Matthew 24:12). All these things, it is said, are undeniably with us today. Jesus said that there would be people who would see all these things, i.e. the events which have taken place since 1914 (Matthew 24:33). In other words, persons alive in 1914 will see the end of the world as it now is. For those who are rejected there will be no resurrection of any kind. The battle of Armageddon is about to take place when Jehovah will utterly destroy all wicked persons and institutions. The adherents of all religions which do not teach what the bible teaches will be destroyed. Faithful Witnesses of Jehovah will live through the battle and the 'great crowd' of believers will be resurrected. The remnant of the 'little flock' will be taken from the earth to reign in heaven with Christ. The 'church' comprises the 144,000 and the term is wrongly used by orthodox Christianity.

Jehovah's Witnesses object to the use of crosses, crucifixes and all religious images for there is no indication that the earliest Christians used these things. There are no such persons as 'saints' in the sense

A mass baptism of Jehovah's Witnesses

of 'spirits of the dead' for the human soul is not immortal. Jesus did not command his followers to celebrate his birth and resurrection; he commanded them to observe only a memorial of his death. For this reason, and because of the secular nature of Christmas and Easter, Jehovah's Witnesses do not keep these festivals. In fact all celebrations which are not enjoined by scripture are frowned upon, for example, Jehovah's Witnesses do not celebrate birthdays.

The bible teaches that animal flesh may be eaten but not the blood (Genesis 9:3-4). Jehovah's Witnesses believe that this law is for Christians too (Acts 15:28-9). Any animal that is to be consumed must first be bled. Human beings are not allowed to have blood transfusions since a true worshipper of God must keep himself free from blood.

All Jehovah's Witnesses must in some way take part in preaching the kingdom. Since the end of the present order of things is very near the work is all the more urgent. Following the New Testament pattern (Luke 8:1; 10:1-6) the Witnesses visit people in their homes and make personal contact. Those who have dedicated their lives to Jehovah make their decision a public matter by being baptized (total immersion).

THE CHURCH OF JESUS CHRIST OF LATTER-DAY SAINTS

The Church of Jesus Christ of Latter-day Saints was founded in 1830 by Joseph Smith II (1805-44). As a boy Smith was in great confusion as to which Protestant denomination he should attach himself to and was on the verge of becoming a Methodist when he became the recipient of a unique experience of the divine. Alone in the woods, Smith was 'seized upon by some power' which quite overcame him. He then saw 'two Personages whose brightness and glory defy all description. . . . One of them spake unto me, calling me by name, and said, pointing to the other—"This is my Beloved Son, hear Him!" ' Smith was told that none of the denominations were right and that he must not join up with any of them.

In 1823 Smith was visited in his room by 'a messenger sent from the presence of God' called Moroni. Moroni instructed Smith that God had a particular task for him to perform. 'He said there was a book deposited, written upon gold plates, giving an account of the former inhabitants of this continent, and the source from whence they sprang. He also said that the fulness of the everlasting Gospel was contained in it as delivered by the Saviour to the ancient inhabitants.' In order to read the plates, which were written in an unknown language (Reformed Egyptian—of which Egyptologists have no knowledge), Smith was provided with 'two stones in silver bows' called Urim and Thummim (Exodus 28:30). With the aid of these divine spectacles he was able to translate the plates and in 1830 *The Book of Mormon* was published. It is from this book that the Latter-day Saints derived their nickname of *Mormons*.

The history which Smith translated told of the descendants of a family which had fled from Jerusalem during the reign of Zedekiah when the city was captured by the Babylonians (c. 586 B.C.). The father, Lehi, built a ship and he and his family sailed to America. From those who landed in the New World two nations were born: the Nephites and the Lamanites. After his ascension Christ visited the Nephites who followed his teachings for many years but as time went on the Nephites forsook God. One of the prophets at this time was Mormon who was keeper of the chronicles of the nation. Mormon prepared an abridged version of the history of his people on gold plates (*The Book of Mormon*) which he bequeathed to his son, Moroni, who survived the annihilation of the Nephites by the Lamanites in A.D. 421. The American Indians of today are said to be the descendants of the Lamanites.

Mormons claim that their Church is not an offshoot from the Protestant churches: it is in fact the Restored Gospel of Jesus Christ. They believe in God as Father, in Jesus Christ as his Son and in the Holy Ghost. God is like a man in appearance and is literally flesh and blood (as in Joseph Smith's vision). He is personal, has spoken to man and still speaks through his Prophet (the President of the Mormon Church). The Father, Son and Holy Ghost are

The Mormon Temple, Salt Lake City

not of the same substance but three quite distinct individuals. Jesus
Christ is God's Son:

> *begotten in the flesh. He lived, died, and was resurrected in a
> literal sense as the New Testament recounts. He was the Saviour
> and Redeemer of men according to the plan formulated before
> the world was created. He yet lives, a being of distinct form
> and personality. The Holy Ghost is a personage of spirit, yet
> nonetheless an individual personality.*[1]

Together these three distinct and individual 'personages' constitute
deity.

God is ultimately concerned for the well-being of man, his greatest creation. Man has free will to choose as he pleases and God does
not force his attention upon him. Mormons believe in the immortality of the soul. The soul exists before entering into a human
body and life on earth is only a temporary sojourn. In the next life
there will still be room for improvement: there is no static idea of
heaven. There is no notion of eternal punishment in hell. Those

[1] *What of the Mormons?* (Church of Jesus Christ of Latter-day Saints, Salt Lake
City, Utah), p. 6.

who have died ignorant of the teachings of Joseph Smith may be baptized by proxy. For example, a Mormon will try to find out the names of his ancestors from registers and birth certificates and, assuming that had they known Smith's teaching they would have responded to it, he is baptized on their behalf. (The New Testament evidence for this practice is said to be I Corinthians 15:29—'There are those who receive baptism on behalf of the dead. Why should they do this? If the dead are not raised to life at all, what do they mean by being baptized on their behalf?')

Mormons believe in the Old Testament and the New Testament as the inspired word of God. However, since men cannot agree as to its meaning it is obvious that the bible is not in itself sufficient. The Latter-day Saints have three books which supplement the bible: *The Book of Mormon*, *The Doctrine of Covenants*, and *The Pearl of Great Price*. It is claimed that these three in no way contradict the bible.

No money is collected at the Mormon meetings but every Latter-day Saint is expected to contribute one tenth of his income to the Church as outlined in the Old Testament. Apart from this the first Sunday of each month is a fast day and Mormons contribute the cost of two meals for charitable purposes. Products which are harmful to health are to be avoided. This includes such things as alcohol, tobacco, meat in excessive amounts, tea and coffee (caffeine).

Many young men have left home to become Mormon missionaries in foreign lands. The usual period of missionary service is two years. The Mormons visit potential converts in their own homes and it is no doubt largely due to this personal contact that the faith is spreading in many parts of the world. Generally speaking, it is true to say that the missionaries are tenacious but do not force themselves on people.

Why I am a Christian

I am a Christian because in the historical figure of Jesus of Nazareth I believe that I have found a satisfactory answer to the problems of the meaning of life. The existence of God is not a question which I have been able to solve. I feel that there is that which is other than man, which is transcendent and that this should have relevance to my own situation. These statements are not easy, and have not been said easily, being the barest outline of a number of years of thought and study which have culminated in an act of faith.

It seems to me that in Jesus of Nazareth there is a revelation of the nature of God, which makes it possible for me to see the relevance of the transcendent as stated in the last paragraph. Jesus' teaching seems ethically to be the best way for mankind, and his life seems to show the way of God. Therefore I have committed myself to this way of life as distinct from any other and say that I believe in Jesus as the Son of God. The company of people who by similar and dissimilar routes have been able to share this commitment make up the Church. We have found ourselves linked together in a mysterious liaison which led us to be called the body of Christ—a metaphor which is best interpreted literally! To this body one shows group loyalty, and to Christ, the Head, devotion. The purpose of all this (Christ and the Church) is to bring the whole created order to the knowledge of that which is other than we are, and yet is God our father.

Rev. P. Coates, B.D., M.Th.

Why I am a Catholic

On the level of biographical accident, I am a Catholic thanks to having been born to Catholic parents and educated in Catholic schools. But the real question, I take it, is why I have remained a Catholic in adult life and why I regard my allegiance to Catholicism as the most basic and important dimension of my life.

This much I can say: the sum total of my experience has tended, finally, to deepen my commitment to Catholicism. Partly, no doubt, this is because my own experience has supported a generically religious perspective and the religious perspective most familiar to me is Catholicism. To this extent I can well understand how a Jew might report the same thing: every experience confirms him in his Judaism. But, I also mean more. Not only has the sum total of my life confirmed me in a generically religious outlook, it has confirmed me in a specifically Christian and Catholic outlook. I find the New Testament believable in a unique way. If it is at all conceivable that God should take it on himself to offer a solution to the human dilemma—to mortality and absurdity, moral impotence and hopelessness—the gospels seem to me to offer the prize candidate, the best imaginable claim, to be that solution.

I do not think of Catholicism in an exclusivist way. The bonds that bind Christians are deeper than their divisions. But, not being indifferent to the divisions, I definitely wish to be Catholic. The reasons for this have to do mainly with the Catholic Church's unabashed, unambiguous acceptance of the whole heritage of historical Christianity.

I am critical of many institutional features of Catholicism and consider the Church to have often been obscurantist and reactionary. Perhaps some non-Catholics admire the Church more than I do, in a way. But when all is said and done, the Church doesn't call for admiration but for faith.

I think that Catholicism has a great mission: not to conquer the world or reign over it as in the High Middle Ages, but to illuminate man's misery and joy and memory and hope, to serve the world in a thousand ways; and in so doing to recognize its main allies—Judaism, for the recovery of the sense of God, and Protestantism for its recovery of the sense of salvation as a gift.

Anon

Why I am a Jehovah's Witness

A detailed study of the Bible produces the undisputable conclusion that it is the Word of the True God. Jehovah's Witnesses believe the Bible from Genesis to Revelation and genuinely love the God who wrote it. However, it goes further than belief, for faith is exercised in Christian works. What other religion exercises faith in the complete Word of God? (I Thessalonians 2:13). The Bible states that God's name, Jehovah, would be declared throughout the earth (Malachi 1:11). Who but Jehovah's Witnesses make known the name of God, even being called by His name (Isaiah 43:10-12)? The Bible, not Jehovah's Witnesses' views, is presented in their meetings and literature and their organizational procedure follows that of the first-century Christians.

These points amongst others convince me that this is the way God wants us to worship Him.

Doing God's will rather than one's own is demonstrated by the preaching and teaching done by all of Jehovah's Witnesses. Matthew 24:14 and Acts 20:20 show that followers of Jesus should do this work. Further, Jesus said in John 17:3 that we need to have knowledge of God and Jesus and we have five congregational meetings each week. Additionally, we study the Bible privately and with our families regularly.

We believe in being Christians twenty-four hours a day. By viewing God's Word as the highest authority, we refrain from things men may require when the two clash (Acts 5:29). Jesus said in John 13:35 that the true followers would have love among themselves. Jehovah's Witnesses will not kill one another by supporting man-made war (John 18:36). I, like many other Witnesses, went to prison rather than support the military, this being done in all countries. Jehovah's Witnesses are not pacifists as God Himself says he will destroy the wicked by war (Revelation 16:14-16). However, because we love our fellow men we want to avoid God's wrath and enjoy the blessings He has in store for those who serve Him. We firmly believe that this is the generation when Jehovah will act, therefore we want to help as many as possible to share our hope (Ezekiel 33:11; Matthew 24; Mark 13; Luke 21).

We have been severely criticized over our stand on obeying God's law regarding eating blood (Acts 15:20, 28-9; Genesis 9:4; Leviticus 17:14) which rules out blood transfusion. However, I have had three major operations, having transfusion of dextrose, without blood and have rapidly recovered. When my son was born prematurely and had difficulty to suck in his incubator, the doctors insisted a blood change was vital. However, having regard for God's law and wisdom, we refused. He is now in his fourth year, strong and healthy without having his blood changed.

Realizing Jehovah knows best, we, as parents, teach our children in religious instruction (Deuteronomy 6:7) and therefore we do not let our children attend religious education classes at school. In regard to God's view of false religion, we do not let them join in any other religious worship (Revelation 18:4). This, of course, applies to ourselves as we recognize there is only one true religion (Matthew 7:13, 14). Seeing that God's Word advocates family worship, Jehovah's Witnesses only marry in the faith (I Corinthians 7:39).

There is no doubt, being one of Jehovah's Witnesses causes changes in one's life—for the better. One is more content trusting in God (Psalm 55:22), honest, long-suffering and kind (Galations 5:22, 23).

Also, it brings one's family closer together, gives a purpose in life and causes one to be humble and obedient.

Jesus said our days would be like the days of Noah (Matthew 24: 37-9) and we remember the only ones who survived the flood were those who not only believed what God said but acted on it. Today, Jehovah's Witnesses recognize the only way to salvation is doing things God's way and unless people come out of false religion and serve Jehovah along with Jehovah's Witnesses, then they cannot receive God's protection; therefore, Jehovah's Witnesses could never join any interfaith movements.

The more I associate and witness the Bible principles being practised and the ever-growing numbers of Jehovah's Witnesses, the more convinced I am that here alone is God's spirit and blessing.

Mr Duncan Willrich
Presiding Minister
Kingdom Hall
Wrenthorpe
Wakefield

CHAPTER THREE

Islam

Islam is the latest of the world's great religions. It has approximately 450 million followers and originated in Arabia. Its founder was Muhammad (A.D. 570-632). The word 'Islam' means 'submission', that is, submission to the will of God, and its followers are called Muslims. Muslims do not like the Western habit of calling them Muhammadans or their religion Muhammadanism. Christians are so called because they worship Christ but Muslims do not worship Muhammad. It is also worth noting that although there are many ways of spelling the prophet's name the strictly correct one is *Muhammad*.

BACKGROUND

To understand Islam properly we must examine the background in Arabia at the time of Muhammad. It is easiest to look at this from three different aspects.

THE POLITICAL SITUATION

The early history of Arabia is clouded in mystery because of the difficulty of communication, the poverty of the land and because the extensive deserts kept it away from the main current of history.

Arabia was inhabited by warlike tribes who were constantly fighting with each other. The two empires of Byzantium in the north and Persia in the south had some influence in Arabia but it was not a conquered nation. There was little sense of unity amongst the Arabs but two events before Muhammad came to power stimulated the rise of patriotic feeling or nationalism. In A.D. 570 Abyssinia made an unsuccessful attempt to invade Arabia and take over the capital city of Mecca. For a brief time, until the danger had passed, the tribes of Arabia, particularly in Mecca, united in the face of a

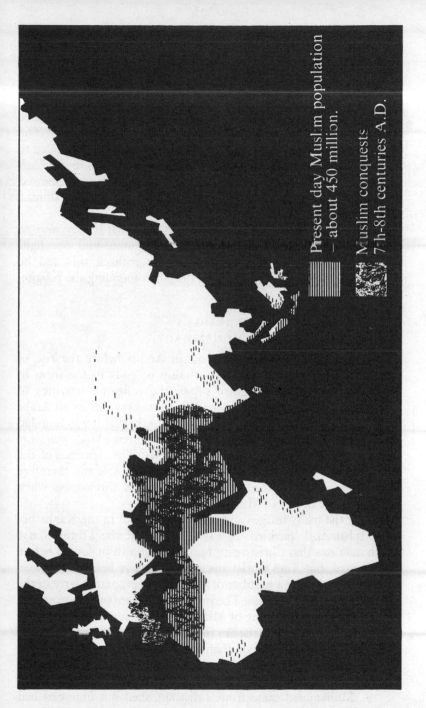

Present day Muslim population
– about 450 million.

Muslim conquests
7th-8th centuries A.D.

The world of Islam

common enemy, forgetting their differences. This demonstrated that the Arabs would unite in the right circumstances but it was not until Muhammad came along that they found the leader to accomplish this unity.

The other event took place in A.D. 610 when Uthman, a native Meccan, tried to rule Mecca and introduce Christianity. The Meccans resented this and drove him out whereupon he appealed to the Byzantine emperor who used force in an attempt to re-establish Uthman, who was eventually murdered. This incident again showed that the Arabs had latent patriotic feeling which Muhammad utilized later on.

The Arabs learned from these two incidents that if they were to be free of foreign domination they had to unite and not fight amongst themselves. Muhammad had also realized this and he appealed to the patriotism of the Arabs when founding the religion of Islam.

THE RELIGION OF ARABIA
AT THE TIME OF MUHAMMAD

The religion most prevalent in Arabia before the rise of Islam was idol worship, i.e. the worship of gods in the form of images. Mecca was the centre of all the religious activities of Arabia. It had a temple, the Kaaba, which was revered by all Arabs and it had a long history. Muslim tradition says that it was founded by Abraham. The god Allah, originally the supreme God, was worshipped there along with many other deities. The influence of the temple at Mecca over Arabian tribes was considerable and therefore Muhammad showed great practical insight and shrewdness when he made it the centre of Muslim worship.

Among the many images and idols to be found in the Kaaba before Muhammad 'purified' it was a picture of the Virgin Mary, which indicates that Christianity was not unknown in Arabia before Muhammad, but Arab Christians appear to have been very few in number. There were a number of Jews, however, particularly in the cities of Mecca and Medina. The influence of these two religions can be seen in the later teaching of Muhammad, most particularly in his condemnation of the polytheism (belief in many gods) of the Arabs and his stress on monotheism (belief in one god).

THE FAMILY BACKGROUND OF MUHAMMAD

Muhammad came from a distinguished but impoverished family. His grandfather was a powerful man in the city of Mecca where he was given the honour of keeping the key of the Kaaba and providing food and drink for the pilgrims. Muhammad's father died before Muhammad was born and his mother took him to Mecca where he lived with his grandfather. Shortly afterwards Muhammad's mother died, leaving him an orphan. After the death of his grandfather Muhammad lived with his uncle, Abu Talib, an influential man in Mecca. Hence, when Muhammad offended the Meccans by preaching against idol worship, Abu Talib protected him from their anger and prevented him from coming to harm.

The political and social influence of the family of Muhammad, together with their interest in the Kaaba, over which they had superintendence, were undoubtedly of help to Muhammad in his preaching and propagation of Islam.

THE LIFE OF MUHAMMAD

Muhammad is revered by Muslims as the greatest prophet of all but he is *not* worshipped by them. Some account of his life is helpful in a study of Islam.

As we have seen, Muhammad was orphaned at an early age and was looked after by his uncle, Abu Talib. He worked on the camel trains for a while and eventually married his employer, a rich widow named Khadija. His first religious experience came when he was about forty while meditating in a cave on Mount Hira during the annual religious retreat of all Arabs. An angel, later identified as Gabriel, appeared to him, ordered him to read a scroll and told him

The angel Gabriel appearing to Muhammad, from a 14th-century MS

that he was the 'apostle of God'. According to Muslim tradition, Muhammad was illiterate. When he told the angel that he could not read Gabriel repeated the command three times until Muhammad miraculously was able to recite by heart what is now sura 96 (*sura* is the Muslim name for a chapter. It begins:

> Recite: In the name of thy Lord who created, created man of a blood-clot. . . .

Muhammad was frightened by all this and rushed back to his wife to tell her about it. Khadija was very understanding and told him not to be afraid; she was later to become his first convert to Islam. For a time, however, Muhammad was very depressed and scared and even contemplated suicide, thinking he was mad. Re-assured by his wife, the depression soon passed and, at the command of the angel Gabriel, Muhammad began his first preaching in Mecca. Muhammad's message was 'There is but one God'; as the city was wholly given to idolatry this roused the hostility of the Meccans—particularly that of the chief tribe, the Quraish—and they sought to do him harm. Fortunately, he was protected by Abu Talib. Muhammad's first converts were his wife, his cousin Ali and Zaid, a slave who had been freed by Muhammad.

In A.D. 621 Khadija and Abu Talib died. Muhammad moved from Mecca to preach in the surrounding towns. He met with little success but did convert a number of pilgrims from Medina, the other large city of Arabia. These pilgrims returned to Medina where Muhammad's message spread rapidly. In A.D. 622 Muhammad migrated with his followers from Mecca to Medina. This is known as the *Hijra* (migration) and it is from this year that the Muslims date their calendar. This is because the Muslims realize that this particular year was the turning point for Muhammad and for Islam. The prophet was soon established in Medina and ruled the city.

Muhammad now began to receive revelations which urged the use of force to spread the faith of Islam. He therefore began to do battle against the unbelievers. The first battle was at Badr where the Quraish were defeated. Victory followed victory until, in A.D. 630, he marched against Mecca and took it easily. His first action was to ride round the Kaaba seven times on a white camel and call the people to prayer. He purified the Kaaba of all the idols and instituted the worship of the one invisible God, *Allah*.

Muhammad died shortly afterwards in A.D. 632, probably as a result of being poisoned. His successor as leader of the Muslims (known as a Caliph) was a man named Abu Bakr.

THE QUR'AN

The holy book of the Muslims, the equivalent of the Christian's bible, is the *Qur'an*. (The word means 'recitation' and is sometimes anglicized as *Koran*.) The Qur'an is said by Muslims to be a collection of the words spoken by the angel Gabriel to Muhammad. The Muslims believe that Allah himself was speaking through the angel Gabriel to Muhammad, therefore to the Muslim the Qur'an is in a very real sense the word of God.

Anyone who attempted to read an English translation of the Qur'an would probably find it very toilsome and boring. There are two reasons for this: firstly, in the original Arabic the Qur'an has a unique literary structure—a kind of rhymed prose which cannot be satisfactorily translated; secondly, the Qur'an has an awkward arrangement of suras (i.e. chapters): except for the first the suras are arranged from the longest to the shortest. It is generally agreed that the first revelations given to Muhammad are the shortest suras (whilst Muhammad was in Mecca A.D. 610-622); the longer ones

The first Qur'an ever printed in Mecca

belong to the Medinan period (A.D. 622-632). So it is better when reading the Qur'an to start with the first sura, then go to sura 114 and work backwards. The Meccan suras (the earlier ones) are concerned with judgment and repentance. The later Medinan suras are concerned more with everyday things such as marriage, divorce, usury, status of women, and so on.

The Qur'an was not immediately written down in the form of a book. In the lifetime of Muhammad some of the revelations were written down and others were preserved in the memories of those who were there. It was Zaid, Muhammad's faithful servant, who eventually collected together the material and compiled the Qur'an after the death of the prophet. The suras of the Qur'an are not known by numbers, as are the chapters of the bible, but by a name which indicates the content of the particular sura, e.g. 'The Opening' (first sura), 'Mary' (about Jesus and Mary), 'Repentance', 'Salvation', 'The Prophets'. English translations, however, usually number them for ease of reference.

JUDGMENT IN THE QUR'AN

The first revelations which came to Muhammad were concerned with the judgment of Allah upon those people who did not repent. Although the picture given in the Qur'an is not entirely consistent, the main outline is clear enough: the world will come to an end, men, restored to life, will come before Allah to be judged according to deeds done when alive, and so will be received into everlasting bliss or cast into everlasting torment. There are interesting similarities between the Qur'anic conception of the Judgment day and that of the Jews and Christians: the day of Judgment comes suddenly, it is heralded by the sound of a trumpet, a cosmic upheaval takes place—the sun is darkened and the stars fall. The idea of the resurrection is closely allied to that of St. Paul.

At the Judgment the books are opened, a man's account is handed to him, he is asked to read it and is judged according to his good or bad deeds; his belief or unbelief is also taken into account. Hell is variously described as 'the Hot Place', 'the Blaze', and 'the Fire'. The torments of the condemned are depicted with a great wealth of imagery. Paradise is described as 'the Garden' or sometimes just 'a garden', possibly an allusion to the garden of Eden. Here the blessed enjoy luxuries—they recline on couches eating fruit and drinking wine.

PREDESTINATION IN THE QUR'AN

Islam has been described as the most fatalistic of all religions because of its doctrine of predestination, i.e. that all that a man does is predetermined by God. The Qur'an teaches that whatever happens is for ever fixed and recorded in the 'tablets of eternity'. One of the reasons that the Muslims were such fearless fighters, and thus able to propagate their faith so quickly, was that Muhammad taught that caution in battle was of no avail because one would die anyway when the destined hour arrived.

THE ETHICS OF THE QUR'AN

1 The drinking of intoxicants is forbidden in the Qur'an.
2 Gambling is prohibited, as are all games which are subject to hazard or chance, e.g. cards, dice. Chess, however, is allowed as it is a game which depends on skill.
3 Usury—the lending of money for interest—is forbidden.
4 The ill-treatment of orphans is especially condemned in the Qur'an.
5 The Muslim is permitted by the Qur'an to have up to four wives, but they are to be treated with kindness and strict impartiality. If a man cannot treat them all alike then he is to keep to one; 'marry such women as seem good to you, two, three, four; but if you feel you will not be equitable, then only one . . .' (sura 4, verse 3).

THE IDEA OF 'HOLY WAR' (JIHAD)

The Qur'an does say that it is both necessary and right to fight to spread the faith of Islam: '. . . fight on until idolatry cease and the religion be God's alone. War is ordained even if it be irksome to you' (sura 22, verse 41). Although this was a major factor in the early expansion of Islam, 'Holy War' today is frowned upon, because Muslims realize that in the present world a 'Holy War' against a Western power is impossible. (Many Arabs think of manoeuvres against the State of Israel as 'Holy War', however.)

WOMEN IN THE QUR'AN

Although the Qur'an does not categorically forbid divorce, it allows it only as a last resort, and legal restrictions were instituted to keep the marriage bond intact, e.g. husbands are required in advance to set up a sizeable trust in the wife's name and in the event of divorce the entire sum goes to her.

The Qur'an presents marriage as a divine institution for the purpose of begetting children. Married life is 'an act of worship'. The actual marriage ceremony is not essentially religious in character: it is not conceived of sacramentally. Rather it is a contractual relationship: the contracting parties are not the bride and groom but the father or other male relative of each. No woman can be married without the consent of her father (or male next of kin). If she has no male relation then someone can act as a substitute. A Muslim man can marry a Jewish or a Christian woman (Jews and Christians are 'people of the book') but a Muslim woman can marry only a Muslim. Every woman must have a dowry. Very often she brings with her a great store of clothes and personal possessions including garments which belonged to her ancestors. A Muslim woman must keep her arms and legs covered.

A Muslim woman wearing the veil

Purdah is recommended in the Qur'an (sura 33, verse 59). Wives and daughters are to wear the veil when outside the house so that they will be safe from attack, but in sura 24, verse 31 women are not explicitly required to wear the veil so long as they are pure Muslims. In some places women are not allowed out of the home at all whereas in others purdah is not strictly adhered to and even wholly discarded. In Algeria there are towns where the woman is allowed two holes in her veil—for both eyes; but a few miles away they are only allowed one hole in the veil—for one eye. It all depends on the location. At Mecca women are veiled by one garment from head to foot. Women do not attend mosques. For them, it is said, the best mosque is the home.

THE FIVE PILLARS OF ISLAM

Arising out of the teaching of the Qur'an there are further principles which regulate the private life of the Muslim and his relationship with God. There are five major principles which the Muslims obey which are sometimes known as the Five Pillars of Islam.

1 Binding on all Muslims is the *Creed of Islam*. The creed consists of one sentence: 'There is no God but Allah and Muhammad is the prophet of Allah.' It is simple and yet it contains the heart of Muslim belief. The first phrase stresses the unity of God—there is only one God, Allah, who revealed himself to Muhammad. This was in direct opposition to the previous religion of Arabia—idol-worship—which had many gods. The second phrase stresses the uniqueness of Muhammad. He is *the* prophet, the one chosen by God to preach to the Arabs and eventually to the world. The Muslims call Muhammad 'the Seal of the Prophets', a phrase which means that Muhammad completed and embodied in himself the work of all previous prophets from Adam to Jesus. Yet although Muhammad is greatly revered he is *not* worshipped. At his death his successor, Abu Bakr, said, 'If there be any amongst you who worshipped Muhammad, he is dead. But if it is God you worship, he lives for ever'. So he quashed once and for all the idea that Muhammad might be divine.

2 The Muslim is urged to be constant in *Prayer*, the second Pillar of Islam. Muslims are required to pray five times daily—upon rising, at noon, in mid-afternoon, after sunset, and before retiring. Although Muslims do not have a Sunday like the Christians, they do meet on Fridays in the mosque for collective prayers and recitals of the Qur'an. When praying in the mosque Muslims must face the

direction of Mecca, and so that they are aware where this is, a niche (called a *mihrab*) is to be found in a wall of the mosque to indicate which way to face. The reason that all Muslims are asked to face one direction is so that in the realization that all Muslims are doing likewise the believer feels he is participating in a world-wide fellowship. When praying the Muslim must make sure that he is ritually clean, and he is required to wash his legs, knees, arms and face. The Muslim usually enters the mosque barefoot as a sign of humility. It is important to note, however, that a Muslim need not go to a mosque to pray but can pray anywhere.

During the act of prayer the Muslim must kneel down, prostrate himself, and then stand up again and repeat the process. As to the content of the prayer he must name God (usually the Muslim recites the phrase 'God is most great'), recite the first sura and then the rest of the prayer may be his own private thoughts.

3   The third Pillar of Islam is *Fasting*. The only fast obligatory on Muslims is in the month of Ramadan. It was at the end of this month, the ninth of the Muslim year, that the Qur'an is said to have been revealed in the Arabic language; previously the original Qur'an, 'the Mother of the Book', had existed only in the presence of Allah. The rule is that during the days of this month no food or drink is to pass the lips, but a Muslim may eat or drink after dark. Nevertheless, as the Muslim calendar is lunar, each month runs eventually through all the seasons of the solar year, so that when Ramadan falls during the summer the long, hot days make the fast very exacting for the Muslim. Certain Muslims are excused the fast —the aged and infirm, children before the age of puberty and pregnant women. Voluntary fasts are recommended by the Prophet especially on certain days of the month which are considered sacred.

4   *Almsgiving* (i.e. charity) is the fourth Pillar of Islam. There are

two types—voluntary and obligatory. The former is donated by the Muslim where he personally feels there is a need. The latter must be contributed by every Muslim as stated in the Qur'an. It is levied at a rate of about 2½% (1/40th) on income and certain kinds of property. The details of the assessment are very complicated and evasion is possible. Although in the early days of the prosperous Caliphate payment was insisted upon and collection of it was highly organized, the tendency now is to leave it to the conscience of the individual. The Qur'an specifies that the money is to be given to the poor, slaves anxious to purchase their freedom, debtors, travellers, etc. It is not to be used for the building or upkeep of mosques.

5   The last Pillar of Islam is *Pilgrimage*. It is obligatory that at least once in his life every Muslim should make a pilgrimage to Mecca. In practice, however, all Muslims do not manage the journey as the Qur'an makes the qualification 'if able to do so', thus exempting those financially or physically unable to make the trip. The details of what the Muslim must do during the pilgrimage are almost entirely taken over from the paganism of ancient Arabia. The three most important rites of the pilgrimage are: to wear the prescribed pilgrim garment—two white cotton cloths; on the ninth day of the pilgrimage the Muslim must stand on Mount Arafat; the Muslim must circle the Kaaba seven times and kiss the Black Stone. Many thousands of Muslims journey to Mecca from all over the world to observe the pilgrimage, and many find it an enriching experience to share fellowship with Muslims from different countries.

THE DEVELOPMENT OF ISLAM

After the death of Muhammad, Islam spread at an astonishing rate. To appreciate this one has only to consider the fact that

A Muslim in the act of praying

exactly a century later, in A.D. 732, the Muslims would have been masters of Europe had they not been defeated by Charles Martel at Tours. It was one of the most decisive battles in history and historians have often speculated what would have happened had the Muslims won: possibly the Qur'an would now be taught in our schools instead of the bible!

The successor of Muhammad was Abu Bakr. The leaders of the Muslims were now known as Caliphs and Abu Bakr was the first.

Chronological Chart of Caliphs

Muhammad	A.D. 570-632
Abu Bakr	A.D. 632-634
'Umar	A.D. 634-644
'Uthman	A.D. 644-656
'Ali	A.D. 656-661
Umayyad Caliphate	A.D. 661-750

(This was the beginning of the split between Shi'a and Sunni sects.)

On the accession of Abu Bakr there was a revolt by many of the Arabian tribes against Muslim authority. However, Abu Bakr refused to be panicked and, with his very able general, Khalid, restored order in a year. Under the rule of Abu Bakr the Arabs began invading and conquering the foreign territories of Syria, Byzantium and Persia. Byzantium and Persia were two main powers at this time but their power was beginning to wane and their forces were no match for the Muslim forces who were full of religious zeal and convinced that they were fighting a 'Holy War'.

Before he died Abu Bakr nominated 'Umar to succeed him. Under 'Umar, Islam went from strength to strength. Damascus was captured in A.D. 635 and Jerusalem in A.D. 637. The Persians were decisively beaten in A.D. 641 and the territory of Iraq fell to the Muslims. Egypt was also conquered by A.D. 641.

'Umar was assassinated in A.D. 644 and was succeeded by 'Uthman. Despite a troubled rule 'Uthman still extended the borders of Muslim rule to Afghanistan in the east and Tripoli in the west. 'Uthman was murdered by the rebellious tribe Umayyad who wished to seize power themselves.

'Ali, the cousin and son-in-law of Muhammad, succeeded 'Uthman but had a difficult reign. He tried to remove Mu'awiya, a prominent Umayyad, from the governorship of Syria. Mu'awiya resisted and civil war broke out. 'Ali was further troubled by a group of people known as the Kharijites who eventually decided to kill both 'Ali and

Mu'awiya. Mu'awiya was only injured and recovered but 'Ali was killed.

'Ali had two sons, Al Hasan and Al Husain. Al Hasan was proclaimed next Caliph but was more interested in the pursuit of pleasure than in the pursuit of power and he abdicated in favour of Mu'awiya. Thus began the Umayyad Caliphate. There was now a split in Islam between those who thought that the Caliph should be a direct descendant of Muhammad and those who would rather a member of the Umayyad tribe rule. Sympathy for the idea that a member of the dynasty of Muhammad should rule was stirred by the death of 'Ali's younger son Al-Husain, who, trying to seize power on the death of Mu'awiya, was brutally slain with his family. This is the origin of the Shi'a schism.

The history of Islam after this is somewhat tedious and complicated. Suffice it to say that Islam continued to spread—to North India, Africa and Spain—and that Constantinople fell to the Muslim Turks in 1453. As recently as 1683 Vienna was besieged by the Turks and only escaped capture as a result of the intervention of John Sobieski of Poland. After this date Muslim political power began to dwindle, although numerically they are still very strong and in all parts of the world.

SECTS IN ISLAM

There are many divisions within Islam, just as there are many divisions within Christianity. In Christianity the main division is between Catholics and Protestants, with the latter subdividing into other sects (e.g. Anglicans, Methodists, Baptists etc.). So also with Islam; there are the Sunnis, to which 80% of the Muslims belong, and the Shi'as, who subdivide into various groups, the most notable being the 'Seveners' and the 'Twelvers'. As the Sunnis are the 'orthodox' group it is perhaps best to see in what way the Shi'as differ from them than to give a detailed account of what they believe in.

The Shi'as are, as we have seen, the followers of 'Ali, the son-in-law and cousin of Muhammad. They believe that 'Ali was the first legitimate Caliph and that the succession was through his descendants. They prefer to call their leaders Imams (rather than Caliphs), a word which lays the stress on spiritual leadership. The Imam is a very exalted figure regarded by many as sinless and the only revealer of truth.

THE TWELVERS

These are the most important of the Shi'a and are so called because they believe that there were twelve Imams, beginning with 'Ali and ending with Al-Mahdi. Legend has it that Al-Mahdi did not die, but has hidden himself and will reappear to restore justice and righteousness to the world. All the Shi'a sects have this hope in common but differ in that they are not agreed as to who will reappear. (This is a very similar idea to the Christian hope of the Second Coming of Christ.)

THE SEVENERS

The Seveners are very similar to the Twelvers, except that they believe that it was the seventh Imam who went into hiding and who will return to conquer evil.

THE AHMADIYYA SECT

Apart from the three major sects there are numerous others, but we will only deal with one more, the Ahmadiyya. They are the most recent sect in Islam and also the best organized and most successful at propagating their faith. They are expanding rapidly and even have mosques in Woking and London. Their beliefs include:

1 Jesus is dead (as are the rest of the prophets) and did not ascend into heaven.
2 There is no eternal hell.
3 Belief in Ahmad, the founder, is essential.
4 Disbelief should not be punished by death.

SOME MUSLIM FESTIVALS

After Ramadan comes the Feast of the breaking of the Fast, called '*Id al Fitr* ('the Little Feast'). It begins with the new moon and is exceptionally popular since it follows a month of austerity. At dawn everyone puts on fresh clothes. The men attend the mosque. It is customary to visit friends, give presents—often delicacies—and send greeting cards. During this festival it is also the custom to offer prayers at the graves of relatives and to provide the poor with food.

'*Id-al-Adha* ('the Great Feast') takes place in the twelfth month, the month of pilgrimage to Mecca. Every Muslim who can afford to do so should purchase an animal (usually a sheep, cow or camel) for sacrifice. This sacrifice is part of the pilgrimage ritual (the pilgrims make the sacrifice at Mina, near Mecca), but even if the Muslim is not going on the pilgrimage to Mecca he should still keep this festival. The sacrifice reminds him of how God provided Abraham with a sheep to sacrifice instead of his son Ishmael (in the Old Testament it is Isaac who is to be sacrificed, Genesis 22:9-13), the father of the Arabs. The actual slaughtering of the animal is performed at home or on an open-air praying ground. Some families employ a butcher to perform the ritual. With its head towards Mecca the animal is killed by cutting the throat with a knife. While this is taking place passages are read from the Qur'an. The flesh is then cooked and eaten by the family and by the poor.

The following is part of an essay written by a seventeen-year-old Pakistani boy living in the north of England. His essay is called 'The Fifth Pillar'.

> When my father and I arrived in Mecca the first thing we did was to visit the Masjid-al-Haram, the Great Mosque. This holy place of the Prophet must be entered with the right foot first. With great difficulty we made our way across the large square towards the Kaaba. At times it was almost impossible to move because of the crowd. Fortunately, we both managed to touch the Black Stone and I was able to kiss it, as did our Prophet. Together with the other pilgrims we walked barefoot round the Kaaba seven times in an anti-clockwise direction making sure that the Kaaba itself was on our left all the time. Each time they go round the pilgrims try to touch it. Next we went over to Abraham's shrine: Abraham and his son Ishmael built the Kaaba. Having paid our respects at the shrine we left the Masjid-al-Haram by another door.
>
> We followed the crowds to a broad street in the city where it is the custom for pilgrims to run from side to side. This ceremony recalls the search of Hagar for water for her son Ishmael, the father of the Arabs. We also visited Safa and Marwa which are holy hills near Mecca.
>
> All this was leading up to the real pilgrimage ceremonies which began on the eighth day of Dhu 'L-Hijjah, the pilgrimage month. First we went back to the mosque to hear a sermon preached by the Imam. An Imam is not a clergyman, for there is no clergy or priesthood in our religion. The Imam usually has an ordinary job: anyone can be an Imam so long as he can read the Holy Qur'an and is knowledgeable about Muslim tradition. This sermon was preached in Arabic.

Next day we all went to Arafat, a hill thirteen miles out of Mecca. We arrived at midday and listened to exhortations until dusk. Many pilgrims walked the thirteen miles but as I had been feeling very hot and sticky since we had been in Mecca my father thought that it would be wiser to go by taxi. Many others went by camel. Together with thousands of pilgrims we spent the whole night under the stars on the plain of Arafat at a place called Muzdalifah: it was impossible to sleep. I cannot really put into words my emotions on visiting the places where the Prophet Muhammad actually lived and walked. Had I been alone I would not have been able to endure it.

The next day we walked on to Mina which is about five miles from Mecca. This is where the famous stone-throwing takes place. We all gathered seven pebbles and threw them at a great pile of pebbles. We do this because Abraham got rid of the devil by throwing stones at him. With this ceremony the pilgrimage ended. But it is followed immediately by 'Id-al-Adha. My father sacrificed a sheep and then we went to have our hair shaved off, as is the custom.

When we arrived back in Mecca we again visited the Masjid-al-Haram and went to wash in the water of the Zamzam well which is holy to Muslims because Muhammad drank from it. The eleventh, twelfth and thirteenth days are called tashriq, which means 'relaxation'. The pilgrim garments can be taken off. The pilgrimage is so exhausting that these three days are really necessary.

The Kaaba at Mecca

The Kaaba itself is approximately thirty-five feet long, thirty feet wide and thirty feet high, the Black Stone being set in the south-east corner. The oval Stone is about seven inches in diameter and is encircled by a silver rim. Covering the Kaaba is a huge black cloth, called the *kiswa*, which is made in Cairo and renewed each year. Qur'anic verses are emblazoned on the *kiswa*. It is not customary for the pilgrims to enter the Kaaba but apparently arrangements are made for distinguished visitors to look round it. Non-Muslims may not enter Mecca.

Much of what Muslims do at Mecca is not required by the Qur'an but is part of tradition. While looking at the Black Stone, 'Umar, the second Caliph, is reported to have said, 'By God, I know that thou art only a stone and canst grant no benefit; canst do no harm. If I had not known that the Prophet kissed thee, I would not have done so, but on account of that I do it.'

After the pilgrimage to Mecca some pilgrims go on to visit Muhammad's tomb at Medina—about two hundred miles to the north of Mecca. Such a journey, however, is not considered to be part of the pilgrimage. Those who can afford it also go to Jerusalem for this city too is mentioned in the Qur'an.

THE MOSQUE

The Muslim need not go to a mosque (*masjid* = 'place of prostration') to pray; all he has to do is wash, find the direction (*quibla*) of Mecca, get out his prayer mat, make the appropriate prostrations and say the *takbir* (*Allahu akbar*)—'God is most great'. (See Prayer, the second Pillar of Islam.) It is nevertheless true to say that the mosque is the focal point of Muslim devotional life. Friday, although not a day of rest like the Christian Sunday, is the day on which mosque attendance is expected.

Most mosques are rectangular in design with an open quadrangle and a covered area, the direction of Mecca being indicated by the mihrab. The construction of many mosques, however, is very simple. Muslims in Bradford, for example, worship in a converted house which makes for a certain warmth and friendliness which is perhaps lacking in greater edifices. Some mosques are converted Christian churches, e.g. Saint Sophia in Constantinople.

As with the synagogue, there are no pictures or statues in the mosque but artists have adorned the walls with splendid ceramic work depicting Arabic texts from the Qur'an. (In small mosques there is often no decoration at all.)

A muezzin calling Muslims to prayer from a minaret

On Fridays the sermon is preached by the *khatib* or sometimes by the *imam*. The sermon is called the *khutbah*. He speaks from the *minbar*, a pulpit at the far end of the mosque. Sometimes the minbar is on wheels so that when it is not in use it can be rolled into a recess. The call to prayer is made by the *muezzin* from one of the mosque's minarets (*minaret* = 'place of light'):

> *The minaret everywhere serves to identify on the landscape the community of the faith of Muhammad. Its form is a silent embodiment of the oral summons which it houses.*[1]

Minarets are towers situated on the four corners of the mosque which project high above the surrounding buildings. The call itself, nowadays often made with the help of a public address system, is singularly impressive as it pierces the morning silence or floats clear above the din of daytime traffic:

> *God is most great. I testify that there is no God but Allah, I testify that Muhammad is God's apostle. Come to prayer. come to security. God is most great.*

For the morning call the muezzin adds the words, *Prayer is better than sleep.* The call of the human voice is far more personal and

[1] Kenneth Cragg, *The Call of the Minaret* (O.U.P., 1964), pp. 124–5.

arresting than the clanging of a bell. In small mosques the rôles of muezzin, imam and khatib are fulfilled by one man whereas in large mosques each of the three officials has an assistant.

The imam's job is usually to lead the prayers although he sometimes preaches. He stands before the mihrab and the congregation follows him in recitals and prostrations: he ensures that everybody is doing the same thing at the same time.

The khatib preaches during the midday prayer-time on Fridays. The sermon, which is meant for believing Muslims, exhorts them to live up to the standards advocated by the Prophet, to live as the Prophet lived. (An example of a typical Muslim sermon is given by Kenneth Cragg, *The Call of the Minaret*, pp. 127-30.) With the exception of the proclamation as to Muhammad's unique position as *the* Prophet of God there is really nothing in Muslim worship which could appear objectionable to Jews or Christians; indeed, Jews and Christians might feel that they can worship along with Muslims.

ISLAM IN THE MODERN WORLD

Christianity is undergoing tremendous changes in attitude and thought due to the scepticism of modern man and wholesale rejection of religious ideas. As it is with the Christian, so it is with the Muslim. After the First World War when Turkey ceased to be a great power and huge areas of her territory were taken away, Islam as a political force began to exert less influence. This, plus the fact that many Muslims now attend Western universities and are influenced by Western ideas, means that recently Islam has had to do a great deal of re-adapting. The position of women, for instance, has been reviewed so that some Muslim countries forbid polygamy and the veiling of women (purdah). Despite this, Islam is responding to the challenge and it is true to say that it is still a vital, vivacious and expanding religion.

ISLAM, JUDAISM AND CHRISTIANITY

The pre-Islamic religion of Arabia had for long been subject to external influences in the form of Zoroastrianism, Judaism and Christianity. The Meccan suras contain little that is entirely original to Muhammad. He taught that which had already been proclaimed by Zoroaster, the prophets of Judaism and the writers of the New Testament. Now these ideas were being proclaimed to Arabs by an Arab: now there was an Arabian Qur'an.

There were political reasons to preclude Meccans from becoming Jews or Christians. If they became Christians they would be identifying themselves with Byzantium. If they became Jews they would be seen as currying favour with Persia, in which country there was a significant Jewish population. Persia and Byzantium were at loggerheads and at the same time Mecca owed her trading prosperity to both. If a monotheistic religion was needed it would have to be a new monotheism: Arabian.

The Jews of Medina were quick to point out that Muhammad's revelations differed in detail from those of the Hebrew prophets and did not accept that he was a prophet of God like Moses. This led Muhammad to maintain that his revelations were at variance with those of the Old Testament because the Jews had 'cooked' their sacred books. This criticism of Islam by the Jews meant that Muslims no longer looked to Jerusalem as their spiritual capital but to Mecca and the Kaaba.

The Muslim debt to Judaism is probably greater than that to Christianity but even the ideas taken from the Jews were tinged somewhat with Byzantine Christianity. In fact Muhammad was profoundly affected by both religions. He no doubt felt that both were correct in their doctrines of resurrection, judgment, paradise, hell and the angelic ministry. But Judaism was far too nationalistic to appeal to Arabians and Muhammad would probably have thought of the Byzantine Christians as idolators.

There was considerable ill-feeling between Jews and Christians. Jews accused Christians of being guilty of blasphemy for believing Jesus to be the Son of God and Christians accused Jews of murdering their own messiah. Muhammad sorted out the situation, as far as the Qur'an is concerned, by stressing the rôle and the religious significance of Abraham rather than that of Moses and the Torah. Christianity already rejected much of the Mosaic Torah and in the theology of St. Paul it is Abraham who features prominently (Galatians 3:7-8). In the Qur'an Abraham is the ideal servant of Allah. Abraham, the saint of both Jew and Christian, was the father of Ishmael who was the father of the Arab peoples: Muhammad took this further by saying that Abraham and Ishmael built the Kaaba. Since the Kaaba was erected long before Muhammad's time, the prophet was in fact calling his people back to the *ancient* religion of Arabia.

HOW MUCH OF CHRISTIANITY DO MUSLIMS ACCEPT?

The words of the Apostles' Creed printed in italics are not accepted by Muslims.

	The Qur'anic position
I believe in God *the Father*	To say that God is Father is blasphemous. God has no children. He has no wife.
Almighty, Maker of heaven and earth:	
And in Jesus Christ	Jesus was a great prophet sent by Allah. He was a human being, not a god.
His only Son, our Lord,	'So transcendent is He (Allah) that He cannot have a Son' (Sura 4, verse 169).
Who was conceived by the Holy Ghost, Born of the Virgin Mary,	Jesus was created by the 'Holy Spirit' of God but this 'Holy Spirit' is not God himself (as he is in Christianity—God the Father, Son and Holy Spirit). In some texts of the Qur'an the 'Holy Spirit' is taken to be Gabriel.
Suffered under Pontius Pilate, Was crucified	'They did not kill him and they did not crucify him, but one was made to resemble him' (Sura 4, verse 155 ff.).
	Jesus was not crucified but some verses in the Qur'an speak of his death.
Dead and buried, He descended into hell; *The third day He rose again from the dead,* He ascended into heaven, *And sitteth on the right hand of God the Father Almighty;*	'I am about to cause thee to die and lift thee up to Me' (Sura 3, verse 41).
From thence He shall come *to judge the quick and the dead.*	The Qur'anic position is not clear. Muslim tradition asserts that Jesus will return to earth before the day of Judgment and presumably will play an important role in that Judgment, but it is Allah who has decided the fates of men.
I believe in the Holy Ghost, *The Holy Catholic Church;* *The Communion of Saints;*	Muslim saints are venerated but this is a feature of popular religion. The idea is not to be found in the Qur'an and there is no teaching with regard to the communion of saints.
The Forgiveness of sins;	Allah is merciful and forgives those who repent.
The Resurrection of the body, And the life everlasting.	Resurrection of the body is an important Qur'anic doctrine. The pleasures of Paradise and the torments of the 'Hot Place' are described in some detail.

The differences are perhaps more apparent to the Muslim than to the Christian : Islam tends to be thought of by Muslims as a correction of Judaism and Christianity. For this reason the differences tend to lie more in what Islam rejects as false rather than in what it asserts as true. The doctrine of the Trinity is quite unacceptable to the Muslim.

THE MUSLIM ATTITUDE TO JESUS

The following paragraph from Professor Geoffrey Parrinder's book[1] will give the reader a good idea of the position Jesus holds in the Muslim faith:

> *The Qur'an gives a greater number of honourable titles to Jesus than to any other figure of the past. He is a 'sign', a 'mercy', a 'witness' and an 'example'. He is called by his proper name Jesus, by the title Messiah (Christ) and Son of Mary, and by the names Messenger, Prophet, Servant, Word and Spirit of God. The Qur'an gives two accounts of the annunciation and birth of Jesus, and refers to his teachings and healings, and his death and exaltation. Three chapters or suras of the Qur'an are named after references to Jesus (3, 5 and 19); he is mentioned in fifteen suras and ninety-three verses. Jesus is always spoken of in the Qur'an with reverence; there is no breath of criticism, for he is the Christ of God.*

Jesus (*Isa* in the Qur'an) promised his followers that another Comforter (Advocate) was to come to them (John 14: 16, 26; 15: 26; 16: 7); this Comforter is taken by the Qur'an to be the prophet Muhammad. So Jesus prophesied the coming of Muhammad who would perfect and complete Allah's self-revelation.

At the resurrection every Muslim will have Jesus as his witness. He will come again from heaven at the parousia to destroy evil and reign upon the earth; this will be followed by the Judgment of all men. The Mahdis of the Shi'a sects are sometimes identified with Jesus. Some Muslims, especially if they live in a Christian country, deem it perfectly right and not in the least at variance with the teaching of their religion to keep the festival of Christmas.

---

[1] E. G. Parrinder, *Jesus in the Qur'an* (Faber, 1965), p. 16.

TIME CHART OF ISLAM

A.D. 570 Birth of Muhammad. Year of the Elephant.

c. 620 Begins to preach in Mecca—message 'There is only one God, Allah'. Encounters considerable hostility.

622 The 'Hijra' from Mecca to Medina. Becomes ruler of Medina.

630 Muhammad takes Mecca. Becomes ruler.

632 Death of Muhammad. Abu Bakr succeeds.

634 Abu Bakr dies. 'Umar succeeds.

635 Damascus conquered.⎫ Illustrates the rapid growth of

640 Egypt entered. ⎭ Islam.

644 'Umar killed—'Uthman succeeds. Official version of the Qur'an prepared. On the death of 'Uthman civil war began between 'Ali and Mu'awiya.

661 'Ali killed. Dispute between his son Al-Hasan and Mu'awiya. Both Al-Hasan and his brother Al-Husain were eventually killed—this was the beginning of the Shi'a schism.

670 All North Africa conquered.

732 Muslims stopped from becoming masters of Europe by defeat at the hands of Charles Martel at Tours.

1258 Baghdad (home of Caliphs) falls to Mongols

1924 Caliphate abolished.

Why I am a Muslim

I believe I was drawn to Islam because of a conviction that God existed, not simply as the distant, elderly father of Christ, nor even as something subtle behind Nature. I was convinced that there were men who were in contact with God; that God could be contacted, and that the Essence of God was that thing which made men into men (good, strong, honest, steadfast, unselfish, peaceful, happy).

I knew men could be 'perfected' because I had read about men who had been perfected. I knew that there were, or had been, saints who shone with the results of certain work they had done, who were not subject to moods and depressions or violence or any of the fits of negative irresponsibility in whose sway one could spend a lifetime unconsciously meandering in a sort of haze, always feeling a little ill, or a little self-conscious, or a little tired. I think perhaps my whole life appeared to me at that time as a chain of revolving problems. Even joy and love and any consistent positive action seemed to me as a once in a lifetime chance rather than a way of life. So often, without knowledge of what I was about, I would kick love and happiness away from me with a sort of bitterness and preoccupation with my own misery, faintheartedness and negativity which were strangling me.

I am aware that in the course of every life, with time and doses of experience, an inner knowledge of how to deal with life situations will to a certain extent emerge. But this seems to me a game of chance: a prayer for guidance will, God willing, bring clarity upon a problem in seconds, but at the time I am referring to I had no true hope of help, no faith to speak of, and had probably with the greater majority, had I sat back with hands folded, feeling passively lost, only the remote expectation of some inspirational flashes in middle age to bring me to the goodwill, charity, maturity, a faith and clarity I felt only the desperate lack of.

How could 'I' be a Christian? 'I' was too fainthearted. 'I' really didn't care two hoots, from the depths of 'myself', about my neighbours' well-being. I really wanted, very deeply, to be able to perform Christian acts—to be able to feel some sort of pure and generous love for another entity; I was yearning hard for Something, something which I did not possess, and without which I could not move. I was in a patent state of disunity, disharmony, and did not know of a way in the world to disentangle myself from the vicious circle.

Free will and the mystery of the knowledge of good and evil presents an immense problem to the comprehension. As God doubtless created trees, birds, flowers, love and little children, surely sewage and bullets were also created by him. St. Augustine said that man is what he loves; man does seem to take on the attributes of what he loves. He will inevitably absorb the qualities of whatever he feeds his heart with—surely high intention is the best food for ascents. If we cannot discern for ourselves what path we should take, then if we can simply hope and wish very hard for the best, then we will be provided with it.

I knew I had to make a firm move in some direction. I had considered learning some form of meditation, but I simply justified this out of existence by saying to myself that if I did not know myself or God how could I contemplate either—and as my tendencies were so passive and laissez-faire I could not trust myself to begin. Islam was introduced to me by an English friend, and intellectually there was no alternative but to practise it. If Muhammad was the most recent Prophet of God, and God demanded through Muhammad that we pray five times a day to him and fast the month of Ramadan, and doing so find the way of drawing nearer to him or else we will go to hell, then there is nothing more to be said. Although I did object, and argued quite lengthily in case I might be able to prove that in some way this was not relevant to me. I shed quite a few tears of petulance at times, but there is no smoothness without a little abrasion, and my suffering in the way is extremely slight.

Creation is not possible without God. This is implicit in the Muslim declaration of faith, La Ilaha Illa Allah. There is no God besides God. God is unity. Wherever unity and harmony exists, be it the harmony of friends, molecules, or unity within man, or the right-working harmony of the universe, the Source of that unity is the same. The illusion that harmony can be found outside this Source is followed at a price, and inevitably turns out a waste of time. Mackeson, health food, the love of an intended mate, money, beauty, might well make the integrated and balanced human being radiantly happy but will not serve to illuminate the dark corners of the mind should a person pin his hopes of salvation upon them. God, however, most certainly will. Man need not fumble around in the dark if he will realize that in fact we have been told quite implicitly a very simple way to save ourselves. Islam means surrender to God. This is often deeply confusing to non-Muslims, but if one examines one's heart, it cannot be confusing. If Muhammad is the messenger of God, and never known to tell a lie, and he passed us certain information about a straight path, upon which we find faith, the love of God and salvation then the highest exercise of our free will is to follow

*that path at whatever seeming temporal inconvenience. We dare not
do otherwise. If we object then our objection stands out clearly as the
faithless meandering that is the opposite of humility. It cannot be that
we are right and God wrong. Or if we consider this is a viable possibility
we might as well give up the whole thing.*

*I have always found a certain amount of inspiration in the Christian
church—literally—in the architecture. In the Christian service I was
never moved, except sometimes by the pure voice of a choirboy, but as
everyone stood up drearily for Hymn 426 I was never moved to consider that we were all gathered together to glorify God. In an Islamic
service, or in any Muslim prayer there can never be any doubt that this
is what is being done. The rites are living. It is strange, now, that when
I think about Christianity I think of people on their own trying to be
self-sacrificing. When I think about Islam I think about men of God.*

*The straight path is the high road of faith, where there is no com-
promise, where one may walk in total safety without stumbling, on
which one is in harmony with the will of God.*

*Islam gives the chance to a man to be on the straight path. Islam
does not need priests or mediators; the believer refers directly to his
Creator for help. Islam needs no complexity of interpretation; if God
wills, the heart of every believer will come to understand whatever it
wishes to understand, and there are no limits to Islam.*

*To me it is more essential than food and drink. I accepted Islam, but
God says that if we take one step towards him, he will take ten towards
us—and so it was. First it was I who accepted Islam, then Islam took
me, expanded my heart, opened my eyes, washed my head out, gave me
the promise of guidance and discrimination, faith, joy, the list can go
on indefinitely. I accepted Islam six months ago.*

Susanne Vincent

PART TWO

India and Southern Asia

CHAPTER FOUR

Hinduism

WHAT IS HINDUISM?

Someone once asked St. Augustine, a scholar of the early Christian Church, to define the meaning of the word 'time'. To this he replied, 'If you do not ask me, I know precisely what it is; but if you ask me, I cannot exactly say.' The word 'Hinduism' presents the same kind of problem to the student of religion as the word 'time' presented to St. Augustine. The reason for this will become clear to you as you read on. But while it is not possible to define what a Hindu is, it is not all that difficult to identify a person as a Hindu.

'Hinduism' is a word with little meaning: it is not to be found in the languages of India. In fact there is not even an equivalent word. If we are to retain the word it might be more meaningful to talk of 'Hinduisms' rather than 'Hinduism' for each 'Hindu' has his own religious duties (*dharma*), his own particular gods. Basically, however, the word 'Hinduism' describes the development of the religion of those people who dwelt in the Indus valley in N.W. India and the word 'Hindu' is used by Westerners to describe a follower of that religious tradition.[1]

Hinduism has no creed like Judaism, Christianity and Islam; it has no historical founder like Moses, Gotama, Jesus, Muhammad; it has no recognizable beginning—we cannot date the rise of Hinduism. It is a religion which has just grown up and represents the largest religious group with a common heritage in any part of the world. There are over 300 million Hindus in India and 15 million outside India.

Indian religion is rich in variety. It ranges from practices which include self punishment as a means of bringing the body into a state in which it can be controlled entirely by the will to those which consider the infliction of any pain on any living creature as sinful—even crushing an insect. Some forms of Hinduism require numerous

[1] A glossary of terms is provided in the Appendix.

priests, rituals and visual aids to worship; other forms foster the idea that religion is a personal matter and that priests are not necessary, neither are distracting objects of veneration.

Religion the world over is constantly changing to suit the needs of the day but nowhere is this more evident than in India. In some parts of the country religion tends to be primitive whereas in other parts it is much more sophisticated and polished. But this notion of change or evolution is an important and vital idea in Hinduism. Everything, the Hindu believes, is in constant change. Nothing is permanent. Even the gods will pass away and others will take their place. In this belief Hinduism shows remarkable insight and tolerance; it admits that truth is understood in different ways at different times and at different places. Ancient Hindu thinkers concluded that the whole universe is in a state of change. Even those things which look as if they will endure for ever, like mountains and rocks, will disappear; all that exists is subject to change. But on the other hand, nothing really comes to an end for the mountains and rocks which will one day be no more were formed out of something else and will become something else. All life is born again; this applies also to the 'soul' which uses living things as a temporary abode. The soul may be found in plants, animals, human beings. This idea of the soul will be explained shortly in greater detail. Since the material world is constantly in a state of change it is, in a sense, not quite real because it is not enduring. For the Hindu the material universe is merely 'appearance'; it is not 'reality'. That which is real must be that which does not change; it is that under-lying cause of all things; it is that which permeates all things; it is that in which all things exist. Hindus call this reality *Brahman*. In Sanskrit, the ancient language of the Hindu scriptures which is no longer spoken, this word is neuter: that is, it is not a 'he' or a 'she' but an 'it'. Brahman, therefore, is not a god in the strict sense, for a person is not addressed as 'it'. Brahman is the *impersonal* unchang-ing reality which is to be found in all things. Some modern Hindus, however, talk of Brahman as the *personal* supreme reality.

Hinduism, then, has one Reality: some Hindus think of this Reality in an impersonal way—an 'it': some think of Reality as a personal being—something akin to the monotheistic view of God. At the same time Hinduism has innumerable gods; the Hindu chooses to devote himself to a particular god or goddess. Some Hindus understand these deities as separate and distinct divine beings whereas others think of them as different ways of looking at the one Reality. If you owned a superb piece of sculpture you would be a rather foolish person if you only viewed it from one angle. Rather, you would want to walk round it and appreciate it from a variety of standpoints. In this way you would be more likely to understand what the artist was trying to communicate to you. So it is with the gods; they are windows into, and varied aspects of, the one Reality. How can you possibly understand 'God' when you only look at him from one angle? Since God or Reality is to be found in all things the Hindu feels quite justified in venerating one particular aspect of this Reality at a time. Looking at 'God' from a number of angles he begins to understand the ultimate Reality, Brahman. Thus, many Hindus believe that there is only one God. '*Ekam sat vipra bahudha vedanti*', declare the Vedas. 'Truth is one: sages express it in different ways.' The expression only is different, not the realization nor the experience.

THE GOAL OF HINDUISM

The Hindu ideal is to be absorbed into 'God'—the one permanent, unchanging Reality—and thereby quit the world of impermanence and change. Most Hindus today believe that this release (*moksha*) from unreality is achieved by leading a good life, a disciplined and orderly existence, non-violence (*ahimsa*), respect for all living things and detachment from the world which is passing. You will remember that, to the Hindu, the world is something less than real. He calls it *maya*, the play of the gods, almost an illusion. However, men and women tend to get so bound up with the things of the passing world that they attach far too much significance to them and consequently are blind to Reality. What they see is maya, not truth. To take a simple illustration: a man looks into the dark corner of his room and sees what he believes to be the coiled form of a snake ready to strike. His immediate reaction is one of terror and he cannot think clearly, cannot see straight: all he can think of is the snake and its bite. Eventually he realizes that it was not a snake after all but only an old piece of rope which someone had tossed into the corner. It was maya. He really believed that the rope was a snake and behaved accordingly. In such a way the world, which is transient and passing and therefore of no ultimate significance, deludes men and women and distracts them from coming to grips with Reality. It is maya!

Since all things are in Brahman, the ultimate truth or Reality, it is easy to see why many Hindus insist on respect for animals and men:

Brahman is to be found in all forms of life: it/he is all-pervading:

> *Thou art woman. Thou art man. Thou art the dark-blue bee*
> *and the green parrot with red eyes. Thou hast the lightning as*
> *thy child. Thou art the seasons and the seas. Thou dost abide*
> *with all-pervadingness, wherefrom all things are born.*

THE ARYANS

The Indus Valley culture began about 2500 B.C. and lasted
for about 1000 years. Since the excavations at Harappa and Mohenjo-
daro have been undertaken, considerable light has been shed on the
relationship between the religion and culture of the Indus Valley
dwellers and that of the invading Aryans who conquered them. It is
surprising to note that the religion of these dwellers was not unlike
that of later Hinduism. The Hindu Vedas describe these people in
unflattering terms; they are primitive, ugly and without religion.
Some scholars have followed the Vedas on this point but archaeology has shown that the Vedas are somewhat off the mark here. In
fact these people had an advanced form of civilization: they were
methodical in the arrangement of their cities; they had advanced
sanitation systems; their cities were surrounded by substantial walls
and there is ample evidence of organized trading. They also had
their own alphabet which has not yet been deciphered.

The Vedas describe the occupants of the Indus Valley as the
Dasas, a word which came to mean 'slave' or 'dark': the invaders
from the north they call *Aryans*, which is Sanskrit for 'aristocrat'.
The people whom the Vedas call Aryans originally inhabited the
area around the Caspian Sea and between 1500 B.C. and 1200 B.C.
(about the same time as the Hebrews were leaving Egypt) they began to leave their homeland and migrate to different parts of the
world. Generally, they migrated towards Europe and India. It is
worthy of note that these people would have spoken the language
from which Latin, Greek and Sanskrit were later derived. We, in
this country, therefore, have a language-link with these ancient
peoples. As already mentioned, the Vedas call those who entered
India the Aryans but because some went in a European direction
and others in an Indian direction it is very convenient to call them
Indo-Europeans. With the aid of their gods, the invading Indo-
Europeans fought and conquered the native Dasas who, it appears,
were much darker than they. This colour distinction is quite possibly
the origin of an important religious distinction between Hindus of

Covered drainage from excavations at Mohenjo-daro

later times. This distinction is known as *caste*. The Sanskrit word *varna*, which means colour, indicates that in early days the distinction was racial and not primarily religious. Caste is an important element in Hinduism and we will be looking at it in greater detail in due course. Nowadays caste has nothing to do with colour.

Hinduism owes much to the conquered Dasas. For example, at Harappa and Mohenjo-daro female images have been unearthed representing the Mother Goddess, giver of life and fertility; in later Hinduism this becomes Shaktism, the worship of the principle in nature associated with the biological function of womanhood. At Mohenjo-daro a seal has been found bearing an image of three faces with a headdress of horns sitting in yogic posture; it looks remarkably like Shiva whose three faces represent his threefold activity of creator, sustainer and destroyer of the universe. Shiva is a very important Hindu god. It would seem therefore that although the Dasas were conquered, their religion was gradually absorbed into the mainstream of the Indo-European culture and emerges at a later date in a modified form.

The Indus valley civilization was urban but this urbanity had most probably been preceded by village organization and it was the village which was the essential unit of Indian society. In fact village life still predominates in India. Where village life is the norm, agriculture is the means of livelihood and one of the religious features of agricultural communities is that its members tend to conceive of deity in terms of womanhood—the village goddess. As a woman conceives and brings forth offspring so does the earth conceive and bring forth from her womb her produce on which man is totally dependent. On the other hand, with nomadic peoples, who depend on livestock, the male principle is more important. For example, the nomadic Semites (Jews and Arabs) conceived of deity in male terms: Yahweh and Allah. Whereas to Jews God is father, to many Indians God is mother. The Aryans, however, who imposed their religion on the Indus valley dwellers, were nomadic and thought of deity as male (the Rig-Vedic deities). After a time, when the cultures had had time to intermingle, deity was thought of as both male and female.

Another (non-Vedic) religious feature of pre-Aryan India was the notion of *karma*, the moral law of cause and effect which determines the status of the individual in subsequent lives (*samsara*).

It becomes evident, therefore, that Hinduism as it came to be known is a merging of Aryan and pre-Aryan (Dravidian) beliefs and practices. Given that the Dravidian religion was based on the village unit, which made for great diversity both in the content of belief and the manner of its expression, and that the process of absorption was gradual (and indeed in some sense is still going on) it will be appreciated that the history of early Hinduism is extremely complicated.

THE SCRIPTURES

Hinduism is a quest for truth by means of three paths and these paths are represented by three groups of scriptures:

The Vedas	The way of action	1200 B.C.
The Upanishads	The way of knowledge	600 B.C.
The Epics	The way of devotion	Early A.D.[1]

1   The way of action is the fulfilling of sacrifices as prescribed by the Vedas. Sacrifice is performed by Brahmin priests in the open, round the sacred fire; the sacrifices do not take place in temples. If

---

[1] Although these Epics were compiled and committed to writing during the early Christian era, they comprise the work of numerous poets of many generations. It is, therefore, virtually impossible to date the origin of the various oral traditions.

the sacrifice is carried out correctly the gods will reward the worshipper with success in agriculture, long life and future happiness. 2 The way of knowledge as represented in the Upanishads is an extension of the thought of the Vedas with their idea that truth is but one Reality which can be understood in a variety of ways. Buddhism owes much to the Upanishads. They teach *samsara* (transmigration of souls). After death the soul is reborn in a new body. The type of person you will be in your next incarnation is directly dependent upon the kind of life you lead now: you will reap the reward of your actions. The soul (*atman*) is identical with the ultimate Reality (*Brahman*)—they are literally one and the same. By meditation you can come to realize this and *know* it to be true. This realization, however, might not be achieved in your present incarnation. A person who has come to this realization escapes the Wheel of Death, Rebirth and Redeath; he becomes absorbed into Brahman and suffers no more incarnations. Since all things are in Brahman it is forbidden to take life.

3 The way of devotion (*bhakti*) is represented by the Epics and in particular by the *Bhagavad Gita* which attempts to harmonize action, knowledge and devotion while laying stress on the latter. Devotion may be offered to the deity in any place by any person; it must be offered with sincerity and from the heart. Even some of the greatest saints have been people of low caste. The way of devotion has become one of the most characteristic features of Hinduism.

THE VEDAS

Veda is a Sanskrit word meaning 'knowledge', 'information': it is information handed down in four sacred books—the Rig-Veda, the Sama-Veda, the Yajur-Veda and the Atharva-Veda. The Vedas comprise the most ancient living religious literature of the world (1200 B.C.). The oldest and by far the most important is the Rig-Veda (Song of Knowledge) which contains 1028 hymns to 33 gods. Written by Brahmin priests, the Rig-Veda was probably completed by about 800 B.C. although the material contained in it was circulated by word of mouth long before that date. In fact, the Aryan Indians preferred to memorize vast passages of the Vedas and it would appear that the actual writing down was due to the influence of foreign rulers of India. The earliest extant fragments in the British Museum were not written until the thirteenth century A.D. The poetry of the Rig-Vedic hymns is of a very high order but unfortunately the English translations available do it less than justice. In size the Rig-Veda is equal to all the works of Homer.

The deities of the Rig-Veda are nature-based, and can be divided into three categories in accordance with the division of the universe:

Gods of the atmosphere or the intermediate region: Indra, Rudra, the Maruts, Vayu (the wind).

Heavenly gods: sky gods: Dyaus, Varuna; sun gods: Surya, Mitra, Vishnu.

Gods of the earth: Agni, Brihaspati, Soma, Prithivi (earth); river deities.

They are invoked with the pouring out of *soma* juice and the fire sacrifice of melted butter. Some have taken the Vedas to paint a polytheistic view, i.e. that there are many gods, but in some of the later Rig-Vedic hymns it would appear that this is not the case. When any particular god is addressed he occupies the mind of the worshipper to such an extent that he is often spoken of as supreme being. Only one aspect of Reality can be contemplated at a time but in contemplating that aspect one apprehends the whole Reality.

Although 33 gods are mentioned, this does not include group-deities like the *Maruts* who accompany *Indra*. And just because they are gods does not mean that they are eternal: they, like all things, will pass away; some are the offspring of others. Heaven and earth are said to be the father and mother of the gods as well as of men. There are some passages where it is said that some gods have become immortal by drinking soma. The gods are usually spoken of as being like human beings in their appearance but the bodily parts are nearly always means of illustrating the particular aspect of nature which the god represents. For example, the limbs and tongue of *Agni*, the fire-god, represent his flames. Some of the gods, such as *Indra*, are warriors. Others, such as *Agni* and *Brihaspati*, are priests. They all travel through the air in horse-drawn chariots. They delight in butter, milk, corn and meat. *Agni* is one of the means whereby the sacrifice is sent to the other gods—he sends it up as smoke. Otherwise the sacrifice is spread out on the grass and left. Their favourite beverage is the highly intoxicating juice of the soma plant. The gods exercise power over the forces of nature and, if favoured, will aid man in the face of natural disasters such as drought, famine and epidemics. These natural disasters are brought about by demons; for example, *Vitra* caused a drought by preventing the rain clouds from opening until he was pierced by *Indra*'s thunderbolt. Generally speaking, the gods are well-disposed towards men as long as men show them due respect. The only one who tends to be somewhat naughty is *Rudra*. The gods are described as 'true' and 'not deceitful'. They are the friends and helpers of decent people and punish guilt. This is especially the case with *Varuna* who is always described as 'righteous Varuna'. On the whole, however, the gods are not unduly concerned about morality.

The Vedic gods, then, are not thought of as distinct from the part of nature they represent; they do not require a moral response. Very often the gods merge into one another or have traits in common. For example, all the sun gods become one. Some of the names of the gods are simply descriptive. The name of one god can be applied to that of another as an adjective. In other words, there is a kind of fluidity of function in naming the gods and in the latest hymns the idea comes to be expressed that all the various deities are but different forms of the one God:

> They call it Indra, Vitra, Varuna and Agni,
> And also heavenly, beauteous-winged Garutman.
> The real is one, though sages name it variously:
> They call it Agni, Yama, Motarisvan.
>   (Rig-Veda I.164, 46)

There is, then, one ultimate Reality to which the later Vedas ascribe various names. This verse is considered to be the starting point of all later Hinduism. It should be pointed out that the above translation takes the Reality as impersonal—'they call *it*'. The Sanskrit, however, can be translated as either 'it' or 'him'. Perhaps the writers (and you will have gathered by now that they were by no means unsophisticated or naïve) intended that the meaning should not be too well-defined. What is clear, however, is that the beginning of Hinduism as we know it from scripture, is *not* polytheistic but holds the possibility of treating the ultimate Reality as personal, each deity representing some essential facet of this Reality.

This coalescence of the Aryan deities is something which is essentially Indian (Dravidian) and is another indication of the resurgence of pre-Aryan ideas in the moulding of Indian religion. No one god can be supreme.

VEDIC MYTHOLOGY

At the beginning of time all was water. *Tvastri*, the universal designer, fashioned the divine pair, Sky and Earth, who are considered to be the parents of all the deities. Their offspring, however, could not get on well together so Indra drank soma and won the civil war. Varuna then laid down the laws.

Near the end of the Rig-Veda there is a late hymn which asks whether perhaps all the deities were made by some greater power:

> *Who verily knows and who can here declare it, whence it was*
> *born and whence comes this creation?*
> *The gods are later than this world's production. Who knows,*
> *then, whence it first came into being?*
>
> *He, the first origin of this creation, whether he formed it all or*
> *did not form it,*
> *Whose eye controls this world in highest heaven, he verily*
> *knows it*, or perhaps he knows it not.
>
> (Rig-Veda X.129, 6-7)

Even the creator himself, if there is such a one, may not know the answer to the poet's question.

THE VEDIC DEITIES DISAPPEAR

The healthy robustness of the Vedas gives way to meditation and self-denial. But, on the other hand, many of the later beliefs of Hinduism may be found in germinal form in the Vedas: 'We drank soma, we became immortal, we found the gods.'

Nowadays the importance of the Vedas is being re-established. For example, the *Arya-Samaj*, a modern Hindu school of thought, draws its inspiration from them. Vedic prayers are still said by pious Hindus. The *gayatri*, which is just as popular among Hindus as the Creed of Islam is among Muslims or the Lord's Prayer among Christians, is recited on rising and before meals: 'Let us meditate on the most excellent light of the Creator, may he guide our intellects.'

The majority of Hindus still venerate the idea of one deity by means of various names and various forms. The important Vedic deities, Varuna, Mitra, Rudra, Indra, Agni, Savitr, lost their positions gradually and some of them, like Varuna and Vishnu, completely changed character. In more recent times sects have arisen; some sections of the community are keen on Shiva[1] and others on Vishnu.

Attention has already been drawn to the fact that there are no passages in the Rig-Veda which express the notion of rebirth which becomes an essential feature of later Hindu thought. Although it was not a part of Indo-European thought the notion began to take form towards the end of the Vedic period.

[1] The Vedic Rudra is the prototype of the important god, Shiva. He is quite probably of pre Indo-European origin (see p. 107).

In the sections which follow we will be examining a number of connected ideas which comprise Hinduism as it came to be known. In doing this we will try to keep the chronological development of the scriptures in mind. The concepts may be roughly represented as follows:

BRAHMAN IS ATMAN	MOKSHA	(Release)	DHARMA	CASTE
	SAMSARA	(Rebirth)	(Caste	Brahmins
	KARMA	(Action)	duties)	Kshatriyas
	YOGA	(Discipline)		Vaisyas
				Shudras

CASTE

To be a Hindu is to be in caste: it is the basis of Hinduism. According to Brahmanical religion, Brahma, the creator, made the first man, called Purusha. From Purusha were taken the four *varnas* or orders; each varna came from a different part of his body. In the Vedic period the community seems to have divided into four classes which represent distinct social and economic groupings. The four groups were looked upon as having been separately created as the outcome of the sacrifice of Purusha. The Rig-Vedic hymn describing this operation is called the *Purusha Sukta* or Hymn of Man. The following is an extract:

> *When they divided Purusha, how many portions did they make?*
> *What do they call his mouth, his arms? What do they call his*
> *thighs and feet?*
>
> *The Brahmin was his mouth, of both arms was the Kshatriya made.*
> *His thighs became the Vaisya, from his feet the Shudra was produced.*
>
> (Rig-Veda X.90, 11-12)

This is the one passage from antiquity referring to caste; for the Hindu it is of eternal making.

To be a Hindu you must be born one. It is not just a matter of being the child of Indian parents: they must be in caste. The child will accept the duties (*dharma*) of his caste because he has been born into it. So to be a Hindu you must have been born into one of the castes as well as into an Indian family. Whatever caste you happen to be born into determines to a large extent your place in society, and requires special religious duties. The Hindu cannot change his caste nor can a person who is not a Hindu 'join' a caste; it is strictly hereditary. Caste, then, is a religious system peculiar to India. There is nothing to be found anything like it in other religions and it means that Hindus are Hindus not by choice of their own but by reason of their birth. Caste still plays a vital part in the community.

A person of one caste should not marry out of that caste: if he does he loses caste and if a Hindu breaks these regulations he is frowned upon. His children, technically speaking, do not belong in the Hindu system for they have no caste. Obviously then, caste can cause serious social problems. For example, there are certain restrictions on eating and drinking with members of other castes. There are several subdivisions between the four castes and many of the sub-castes have fixed occupations. There is social prestige in belonging to the Brahmin caste, in fact the whole system has turned on this prestige. Since religious speculation was the dharma of Brahmins it is reasonable to assume that this hymn is Brahmin-inspired. According to some scholars the Kshatriya philosophic reaction can be seen in the thought of the Upanishads. Although caste really has nothing to do with skin pigmentation many Brahmins are in fact concerned about colour.

There are more than 3000 sub-castes and millions of outcastes (Pariah) who are considered by some to be the descendants of the native Dasas. The outcastes used to be called 'untouchables' but nowadays such a word suggests discrimination and this kind of discrimination is not allowed in India.

But from the religious point of view caste is not a system in which one caste is more important than another for all are part of the same Purusha: Purusha is one and it is only when you look at different parts of the one that you can say that there is a mouth, that there are arms, thighs, feet. All these are part of the one and all groups are needed in order to have the one Purusha. This is the Vedic point of view. By the third century A.D. the *Laws of Manu* laid down certain functions of a social and religious nature for each of the four groups. The Brahmins were created to teach the Vedas and to be priests. The Kshatriyas were to protect the people as warriors, to offer sacrifices, to study the Vedas and to lead respectable lives: Gotama, the founder of Buddhism, was a Kshatriya. The Vaisyas were to tend cattle, cultivate the land, trade, lend money, offer sacrifices and study the Vedas. The Shudras had one assignment only—to be subservient to these three castes.

THE RELATIONSHIP OF CASTE AND PURUSHA

CASTE—THE FOUR VARNAS

Mouth — Certain human beings came from his mouth and were given understanding so that they could teach the Vedic knowledge. They were called BRAHMINS.

Arms — Some came from his arms; they were muscular, good fighters and were called KSHATRIYAS (warriors).

Thighs — Those who came from his thighs were energetic, hard-working people; they were non-professional workers such as farmers and traders and were called VAISYAS.

These three are dvija castes (twice-born) who all study the Vedas but only Brahmins may teach them. They are so called because of the initiation or introduction to full participation in religion and the responsibilities which go with it, which takes place through certain ceremonies at which a young person is 'reborn' and assumes the sacred thread. The ceremony is for males only (but not Shudras) and they will wear the thread for the rest of their lives.

Feet — From his feet came the SHUDRAS. Their task was to be subservient to the other three castes.

PURUSHA

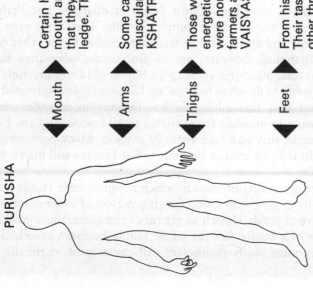

OUTSIDERS
(no part of
Purusha)

The outsiders—PARIAHS—are those who are outside the caste system and are therefore, strictly speaking, not Hindus.

The Brahmins, Kshatriyas and Vaisyas are referred to as *dvija* or 'twice-born'. This is because when a boy reaches a suitable stage in his religious development (about 7 to 12 years of age) he takes part in a ceremony in which he is said to be reborn. He sits in a garden by the sacrificial fire with his *guru* (his religious teacher) who prepared him for the occasion by teaching him Hindu philosophy and yoga. The climax of the ceremony comes when the boy receives from his guru the *sacred thread* which he then wears diagonally across the shoulder for the rest of his life. The guru then prays that the boy might continue in spiritual growth. The boy's first birth was into life: now he has been born into full membership of his caste and acknowledges all the responsibilities and duties (dharma) which go with it. Religiously speaking, he has become a man.

The caste system remains a permanent feature of Hinduism and it will not disappear until there is in India a new concept of man entirely different from that of the Rig-Veda.

I was not born in one of the twice two castes;
I am not learned in the four sacred Vedas;
I have not conquered the five senses;
Save thy shining feet alone, O Lord,
I have no other hold.

(A Shudra prayer to Vishnu)

DHARMA

Each caste has its own duties or dharma. The Brahmins have to carry out the most complex rituals. They must pray three times a day and spend time in teaching religion to the other castes. Many Brahmins, however, are in professions other than that of religious teaching. Some years ago, a boy would know precisely what he was going to do when he grew up because caste determined your work but now that education has become more widespread in India many professions are available to all castes. And the Pariah, for example, may now take virtually any job. Many priests working in Hindu temples are not Brahmins. But Hindus still marry within their caste.

There is a variety of ways in which a higher caste Hindu may be defiled by coming into contact with a person of lower caste and he may have to purify himself to get rid of the contamination. When a member of a family dies the whole family becomes ritually defiled and they must purify themselves. All castes must be ritually clean when they take part in any kind of religious activity. If you happen to know any Hindus you will no doubt have been impressed by their great attention to cleanliness; they bathe frequently and chauge their clothes often. We will not examine all the religious duties of each caste: some indeed are no longer of consequence, e.g. the fighting duties of the Kshatriya. A conscientious Hindu will, however, try his best to keep the dharma of his caste.

Apart from the notion of dharma based on caste there is also that of dharma based on *guna*. The concept of guna is basic to Hinduism and determines its doctrine to a significant extent. It is a complicated idea but put in simple terms it means that there are three basic qualities which make up human nature. These qualities are known as *satva* (a state of equilibrium—the balanced personality), *rajas* (when the self-assertive part of the personality subjugates other qualities) and *tamas* (where evil qualities predominate). As a result of the law of *karma* these qualities are manifested to different degrees in different people, according to their attention to dharma in previous existences. Environmental factors are also taken into account.

Brahman alone is without gunas for Brahman is ultimate. Brahman is *Nirguna Brahman*, that is, without any 'qualities' whatsoever. As soon as Brahman is attributed with 'qualities' then Brahman ceases to be ultimate. When, for example, Brahman is manifested as the god Isvara he is endowed with gunas. Any god that is worshipped has gunas.

THE UPANISHADS

Upanishad is a combination of three Sanskrit words which mean 'near down-sit'. These scriptures take the form of a 'teach-in' or seminar, the pupil sitting down at the foot of the teacher to receive instruction. Much of the Upanishads is in fact in dialogue form between pupil and teacher and these sacred writings were later called Vedanta, the 'end' of the Vedas. Like the Vedas, the Upanishads were originally circulated by word of mouth and were not written down for some considerable time after they had taken shape. The thought of the Upanishads was developed between 800 and 600 B.C. As in the case of the Vedas, the Upanishads are considered too noble to be recited or read by those of lower caste.

The Upanishads develop the notion of *Brahman*, the cause and reason for all that is; it is the underlying force of all being, the supreme being. All that is is in Brahman. The only way Brahman can be described is as 'it': it represents the impersonal character of the universe and the Hindu believes that one day his soul will become merged or absorbed into this impersonal 'it'. This idea of merging into Brahman or Reality lies behind all Hindu thought. Brahman is that which is in all things: all things that exist exist in Brahman. This teaching is sometimes called pantheism (i.e. all is God). But to say that Hinduism teaches that everything is a bit of God is a ridiculous simplification. Rather, the Hindu wants to say that *all is in Brahman*; even the individual soul is in Brahman.

ATMAN AND BRAHMAN

The word *atman* means the soul of man: all men have atman. Brahman is the universal impersonal soul that pervades all things. Since 'it' pervades all things 'it' must also pervade the atman. The Hindu then concludes that atman and Brahman are one and the same. They are just different words which express the same idea. If we distinguish Atman as the supreme soul we may use atman for the individual soul. In the following extract from the Chhandogya Upanishad the water is atman and the salt is Brahman. Svetaketu learns that atman and Brahman cannot be distinguished: they are identical, they are one and the same—just as the salt cannot be distinguished from the water in which the former is dissolved. The salty taste shows that the universal soul (Brahman) is to be found in all that exists and is yet present in the individual human being.

> '*Place this salt in water, and come to me tomorrow morning.*'
> *The son did as he was commanded.*
> *The father said to him: '*Bring me the salt, which you placed in the water last night.*'*
> *The son having looked for it could not find it, for, of course, it was dissolved.*
> *The father said: '*Taste it from the surface of the water. How is it?*'*
> *The son replied: '*It is salt.*'*
> '*Taste it from the middle. How is it?*'
> *The son replied: '*It is salt.*'*
> '*Taste it from the bottom. How is it?*'
> *The son replied: '*It is salt.*'*
> *The father said: '*Throw it away and then come back to me again.*' He did so; but salt exists for ever.*
> *Then the father said: '*Here also, in this body of yours you do not perceive the True (Sat), my son; but there indeed it is. In that which is the subtle essence, all that exists has its self.*

That is the True, That is the Self, and thou, O Svetaketu, art That.'
'Please, Sir, inform me still more,' said the son.
'Be it so, my son,' the father replied.
(Chhandogya Upanishad, Prapathaka 6, Khanda 13)

('That', i.e. Brahman, is the Self, i.e. the atman, and thou, O Svetaketu, art 'That', i.e. Brahman.) 'Thou art That/It': this is a notion which crops up time and time again in Hindu religious writing. For example, the same kind of sentiment is expressed in the marriage ceremony as laid down by the ancient lawbooks:

> *Leading her three times round the fire and the water-pot, so that their right sides are turned towards the fire, the bride-groom murmurs, 'This am I, that are thou; that art thou, this am I; I the heavens thou the earth. Come let us marry, let us beget offspring. Loving, bright, genial, may we live a hundred autumns.'*

To the Hindu, Brahman, atman and Reality are one. He can there-fore say, *'Aham Brahman asmi'*: 'I am Brahman'. 'It' pervades all things as butter is contained in cream. 'It' is indescribable; who can hope to describe Reality (something *not* limited in meaning) with mere words (which *are* limited in meaning); it cannot be done. The Hindu can only hint at what he means by Brahman.

'It' moves.
'It' moves not.
'It' is far.
'It' is near.
'It' is within all this.
'It' is outside all this.

Brahman is all-inclusive, all that is exists in 'it'. 'Brahman before, Brahman behind; to the right and to the left; stretched out below and above. Brahman indeed in the whole world; this widest extent.' Sacrifices are not necessary because you achieve peace by realizing that you are in Brahman. In any case, Brahman is all gods.

It should be understood that the Hindu does not think of, say, the ashtray on my desk as a piece of Brahman. I cannot say, 'There is Brahman in the ashtray. You are now looking at Brahman.' The Hindu would rather wish to say, 'You can realize the presence of Brahman in the ashtray but you cannot say precisely where or how "it" is there.' In the same way Svetaketu could not tell how the salt pervaded the water; he did, however, realize that the one did exist within the other.

You cannot examine Brahman because 'it' is an abstraction. 'It' is something which has no being and yet at the same time it is everything that has being. 'It' is beyond explanation. 'There is nothing that Brahman is not. Brahman is everything that is thought of as being, yet is no being.' The Upanishads teach that because atman and Brahman are identical it follows that the more you understand yourself the more likely you are to understand Brahman. This is why meditation and looking inside oneself is so stressed in Indian religion. Meditation was practised in pre-Vedic times and we shall be examining it later. Sometimes holy men would practise *tapas*, that is, bringing the body into subjection by fasting and hardship in order to concentrate on the soul. Striving after Reality became an individual quest. You can only contemplate Reality alone; it is a personal experience. The result is that Hindus have never been particularly keen on corporate worship. Temples are used for private meditation.

MOKSHA

The goal of Hinduism, that is, release from the Wheel of Rebirth, is called *moksha* and attainment of moksha is a highly personal matter: it is your own soul and not those of others that you must first seek to release. If you achieve release yourself you may then go on to help others do the same. Release comes when it dawns upon you that your atman and the universal Brahman are identical. Hindus say that the experience of moksha is of such a kind that you are quite certain as to whether it has taken place within yourself. You not only feel that you are one with Brahman but you *know* it.

Since moksha is the goal of Hinduism, for it is absorption into Brahman and the end of rebirths, it follows that death is of considerable consequence to the Hindu. It means either the beginning, at some uncertain time in the future, of a new life in a body or it means complete union with Brahman. Many elderly Hindus make a journey to Benares to bathe in the river. It is a symbolic way of washing away *karma* (action, guilt) for it is karma which will determine your next incarnation.

At death the body is usually cremated on steps leading down into the river; these steps are called ghats. The ashes are then sprinkled over the water. If the friends of the deceased are sure that he has attained moksha he need not be cremated. Instead the body is weighted and dropped into the river—rather like burial at sea. As the body sinks horns are sounded in gladness that the deceased has been united with Brahman.

Cremation on the ghats at Benares

> *My father wind and you my mother earth,*
> *Fire, my friend, water my near relation*
> *And you my brother sky; in this last breath*
> *Of mortal life I send you salutation.*
> *From living ever with you comes this birth*
> *Of uncontaminated wisdom, with increase*
> *Of goodness, that all darkness and all folly cease,*
> *As now I live in Brahma in my death.*

SAMSARA

Having read about the teaching of the Upanishads on atman and Brahman the reader will no doubt appreciate why it would not, by itself, have a very wide appeal. It is a highly intellectual view of life. In order, however, to make it more acceptable to ordinary folk a number of other ideas were introduced.

Hindus believe in *samsara* or rebirth (also called transmigration of souls, reincarnation, metempsychosis). When the body dies the soul (atman) which cannot die, because it is Brahman and eternal, lives on and will be reincarnated in an unending series of bodies. Whereas this belief is not unknown elsewhere it is in India that it has become a highly developed and essential religious doctrine. As far as we can tell from the Vedas the Aryans did not believe in rebirth and so samsara must be an ancient Dravidian notion.

Each soul may be reincarnated innumerable times, the bodies, of course, being different every time. Samsara is an assumption; it can never be proved. Nevertheless, it has been very strictly and formally held to since the period of the Upanishads. It bolsters up the atman/Brahman teaching. You are not likely to realize that you are Brahman in one incarnation, but if you strive to live a pious life you may come back in a higher caste and therefore be in a better position to reach moksha and achieve the state of realization so that you will not be reincarnated any more.

> Those whose conduct has been good, will quickly attain some good birth, the birth of a Brahmin, or a Kshatriya, or a Vaisya. But those whose conduct has been evil, will quickly attain an evil birth, the birth of a dog, a hog, or an outcaste.
>
> (Chhandogya Upanishad, Prapathaka 5, Khanda 10)

The kind of life (caste) you will be born into in your next incarnation depends on the life you live now. This appealed to ordinary people whereas the highly intellectual atman/Brahman idea would have been somewhat above them. With samsara the Hindu feels that he is trying for something which he can attain, a better birth, whereas he is not certain that he can reach moksha and might therefore lose his stamina. Samsara, then, is vital to making sense of the atman/Brahman ideal to the ordinary Hindu.

Rebirth is to be avoided because life and the world partake of maya; matter is inferior. Since life is evil or inferior it is not a pleasant thought that you might be reborn time and again but it is most desirable to be united with the only thing which is not maya and which will not pass away, i.e. Brahman, the only *real* thing in existence. It is desire for existence in the world of maya which causes you to be reborn because you build up *karma* (action, guilt) which prevents you from realizing that atman and Brahman are one. If you can stop taking part in the world of maya you will have no karma or actions to tell against you. The Hindu therefore strives towards a life in which he has as little karma as possible. In order to understand Hinduism and Buddhism it is absolutely essential to grasp the meaning of the word *karma*.

KARMA

Bound up with samsara is the doctrine of karma which is the most religious feature of Hinduism because it links the rather abstract idea of atman/Brahman with the notion that your actions are all-important in determining whether you achieve moksha. If you do not achieve moksha then your karma determines your next incarnation. When you live a life without karma you realize that atman and Brahman are one, i.e. moksha. Hinduism teaches that whatever you do, however trivial it might appear to you at the time, is important because it will affect you for all time, in every incarnation. Your station in this life is the result of the karma, or the lack of it, which you have been building up in your previous incarnations.

It is karma, then, which determines your caste and since it determines your caste it also makes it more or less difficult to achieve moksha. It is probably easier for a Brahmin to realize that he is one with Brahman than it is for a Shudra; the Brahmin has the advantage of being able to study the scriptures at first hand. You should rise in caste incarnation after incarnation as the weight of karma against you is lightened. Every bad Hindu has the possibility of one day becoming a good Hindu and achieving moksha; you always have another chance. Birth into a particular caste indicates the progress your soul has made but just because you are at the bottom of the caste scale (a Shudra) does not mean that you cannot achieve moksha; the truth of union with Brahman may come to anyone in a flash. You can keep down the weight of karma against you by keeping the dharma of your caste—this idea is taught in the Bhagavad Gita. The higher your caste the greater, of course, are your responsibilities. For example, a bad Brahmin will build up more karma than a bad Pariah; he ought to have known better. The bad Brahmin may well end up well down the caste scale or even as an animal in his next incarnation.

The Hindu ideal is, then, to live a karma-less existence. If you do this you will achieve moksha and, at death, be absorbed into Brahman to be born no more.

It should be pointed out, however, that the development of a rigid caste structure cannot be put down entirely to religious influence. The doctrines of karma and samsara went a long way towards providing a neat solution to the problem of social inequality: it was all due to karma; and in any case there was always the possibility of achieving a better state so long as you behaved in the manner expected of your group. It is perhaps not without significance that the Pariah (outcastes) are the most socially and economically depressed group in India.

THE INDIAN IDEA OF TIME

In the Western world and in all those countries influenced by Judaism, Christianity and Islam, we tend to think of time as existing in a straight line. Along this line we can mark events which have taken place in the past, put a point to represent the present and also, to some extent, indicate certain events which will take place in the future. In other words, there is a beginning and an ending of things. Hindus, however, do not think of time as working towards a goal. It is rather like a revolving wheel for life consists of endless repetitions. Although life constantly repeats itself those who are caught up in time can free themselves from the wheel by union with Brahman.

YOGA

The word *yoga* means 'yoking', 'disciplining', and is really a way of achieving mastery over the mind and body by means of exercises. The idea is to cut yourself off from the passing world which is maya and concentrate on that which is neither passing nor maya but eternal and real—Brahman. Yoga is not mentioned in the Vedas but there is archaeological evidence to suggest that the postures used by yogis today were in fact practised in the Indus Valley thousands of years ago. Seals which have been unearthed show individuals practising yoga. There are many forms of yoga but we need only take a brief look at the simplest form.

You will remember that the devout Hindu tries to live a life in which he builds up as little karma as possible. Karma is acquired by activity in the world of maya—by living a worldly life. So if you can cut yourself off from the world and focus your attention on Brahman you will not build up karma, at least while you concentrate. This concentration is yoga.

The Hindu will sit cross-legged on a low platform. He makes himself as comfortable as possible; it is necessary to be relaxed in order to concentrate, but not too relaxed. He straightens his back and then focusses his eyes on the tip of his nose. If you try this you will find that, although you are aware of what is going on around you it is, for the most part, out of focus and so does not distract you. If you closed your eyes instead you would find that your mind would begin to wander and all concentration would then be lost. The yogi can, therefore, cut himself off from the world about him and concentrate on Reality. Some yogis have developed such perfect control that they can very easily slow down the beating of the heart. Some appear to stop breathing altogether for an alarming length of time. Basically, then, yoga is a means of quietly looking within yourself to discover atman and therefore Brahman: it is a means of discovering God within yourself.

Some Yogis go to extremes of self-mortification. This man has been lying on thorns in a trance for some hours

The following is a quotation from the Bhagavad Gita: it shows that the same kind of discipline as used in meditation should be applied to all aspects of life; for example, eating and drinking. It is the Lord Krishna who is speaking:

> *The man of the Rule (yoga) shall ever hold himself under the Rule, abiding alone in a secret place, utterly subdued in mind, without craving and without possessions.*
>
> *On a pure spot he shall set for himself a firm seat, neither overhigh nor over-low, and having over it a cloth, a deer's skin, and kusa grass.*
>
> *On this couch he shall seat himself with thought intent and the working of the mind and sense-instruments restrained, and shall for purification of spirit labour on the Rule.*
>
> *Firm, holding body, head, and neck in unmoving equipoise, gazing on the end of his nose, and looking not round about him,*
>
> *Calm of spirit, void of fear, abiding under the vow of chastity, with mind restrained and thought set on me, so shall he sit that is under the Rule, given over to me.*

(Bhagavad Gita 6: 10-14)

In India you sometimes see yogis on the side of a busy road completely oblivious to what is happening round about them. Yogis say that when they meditate they are beyond hearing, seeing, tasting or smelling; beyond good and evil, time, space; the yogi is at one with Brahman.

In Hindu schools time is set aside for the study of yoga and the students are given special breathing exercises to perform and must accustom themselves to various yogic postures.

BHAKTI AND THE EPICS

In the Vedas we have seen belief in a variety of nature deities who are means of looking at the one central deity. In the Upanishads we have come into contact with a highly intellectual and somewhat complicated set of religious beliefs; what makes the Upanishads difficult is that you do not understand the meaning of any one of these ideas—samsara, karma, moksha, caste, dharma—unless you understand them all. We now come to the Epics with their stress on *bhakti* or personal devotion to a particular god. The god of the Epics is Vishnu and in the *Bhagavad Gita* Krishna, Vishnu's incarnation, develops the Upanishadic notion of Brahman while at the same time laying stress on the idea of devotion to himself as the divine in personal, human form. The popularity of the way of bhakti led to its incorporation into the worship of the other important Hindu deity, Shiva, who is not, however, the subject of the epic literature. Bhakti, therefore, is a term which is applicable both to Vaishnavism (the worship of Vishnu) and to Shaivism (the worship of Shiva and of his consort, Shakti). The impersonal Brahman of the Upanishads is too distant and abstract for many; indeed the Upanishads themselves show a drift towards bhakti when Isvara, a personal deity, takes the place of Brahman.

The notion of bhakti is expressed in the two great epics or legends which form the 'popular' basis for Hinduism today—the Ramayana and the Mahabharata. The development of these scriptures is reckoned by some scholars to have continued for over a hundred years. It is perhaps safe to say that the two legends reached their final written form around A.D. 200 but, of course, they were circulated orally for many years before this time. In the bhakti movement the common people put the thought of the Upanishads into practice in a personal and practical way. The Epics do not contradict the thought of the Upanishads but rather complement it.

AVATARAS

Before we look at the legends we must take into account a now and important idea. Every so often, it is believed, a deity allows himself to be reborn on earth in order to conquer evil and restore peace and order. An incarnation of a god is called an *avatara*. Since Vishnu is the protector and sustainer of the universe it is only reasonable that the avataras mentioned in the legends should be of him rather than of the other two members of the 'trinity': Brahma the creator and Shiva the destroyer.

> *Whenever there is a decline of dharma and rise of adharma (unrighteousness) I incarnate myself.*
> *For the protection of the good, for the destruction of the wicked and for the establishment of righteousness, I come into being from age to age.*

(Bhagavad Gita 4:7-8)

It should be pointed out that these avataras of Vishnu are not thought of as actually having taken place in history; the avataras were not necessarily real people or animals. Therefore, it is not very apt to compare them with the idea of God being incarnated (enfleshed) in the Jesus of history as taught in the Christian gospels.

Hindus recognize ten avataras of Vishnu (although some put the number as high as twenty-four).

1   The fish (Matsya). In the form of a fish Vishnu is meant to have saved early man.
2   The Tortoise (Kurma). The Tortoise, it was imagined, had the ability to find mislaid belongings.
3   The Boar (Varahavatara). In the form of a boar Vishnu pulled the earth from under the waters where the demons had buried it.
4   The Man Lion (Narasimha). When Vishnu takes this form he delivers man from his oppressors.
5   The Dwarf (Varnana). Vishnu paraded before a demon called Boli as a dwarf. Boli thought that he could easily overpower a dwarf but when he went for Varnana the latter expanded himself and defeated the demon.
6   The Porasurama is a hero who saved the Brahmins from the hostility of the Kshatriya warriors.
7   Rama, who appears in the Ramayana, is a model son and husband. As Rama, Vishnu destroyed the demons who took Sita.
8   Krishna. In the Bhagavad Gita Vishnu appears as Arjuna's charioteer.
9   The historical Buddha.

Rama, the seventh
avatara of Vishnu,
with his bow

10   Kalki. This is an avatara of Vishnu which is expected in the
future when he will appear in the sky astride a white horse,
brandishing a sword. He will have come for the final destruction of the wicked and the establishment of law.

These avataras may be compared to the Bodhisattvas of Mahayana
Buddhism who, instead of completing their release from the world,
remain in order to help others reach enlightenment.

Although Rama and Krishna were meant to be merely the instru-
ments of Vishnu they were made into gods in their own right. In
fact, in N. India the gods Rama and Krishna are of more importance than Vishnu himself.

THE RAMAYANA

The Ramayana (*Career of Rama*) is a lengthy Sanskrit poem
written by Valmiki[1]. It exists in various versions, has been translated

[1] About the second century B.C.

Hanuman, the monkey god

into most of the Indian languages and is loved all over India. The most common (Hindi) version is by Tulsidas, a sixteenth-century poet. It is a delightful family story of the love of a husband, Rama, for his wife, Sita. Rama is described as the king of the northern area.

Sita was kidnapped by Ravana, the demon, who took her to Lanka (Ceylon). She was discovered, however, by Hanuman, the chief of the monkeys, and his fellow monkeys constructed a bridge of planks and rocks across from the mainland to Ceylon. Rama used this bridge to rescue Sita. At the end of the story, Rama and Sita return to their country from which they have been exiled and Rama ascends the throne. Since Hanuman helped the couple Hindus now consider monkeys as sacred and they are treated with great respect in various temples.

Rama is said to be the seventh avatara of Vishnu. The Ramayana tale is retold in the modern languages of today and is a favourite of both educated and uneducated alike. The story is part of every literary textbook in every school. It is related on all festive occasions. It is often acted. It has been produced as a film in several different Indian dialects and wherever the film is shown a 'full house' can be expected. The story teaches purity of motive and action and is a kind of bible for 150 million people in North India.

THE MAHABHARATA—THE BHAGAVAD GITA

The Mahabharata is the longest poem ever written, containing 100,000 verses. It stresses morality and devotion (bhakti) to God. The story is about the struggle between two families, the Kurus and the Pandavas. These two families were related. They fight a battle at Kuru Kshctra (the Kuru field) near Delhi.

The most important section of the Mahabharata is the *Bhagavad Gita* (the Lord's Song) which is probably the most cherished writing of all Hindu literature[1]. It represents virtually every point of view within Hinduism.

Arjuna, son of Indra (the Vedic god), and a Pandava prince, cannot make up his mind whether it is wrong to fight and kill members of the Kuru family to whom he is related. He holds a conversation with his charioteer, Krishna, who turns out to be an avatara of the god Vishnu. The two armies are facing each other but Arjuna dare not give the sign for battle to commence; he does not wish to be guilty of murder, not even when the reward is fame and glory. His bow falls from his hand. Then Krishna tells him that not only may he kill but he *must* go to battle. He is a Kshatriya and it is therefore his caste obligation.

Arjuna, says Krishna, is making a mountain out of mole-hill; in fact there is not even a mole-hill, for dying is not a reality because the soul cannot be killed; it will either be reincarnated or absorbed into Brahman. The one who kills and the one who is killed are both Brahman and, of course, Brahman cannot be destroyed.

> *He who thinks the soul is the slayer and he who thinks it is the*
> *slain do not understand.*
> *It neither slays nor is it slain. . . .*
>
> *It is never born and never dies, nor, once it exists, does it cease*
> *to be.*
> *Unborn, eternal, abiding and ancient, it is not slain when the*
> *body is slain.*

[1] Possibly inserted into the Mahabharata during the first century A.D.

As a man puts off his worn out clothes and puts on other new ones, so the embodied soul puts off worn out bodies and goes to others that are new.

(Bhagavad Gita 2:19-22)

There is, then, no real killing, no real death. Arjuna, therefore, must do his duty without wishing for reward or recognition but simply because it is his duty, i.e. it must be done by yoga or discipline; it must not be done for selfish or personal reasons, otherwise it is sinful. Yoga, Krishna says, is most important but the best kind of yoga is that of devotion to the Lord Krishna:

Have thy mind on me, be devoted to me, sacrifice to me, do reverence to me. To me shalt thou come; what is true I promise; dear art thou to me.

Abandoning all duties come to me, the one refuge: I will free thee from all sins: sorrow not.

(Bhagavad Gita 18:65-6)

The way of bhakti to Krishna is the best form of worship you can offer. In Krishna, the impersonal Brahman becomes a personal, loving God. Krishna, because he is kindly, accepts all devotion, even though it might be offered to other gods. Any sincere and honest man who is devoted to truth is dear to the Lord Krishna. Anything which is offered with devotion is accepted by him—'even a leaf, a flower, fruit or water, if offered with devotion'. Krishna does not require elaborate Vedic sacrifices.

At the end of the Gita Arjuna asks to see Krishna in all his glory; he then reveals himself in terrifying form. In order that he might see this form without being completely overcome by it, Krishna gives Arjuna a 'Divine Eye'; human vision could not stand the sight. Quaking with fear, he asks Krishna to show himself in human form so that he might become collected in mind and restored to normal. Seeing Krishna's human form, Arjuna is no longer afraid.

The poem ends with Arjuna making a confession of faith in the Lord Krishna:

My bewilderment has vanished away; I have gotten remembrance by thy grace, O Never-Falling. I stand freed from doubt: I will do thy word.

(Bhagavad Gita 18:73)

The Gita is not just a story about a peace-loving warrior but deals with man's attempt to make sense of the world in which he finds himself and in which he meets with suffering and death on every side. The Hindu finds consolation in the notion that the essence of the living person, the soul, even though the body suffers and passes away, is eternal and real. The Upanishads suited the needs of the thoughtful man; the Gita, by introducing Krishna-devotion, enables the ordinary man to become involved. Modern Hindus are enormously fond of the Gita.

We shall be looking at some important developments from traditional Hinduism when we examine the religion of the Sikhs and the most important product of Hinduism, that is Buddhism, which is no longer to be found to any extent in its homeland.

MOHANDAS KARAMCHAND GANDHI

During the last hundred years there have been numerous reformers at work within Hinduism but none have had such wide and immediate appeal as Mahatma (Great Soul) Gandhi (1869-1948). Hinduism represents a multitude of different religious quests and ideas; in Gandhi's life can be seen a magnificent practical expression of this diversity and the issues of his teaching and example are with us to this day. He is considered the most significant modern commentator on the Gita.

His main doctrine was that of *ahimsa* (non-violence) by which all obstacles could be overcome. Ahimsa would eventually lead to the apprehension of *Sat* (Truth). 'Truth is God.' The method involved is *Satyagraha* (holding on to Truth). Truth is vindicated not by inflicting suffering on one's opponent but on oneself. This is why Gandhi fasted to gain his political ends (Indian Independence). By fasting he exerted a kind of mental pressure on the British Government; if he did not have his way he would fast to death. (Perhaps the ethics of Gandhi's interpretation of ahimsa might be questioned.)

He championed the outcastes and called them *Harijan*—children of God. His intention was not to abolish the caste system but rather to spiritualize the concept, to reinterpret it in the light of ahimsa. The claims and needs of the poorest peasant were as great or equal to those of the Brahmin caste. Untouchability, for Gandhi, was quite alien to the spirit of Hinduism. He did much to improve the condition of the Harijan people and it is thanks to him that they are now able to enter temples. Gandhi also saw that truth was revealed in other religions but chose to reform Hinduism from within rather than introduce doctrines alien to India.

Gandhi believed that all these ideas are inherent in the Bhagavad Gita. Some would argue, however, that it would appear that

Mahatma Gandhi among his people

Arjuna, in fulfilling his caste duty, must resort to violence. On the other hand he is presented as doing his duty with non-attachment and without desire or trace of self and with his mind in union with God. Perhaps to fight without passion (i.e. with non-attachment) is to have no violence, for himsa (violence) is the product of passion. For Gandhi, if the Gita ideal is fully realized, violence would stop of its own accord and Satyagraha would be the logical step. Arjuna used the weapons at his disposal; for Gandhi, Satyagraha should be used to gain what is just and true (Sat). Gandhi did not merely interpret the Gita; he put his interpretation into practice. He preached the way of life by which he was living and men could judge by what they saw, not merely by what they heard.

It was much to Gandhi's regret that when independence was achieved in 1947 it meant also the religious partition of India into Hindu and Muslim countries—the Republics of India and Pakistan. (Perhaps the existence of the Sikh religion is a reminder that Hinduism and Islam are not entirely incompatible. It is also sad to reflect that it was the Sikhs for whom Partition was to prove the greatest hardship.) He fasted as a protest against the tragic separation but in so doing evoked the open madness of a Hindu fanatic who, on 30th January, 1948, shot and killed the Mahatma at an open-air prayer meeting.

In many villages of India Gandhi is venerated as an avatara in his own right. His follower, Vinoba Bhave, continues with Gandhi's work of distributing land given by the rich to the Harijan people.

PRACTICAL RELIGION, CUSTOMS AND FESTIVALS

THE SECTS

Vishnu and Shiva gradually evolved as the principal deities of Hinduism; both exhibit non-Aryan features. Many hymns were composed in honour of both gods. The hymns of the Nayanars to Shiva and those of the Alvars to Vishnu are still popular throughout Southern India. During the early Christian era Hinduism became established in the form ('classical Hinduism') which we find today. Roughly speaking, although there are *two* main deities there are *three* groups (but the lines of demarcation are by no means unambiguous). These groups are known as *Vaishnava*, *Shaiva* and *Shakta* and comprise devotees of Vishnu, Shiva and the Shakti, the active, female side of Shiva, respectively.

The beliefs of each sect and their outward ritual expression vary considerably yet in spite of this there is no real friction between them. One group will believe that the other's god or goddess is merely a lesser deity or a secondary manifestation of their own deity. The three sects are to be found throughout India but the numerical strength of each varies according to location. Vaishnavism is predominant with the exception of Tamil land in the south and Kashmir in the north. Shaktism is not predominant in any particular area but enjoys considerable popularity in Assam and Bengal. One's choice of deity is usually a matter of family tradition but it is not uncommon to find devotees of one god worshipping at the shrine of another. The educated tend to think of all the gods as various aspects of the one God whereas the less sophisticated think of their god as more powerful than any other.

Judaism is monotheistic in that it excludes all other deities. Yahweh is Israel's God and beside him there is no other; he alone is God. Hinduism, on the other hand, has not singled out a particular deity with an exclusive prerogative on the allegiance of all sons of India; instead it has gradually merged together the lesser deities and these have become assimilated to one or two of the greater deities. This is why Hinduism can tolerate beliefs which might appear opposed, if not contradictory. This is why the Hindu can pray to more than one god. In doing this he sees no inconsistency.

SHIVA AND ASSOCIATED DEITIES

Vishnu, as we have seen, is kindly and willing to help man when the need arises. Shiva, on the other hand, is a god who exhibits

Shiva as
Lord of the Dance

many facets of his personality, some pleasant and some not so
pleasant. In some sculptures he is seen as destroying time, with a
string of skulls round his neck, performing the dance which ter-
minates all things and brings about the end of the *Kalpa* (the Hindu
era).

Shiva is also represented as Lord of the Dance (Shiva Nataraja).
In this form the four-armed god performs the cosmic dance. In his
upper right hand he holds a small drum which represents sound as
the primal element in creation. In his upper left hand he bears a
flame, for fire is the means of the final destruction of the universe.
The gestures of his other two hands show how life and death are for
ever held rhythmically in a state of balance. The right foot treads on
the back of the demon of forgetfulness, who grasps a cobra, and the
left is raised in dance. This is meant to symbolize the stream of
consciousness from knowledge to ignorance to knowledge, from

birth to death to rebirth. The arch represents the whole universe which depends entirely on Shiva's function as creator and destroyer —all life is dissolved to be recreated.

Shiva is also Lord of Ascetics (*Mahayogi*). It will be recalled that the citizens of Mohenjo-daro possibly thought of him in this form. He keeps the world intact by virtue of his meditations and in this sense shares the preserving characteristics of Vishnu. At the same time he is the god of fertility and called *Pasupati* (Lord of Beasts). In this form his symbol is the male reproductive organ, the *linga*, suitably disguised, set in a female *yoni*.

Vishnu's partner is the goddess *Shri* or *Lakshmi* but these are relatively unimportant compared with Shiva's wife, *Shakti*. Shakti is known by various names: in her fierce and ugly form she is called *Durga* or *Kali* and in her beneficent form she is known as *Parvati* or *Uma*. The majority of Hindus venerate her as a deity of secondary importance but the Shakta sects treat her as the supreme deity. She is referred to as *Mahadevi* (Great Goddess) or simply 'the Mother'.

The Shakta sects believe that since his great act of creation Shiva has remained inactive. His active energy (his *shakti*) is now embodied in his wife. The actual act of creation was the coitus of Shiva with Shakti. It is because of this that the ritual and symbolism of Shaktism leans rather heavily on sexual imagery. Since Shakti is the active side of Shiva it is natural that the worshipper's attention should be centred on her rather than on her passive husband. The Shakta feel that Shiva does not need worship; it is the Great Goddess, the Mother, to whom all worship should be offered for she is supreme. As Durga or Kali she personifies death and darkness. As Parvati or Uma she often appears as a singularly attractive woman. It is still common for her devotees to make animal sacrifices to her, especially when she appears as Durga or Kali, and there is evidence to suggest that human sacrifice was occasionally practised in the past.

There are also a number of less significant deities associated with Shiva, the best-known of which is *Ganesha*, Shiva's son. He is the good-natured, potbellied, elephant-headed god who brings good luck and it is customary to pray to him before tackling any new task.

Some deities are popular among particular groups of people who might belong to a variety of sects. For example, *Sarasvati*, the goddess of study, is prayed to by students at examination time. *Hanuman*, the monkey-god of the Ramayana, is particularly popular among the poorer people of North India. There are numerous village gods and goddesses—deities associated with, and only worshipped at, one particular place. Whereas the great gods are always busy the village gods, it is believed, will have time to deal with the poor man's problems.

Divinity is manifested in many material, common things. Possibly the best-known symbol of divinity in India is the cow. It is difficult to trace the origins of cow veneration in India for it is an ancient cult. The cow is not venerated because of any economic value that might be attached to her but because she is the embodiment of Mother Earth. She wanders at will through busy traffic, enters temple precincts where only priests are admitted and is never injured. Gandhi encouraged cow veneration as he thought that it entailed a practical illustration of the essential oneness of all life and therefore of the sacredness of all life—the idea that in all that is, there is that which is God. He also said that the condition and treatment of many cows in India was a disgrace and thought it not improbable that cattle in India were treated worse than anywhere else in the world. On one occasion he ordered that a suffering calf be destroyed.

Several other animals receive homage. The bull-image, Nandi, is sacred to Shiva and can be seen in most temples dedicated to this god. Monkeys are sacred to Rama and must not be killed. Snakes are also considered to be holy and should only be killed in an emergency. Those who kill a snake should go into mourning.

Certain trees and plants are the embodiment of the divine in nature. Banyan and pipal trees are not to be felled. The *tulasi* plant is holy to Vishnu. Each village has a sacred tree and many of the pious cultivate sacred plants. The Ganges and several other rivers and streams are considered sacred and so are certain types of stone and rock.

In other words, the Hindu cannot escape coming into contact with the divine; the divine is to be encountered and confronts man in all things, both animate and inanimate. Whereas Judaism's God is transcendent, categorically indivisible and so other than man that man dare not mention his name, the Hindu finds God in all forms; the God at the centre of things is to be felt in all things. All that is points to the reality of God. Life itself is a symbol. Even the illiterate peasant intuits that beyond all these objects of veneration there lies the one Reality; the name is immaterial.

CUSTOMS

To the educated Indian it is probably the Hindu philosophy which is most important but to the ordinary person, unversed in the intricacies of the Upanishads or the interpretation of the Gita, it is largely customs and ceremonies which make up the Hindu religion. Apart from marriage and cremation the old Vedic rituals have mostly disappeared.

HOME AND TEMPLE

Many families keep an image of their deity in the home where it is treated as a visitor of great consequence. In temples the image is treated as a king or queen. Most Hindu acts of devotion take place in the home and there are family rites for every kind of occasion, from conception to years after death. There are ceremonies to ensure safety in child bearing and rites for the veneration of ancestors. A strict Brahmin should perform the *samskaras* (about forty rites) during the course of his life. It is only the old-fashioned Brahmins, however, who observe all these rites. A rich Brahmin will probably pay a priest to perform them for him. All three of the dvija castes are required by their dharma to perform special ceremonies, but again it is only the most conservative and financially independent Hindus who have the time to observe their dharma to the full. Be this as it may, it is nevertheless still generally true to say that the average Hindu devotes far more time to meditation and religious observances than does the average European or American Christian.

The observant Hindu begins his devotions before sunrise by uttering the sacred and numinous word *Om* from the Vedas. This sacred word is said or sung before and after all prayers, recitations and religious discourses. It is said to attune the soul of the worshipper to the infinite; it can fill him with awe and wonder. Having uttered this sacred syllable he repeats a mantra on the name of his personal deity, mentions the name of his guru (to whom he owes his religious understanding) and then says a prayer identifying himself with the ultimate Brahman.

After tying his hair up in a knot he says the gayatri mantra. Devotees of Shiva paint the white *tilaka* marks horizontally on the forehead and those of Vishnu make them vertically. Wearing the sacred thread across his bare trunk he sits, bare-footed, in yogic posture, facing east to greet the sun which reminds him of the regeneration of all things. Sipping water, he continues to utter the name of his god while he touches his body in six different places to identify himself with the divine. He makes an oblation of water to the image of the god, recites verses from the Vedas and repeats the gayatri mantra numerous times. Midday and evening worship is similar in nature. All Hindu ceremonies end with these words:

> Peace be in the higher worlds, peace be in the firmament, peace be on earth. May the waters flow peacefully, may the herbs and shrubs grow peacefully; may all the divine powers bring unto us peace. Brahman, the Supreme, is peace. May all be in peace and only peace; and may that peace come unto me. Om. Peace. Peace. Peace.

Sometimes a room is set aside for puja (worship) but more usually the rites are performed in the corner of the living room where a small image or symbol is set up. These images will have gone through the

A Hindu symbol, the sacred syllable *Om*

pranpratishta process whereby they become the direct means of contact between the worshipper and the deity symbolized. Their function, in a sense, is not unlike that of the consecrated host of the Roman Catholic Mass. The symbol for Vishnu is the *shalagrama* stone (fossil ammonite) and that of Shiva is the stone *linga* (phallus). Shalagramas are small worn stones from a riverbed. A river goddess once asked that Vishnu be reborn in her womb as one of his avataras. The stones are gathered from certain streams and rivers in memory of this request. The origin of linga veneration is quite obviously sexual. The story is that while Shiva and his beautiful wife, Parvati, were engaged in the act of intercourse they were visited by Parvati's father, Brigu. Shiva refused to be interrupted. Brigu was so incensed by this lack of respect that he cursed Shiva to be worshipped as a phallus. The phallic symbolism of Shiva has, however, been sublimated and the linga is hardly recognizable as such.

A linga of ice in a cave in the Himalayan foothills which is regarded by Hindus as the living symbol of Shiva. Pilgrims throw offerings of flowers, clothing, etc, some of which freeze on the symbol

Shaivite ascetics often carry a trident called a *pinaka* which is the symbol of lightning and characterizes Shiva as the god of storms. The pinaka was originally one of his weapons. His other symbols are the sword, bow, a club with a skull at the end and three serpents. He wears one of the serpents as the sacred thread.

If the family owns an image (as distinct from a symbol) of the deity it is always pampered. It will be washed, receive changes of clothes and be offered fresh fruit. Raw food and lights are arranged on the left of the image and cooked food on its right. There are some occasions when the family will wish to hold a special ceremony in the home and will employ a priest to officiate. Bells are rung, conch shells blown and a variety of offerings made to the image. Rich families will often employ a priest on a full-time basis and in such homes the caste obligations are usually observed in their entirety by proxy. This, however, is the exception rather than the rule.

With the exception of those who have chosen the ascetic life, marriage is considered a religious duty for the production of sons. The main part of the wedding ceremony, which usually takes place at home in the garden, is when the couple walk hand in hand around the sacred fire and take seven steps together. Although divorce has been legalized in India most Hindus believe that once the seven steps have been taken the bond is indissoluble—this constitutes consummation. The union is said to continue in the afterlife.

Many Hindus believe that, according to the working out of the law of karma, a special partner is destined for them. It is the duty of the parents to find that special partner; they decide on the kind of match they feel will suit their son or daughter and then make enquiries.

The scriptures clearly indicate the place of women in society. A girl must be obedient to her father: in marriage a woman must be obedient to her husband: in old age she is subservient to her sons. She is allowed personal possessions such as jewellery but cannot hold real estate. She must obey her husband's every whim. In North India many women follow the Muslim custom of *purdah* (veiling of women).

> *No act is ever to be done according to her own will by a young girl, a young woman, or even by an old woman, though in their own houses.*
> *In her childhood a girl should be under the will of her father; in her youth, of her husband; her husband being dead, of her sons. . . .*
> *She must always be cheerful and clever in household business, with the furniture well cleaned, and with not a free hand in expenditure. . . .*
> *The good wife of a husband must never do anything disagreeable to him. . . . She must be till death subdued, intent, chaste. . . . Wife, son and slave, those three are said to be without property: whatever property they acquire is his to whom they belong.*

(Laws of Manu)

Polygamy is permitted but not encouraged. The Hindu ideal is to be found in the Ramayana where Rama and Sita were faithful to one another. If, however, the wife proves to be sterile or only produces daughters then it used to be considered a man's duty to take another wife to ensure the continuance of the family and the attendance to ancestral rites after his death.

Although the status of women in India is, for the most part, secondary to that of men, this is not to imply that women are not treated with respect. In the home a girl is called *kanya devi*, the 'girl-goddess'. The equivalent of 'Mrs' is *Shrimati* which means 'graceful lady'. After her surname the word *devi* is added, meaning 'goddess' and the word *ji*, a term of great respect, is added to it—*Deviji*. The woman has complete control of the home. Her husband will give her all the money and she will hand back as much as she can spare.

The great reformer, Gotama Buddha, included nuns in the Buddhist Sangha. In South India, where society is based on Dravidian rather than on Aryan ideals, there are some areas where property is handed down to daughters, not to sons, and where a bride does not go to live at her husband's home but he comes to live with her.

Today, educated Indian women enjoy international prestige and no candidate of any political party in India stands much chance of winning an election against a woman candidate.

> *By woman we are conceived and from her we are born;*
> *With her we are betrothed and with her we are married.*
> *It is woman who is our friend and she who perpetuates the family.*
> *When one woman dies, man seeks another.*
> *And with her he is established in society.*
> *Out of woman comes woman herself: without her no other exists.*
> *Why call woman evil when she gives birth to kings.*
>
> (Guru Nanak. Asa di Var slok 2:19)

The lawbooks say that life should be divided into four stages, the last of which is to give up all possessions and become a religious mendicant (*sannyasi*) in one's old age, but only a small minority of Hindus in fact do this. However, many elderly men do devote considerable time to meditation.

From Vedic times it has been customary to dispose of the dead by cremation. Members of the low castes often bury their dead and young children are usually buried. For ten days after the death all those who have been in contact with the corpse are unclean and must perform purification rites. Prayers are said asking that the soul of the departed might be reclothed in a suitable body for his next life. If the funeral ceremonies are not properly observed it is believed that the soul will remain attached to its old haunts and become a ghost. This is why all Hindus want to have a son for, technically, only sons can perform the funeral duties (*antyeshti* ceremony). A substitute may be employed but he can never perform the task so well as a son. From time to time further offerings called *shraddha* are made by the son. As in China, this kind of ancestor veneration makes for corporate solidarity.

The temples of Southern and Central India are buildings of considerable beauty whereas those of the North are usually comparatively modern, small and unspectacular. All temples are built on

A feast day at a Hindu temple in Delhi

the same plan which consists of a central shrine, housing the image of the deity, over which is erected a tower. Before the shrine is the congregational area around which runs a covered ambulatory for processions. There is also a pool for ritual bathing. Priests officiate at temple ceremonies but the laity come and go as they please and worship in the manner they choose. The shrine houses the image and symbols of the deity to whom the temple is dedicated and these are treated in the same kind of way, but perhaps with more pomp, as the images at home. Visitors light lamps in honour of the deity and walk round the shrine keeping the right side towards the image. It is common to see Hindus prostrating themselves in various parts of the building.

The god is woken up at dawn in his bedroom where he has been asleep with his wife. He is then carried ceremonially to the shrine where he is washed, dried and dressed. Offerings are made of flowers, perfume, fruit, incense and lights. He consumes the spiritual aspect of the offering and the rest is distributed to the poor. The god is fanned with peacock-feathers and is entertained with music.

Animal sacrifice is not common in the North but it is a feature of several Southern temples. Devotees of Durga will decapitate a goat or cockerel before her image so that some of the blood touches it. Sacrifices to Kali are offered daily in the Kaligat temple in Calcutta. She is thought of as the source of fertility and women kiss the stonework of the Kaligat in the hope of conceiving. The devotees of the goddess form two sub-groups known as the 'right hand' and the 'left hand'. Numerically the 'right hand' group is superior and its members perform their worship publicly. The 'left hand' group is somewhat esoteric and its adherents seek salvation by means of the five M's : *madya* (liquor), *matsya* (fish), *mamsa* (flesh), *mudra* (gestures) and *maithuna* (copulation). The idea behind their ritual is to overcome evil by the application of evil. The 'left hand' (*Vamacharis*) conceive of the five M's symbolically: in non-liturgical life they are considered to live virtuously. The special scriptures of the 'left hand' are Tantras which were possibly the product of late Mahayana Buddhism in India. Before the Westerner turns away from such beliefs and practices in disgust it is as well to reflect that the Shakta cult has points of similarity with religious (devotional) phenomena elsewhere, e.g. the Christian religion where the female element is represented in the Roman Catholic cult of the Virgin Mary.

Many Hindus object to any kind of animal sacrifice and regret that it persists within Hinduism. Those who offer an animal for sacrifice are allowed afterwards to eat it so it is possible for a Hindu to eat meat without breaking the rule of non-violence (*ahimsa*). The soul of the sacrificed animal is meant to achieve immediate bliss; selection for sacrifice is a great honour.

Although the most important Hindu rites are performed in the home Hindus do look on their temple as the centre of religious life. The temple is not merely a place of worship but the hub of social life. For example, when religious plays are performed the temple becomes a theatre.

FESTIVALS

In India festivals are very popular and play an important part in community life. They are accompanied by parties and the performance of Indian classical and folk dances. Festivals occur at all times of the year and many are peculiar to particular districts. Some, however, are held all over India. *New Year* occurs in March or April. In October there is *Divali*, the festival of lights, in honour of Vishnu and his wife Lakshmi, when fireworks are let off to scare away evil spirits. Also in October is *Dasara* in honour of Durga. This festival recalls how Rama defeated the demon Ravana, the kidnapper of Sita, by shooting off each of his ten heads. The goddess is said to have assisted Rama in this noble victory. Models of Ravana filled with fireworks are paraded through the streets and set alight. *Holi*, the festival of colours, occurs in February or March. People squirt each other with coloured powders and dyes and special attention is given to the amorous conquests of Krishna. All these festivals are occasions for great joy and merrymaking.

Why I am a Hindu

I was born a caste Hindu and for me my religion holds within itself the questions, and some of the answers, which man asks about his own nature and ultimate reality. It is not inflexible, like so many other religions, but is tolerant of a great variety of beliefs and practices. Hinduism, in the words of the great Christian teacher, Paul, is 'all things to all men': it is a religion which caters for all kinds of people, from the most simple to the highly educated. I would find it almost impossible to belong to a religion with a defined creed or body of dogma, for dogmatic statements mean that there can be no change in thinking but since, as I believe, all things are in a state of change, the only sensible religion is one which admits that as civilization changes men will have different needs. Hinduism is such a religion.

I am often asked about the Hindu belief in samsara and karma. 'Do you really believe that?' ask my friends. The answer is, 'Yes, I do.'

By profession I am a research physicist. One of the laws of science and one which all scientists will accept, is that everything which happens has a cause: it is the law of cause and effect. All my friends agree that this law is operative in the universe. Why then does it apply to the physical world but not to man? Why is X born into a rich family, why does he grow up happy and live a good life while, on the other hand, Y is born in poverty, lives a life of crime and dies miserably? Is all this simply a matter of chance, effects without causes? Is there not some law, similar to the one which applies to the physical universe, which applies to man also? I am not talking about the laws of genetics (obviously these laws cause us to be what we are directly) but about a moral law (karma). My present mode of existence is the result of some cause, i.e. a previous mode of existence. It would seem to me that the Hindu reasoning on this subject is logical. If I belonged to the Jewish, Christian or Muslim traditions the only conclusion I could come to would be that God causes one man to be born happy and another miserable, and I am afraid I do not wish to be intimate with such a God. Hinduism is more compassionate than this. Because of rebirth the people of India believe that even the most evil Hindu may one day become a good Hindu.

Another thing about which my Western friends ask is yoga. I imagine they think it is some kind of magic. How can a scientist believe in it? To me it is the way to self-realization. Yoga has a great calming influence which does not leave one even when hard at work; it certainly aids my concentration but for me, first and foremost, it is a means of being at one with ultimate reality.

I am proud of my religion; it plays a most important part in my life. I find in it all the teaching of other religions but in a more compassionate and sympathetic form: Hinduism is persuasive, not coercive. Hindus are the brothers of all those who seek after the truth for 'truth is one'.

Dr L. P. N. Chottai.

Why I am a Hindu

I have been asked why I profess the 'Saivite faith' in Hinduism. When I say I am a Saivite[1], I do not mean I am opposed to the other forms of Hinduism; far from it. In fact, Saivism is liberal enough to embrace all other forms of Hinduism. I believe in Saiva Siddhanta philosophy which is a system which names the God-head as 'Sivam' in preference to any other term. This is a system of thought practised in its pristine purity by a majority of Hindus in South India and North Ceylon. It is monotheistic and pluralistic in character and realistic in approach. According to it 'God is one and is nameless and formless, but men have given him name and form to suit their ideals and experiences.'

This system of thought goes to pre-Vedic times (5000 B.C.). The findings of the excavations of Mohenjo-daro and Harappa show that Saivism is the most ancient of all living religions and that Siva-linga (Shiva), which is found in many places in the world, symbolizes Siva as the Supreme Spirit radiating spiritual effulgence. The sacred books of Saivism and Puranic lore refer to Siva-linga as the Pillar of Fire. The idea that this Supreme Spirit (Sivam) is the self of the Selves is the very foundation of the philosophical structure of this system. 'Remember Siva is the indweller of every living being and be loving towards every one of them.' Saiva Siddhanta recognizes three eternal categories, viz, God (Pati), Soul (Pasu) and Bondage (Pasam).

The Vedas speak of Lord Siva (the God-head) as Visvadhika (one who transcends the universe), Visvakarana (the cause of the universe), Visvarupi (one who has universe as his form) and Visvantaryami (indweller and primary source of motion of universe). The Saiva Siddhanta system presents a noble and lofty conception of God-head which is both absolute of philosophy and God of religion. The name and form of Siva (Vedic Rudra-Siva) is always referred to in this system as

---

[1] The writer prefers the spellings Saivite, Saiva, Sivam, Siva instead of the version used by the authors.

the Supreme Being who is the first cause of the entire universe, who transcends the very consciousness-force of the individual self, who has no birth and death and whose grace and realization alone will lift the individual self above the vicious circle of birth and death.

Evolution is intended for the soul's spiritual growth and its ultimate salvation. The Supreme Being and individual selves are distinguished by the fact that the former never gets himself entangled in the law of karma and in birth and death nor brought down to the level of the suffering multitudes of the souls. He is the 'One, not being the second'. Puranic literature is singularly free from attributing birth or death to Lord Siva.

The Souls are sentient beings who require to be energised by the consciousness-force of God. Their intellect is covered with and limited by an inherent pre-cosmic evil called Anava (spiritual ignorance). For the removal of this ignorance God has bestowed on the bound souls the organism called body and has placed them in the orbit of birth and death subject to nature's laws.

The relationship between God and his consciousness-force is known as Tadatmya (Duality in Unity). It is the relation that exists between a substance and its quality or between the whole and its part. Pure consciousness is the very form of God. This consciousness-force is called Light of Grace. Saivites believe that the Supreme Being, being light, love and bliss, reveals himself to matured souls. This is evidenced by the sacred utterances of the four great Saiva Tamil Saints, Manickavasagar, Sambandar, Appar and Sunderar. The Lord appears before them either in human form or in form divine and makes them purified and perfected souls. They meditate on the spiritual form that was vouchsafed to them and thus establish themselves in tune with the Infinite. The inspired utterings of these God-men or spiritual leaders are the Scriptures and Revelations of the Saivites.

The innumerable Siva temples in South India are the repositories of the religious forms of worship which are the visual expression of the system. The Siva-linga, Nandi (Bull) facing it and the Altar in the temple represent the Supreme (Pati), the released soul, and Malam (bondage-evil principle) respectively. The Nandi representing the Atman turns away from the Altar (world and illusion) and gets released from bondage and directly perceives and enjoys the Supreme in the form of effulgent Bliss. This is the essence of the Saiva Siddhanta philosophy which has kept me enraptured in devotion.

Mr Sabapathipillai, M.A., LL.B., F.R.A.S., F.T.I.I.
President of the Federation of Hindu Organizations in U.K.
President of the Hindu Association of Great Britain

CHAPTER FIVE

Buddhism

Early Buddhism is part of the complex of what may loosely be defined as 'Hinduism'. Some of its doctrine and much of its mythology is derived from this complex of belief in which it originated. However, there is considerable debate today as to whether the original Buddhist movement was unique and independent, or whether it was an offshoot from the main body of Hinduism. Some scholars contend that Buddhism was a child of Brahmanism and never really extricated itself from its source. Others point out that the Buddha did not claim to form a new religion, nor did he reject the old, so that Buddhism originated as a schism intent on reforming Brahmanical religion. Yet others say that although one cannot separate Buddhism from the Hindu complex of that time —for it is the religious and spiritual atmosphere in which it originated—Buddhism was an original creative development that presented religious understanding in a new way.

Like Jesus, the Buddha did not leave his teachings in written form—they were memorized by his disciples and written down many years later after being passed on orally. Because of this many people doubt whether we can say with any confidence that the Buddhist scriptures we now have are reliable historically. For instance, it is very difficult to maintain that the birth stories of the Buddha are credible historically. Yet this is only the same problem as many Christians face with the bible; many believe that the birth stories about Jesus are a mixture of legend and fact. We must investigate the validity of the Buddhist narratives in the same way in which we examine the bible narratives. Many scholars who have done this have come to the conclusion that we can certainly say that the teaching of the Buddha in the Three Universal Truths, the Four Noble Truths and the Noble Eightfold Path is genuinely original to the Buddha and historically accurate.

Buddhism is different from Hinduism in having a historical founder, Gotama Buddha, who probably lived from 563 to 483 B.C.

THE LIFE OF THE BUDDHA

Careful examination of the Buddhist scriptures shows that we can divide the life of the Buddha into three stages: early family life, the Buddha seeking Enlightenment and the preaching of the Buddha to his fellow men.

THE FAMILY LIFE OF THE BUDDHA

There are many legends in the accounts of the early life of the Buddha and some of them make Gotama the son of a powerful king. In fact he was probably the son of a rajah of a small tribe, the Sakyas. He was born a Hindu of the Kshatriya caste. One of the names of Gotama is *Sakyamuni*, which means 'the sage of the Sakyas'. He did not assume the title of 'the Buddha' (i.e. 'the Enlightened One') until after his experience of Enlightenment. His birth place cannot be identified exactly but it is believed to be somewhere in present Nepal.

It would appear that Gotama was a sensitive boy for although he was well cared for and had everything wealth could supply, he was troubled by those things which made life unhappy—the inequality of the caste system in that one is in caste by virtue of birth and not by virtue of merit in one's present incarnation, sickness, old age and death. He married and had a son but remained unhappy. Legend says he saw on successive occasions a very old man, a sick man, a dead man and finally a monk and these four sights determined him to leave his family and set out to find the answer to life's problem, the problem of suffering. At the age of 29 Gotama left his wife and son and started out on his quest.

GOTAMA SEEKS ENLIGHTENMENT

The Buddhist scriptures are vague about the first six years of Gotama's quest but it would seem that he studied under two ascetic teachers and practised *tapas*, that is, bodily austerities. The object of these austerities is to reduce the physical life and thus set free an expansion of spiritual power. Gotama then appears to have practised extreme mortification and fasting, enduring great physical discomforts such as standing for days in one position, wearing irritating garments, letting dirt cover his body and sitting on thorns. He says of his condition at this time: 'When I went to touch my stomach I actually took hold of my spine.' During this period five ascetics were so impressed by his self-discipline that they decided to follow him. He tortured himself so much that he eventually

A pilgrim in meditation at the site of Buddha's enlightenment

collapsed and was assumed dead. He recovered, however, and took food, realizing how foolish bodily austerities were. The five ascetics left him in disgust because he had given up the ascetic way of life.

Gotama continued on his way and when he came to Uruvela he sat under a Bo-tree and vowed never to leave until he attained Enlightenment. Under the Bo-tree Gotama did attain Enlightenment and from then on was known as 'the Buddha'. Gotama sat under the Bo-tree for some time wondering whether or not to preach what he had learned in his Enlightenment. Eventually he decided that he would preach to his fellow men and so began his preaching mission.

THE BUDDHA PREACHES TO HIS FELLOW MEN

The Buddha's first action was to find the five ascetics who had left him. He found them in Benares and preached to them his first sermon which is usually called 'Setting in Motion the Wheel of the Law'. In it the Buddha expounded the 'Four Noble Truths' and the 'Noble Eightfold Path' for the first time. The five ascetics were impressed and became his first disciples.

There is no connected account of the Buddha's preaching career but Buddhism was spread by the journeys of the Buddha and his five associates in North-east and Central India. Later it spread to the west, north and east of the Ganges Valley. The Buddha's decision to preach made Buddhism a missionary religion (compared with Hinduism which is not).

Buddhism spread rapidly and a community known as the *Sangha* was formed. The members lived together for three months of the year, during the rainy season, and for the rest of the year they went out and preached. The essential rules for entering the Sangha were simple—the monk needs to have his head shaved and must wear a yellow robe. Newcomers must confess, 'I take refuge in the Buddha, I take refuge in the Dharma, I take refuge in the Sangha.' This means simply that they believe the Buddha to be their spiritual guide and helper, that they believe in the doctrine (Dharma) of Buddhism and find sustenance and strength in the Buddhist community (Sangha).

The lay Buddhist needs to observe five rules which are:

1   Do not destroy life.
2   Do not steal.
3   Do not be unchaste.
4   Do not lie or deceive.
5   Abstain from intoxicants.

In addition, Buddhists have to observe five more on special fast (*Uposatha*) days:

6   Eat moderately and not after noon.
7   Do not look at dancing or drama.
8   Do not use perfume or ornaments.
9   Do not use a comfortable bed.
10   Do not accept gold or silver.

The Buddha died an old man. His last reported words were, 'Sorrow not, lament not, have I not said . . . in all things there is the element of change, of separation, of otherness. . . . I remind you that the elements of being are transitory.' His body was cremated. He did not claim to be a god although later Buddhism bestowed upon him that honour. Many would dispute that he was a god but few would dispute that he was one of the greatest men who ever lived. His life and thought have been an inspiration to many throughout the centuries.

BASIC BUDDHIST IDEAS

Before we examine in any detail the teaching of the Buddha we must endeavour to understand the Buddhist outlook on life by examining a few basic Buddhist ideas.

Early Buddhist doctrine is rooted in the thought of the Upanishads. The writer of the Maitri Upanishad says, 'In this sort of cycle of existence (samsara) what is the good of enjoyment of desires, when after a man has fed on them there is seen repeatedly his return here to earth?' In this passage there are two basic ideas in Hindu thought which are carried over into Buddhist thought. They are called *samsara* and *karma*.

SAMSARA AND KARMA

Samsara literally means 'continuation' or 'carrying on' and to the Buddhist it is the idea that man has more than one existence—when he dies he is reincarnated or born again. Life to the Buddhist is just an endless round of existences: man is born, dies and is born again. This is known as the *samsara cycle* and it is useful to think of it diagrammatically.

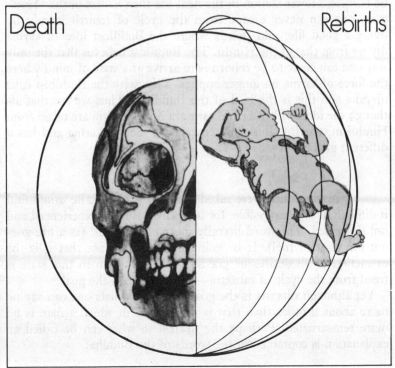

The Samsara cycle

It can be compared with the Christian idea of time:

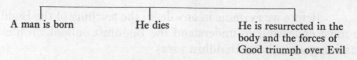

| A man is born | He dies | He is resurrected in the body and the forces of Good triumph over Evil |

Although this may seem strange to the Westerner the Indian regards this cycle of existences as intolerable, for it means that man will never be free from existing in a world which is full of trouble' sorrow and misery. Therefore all Indian philosophies and religious systems are aimed at providing a means of escape from constantly being reborn; the Hindu, it will be remembered, aims to be absorbed into Brahman, the Buddhist aims to reach *nirvana*.

The force which keeps this 'wheel' of samsara turning is called *karma*. It is karma that is the cause of rebirths. Literally karma means 'deed' or 'act' and the Indian believes that everything a man does, in deed or word, creates a kind of force which is carried over when the man dies and leads to his being reconstituted in another body; in other words, born again. Like the Hindu, the Buddhist believes that if a person's acts when he is alive are bad then he will be born in a lower station in the next life than he has in this. However, one can never escape from the cycle of rebirth merely by living a good life; and this is where the Buddhist idea of karma differs from that of the Hindu. The Buddhist believes that the only way one can cease to be reborn is to arrive at a state of mind where the force of karma no longer applies. That state the Buddhist calls nirvana and this is the goal of the Buddhist. Thus we see that although the ideas of karma and samsara in Buddhism are taken from Hinduism, the Buddhist reinterprets the idea of karma and has a different goal in nirvana.

NIRVANA

If a Buddhist were asked to describe nirvana he would find it difficult, if not impossible, for basically it is to be experienced and not described. The word literally means 'going out' (as a fire goes out for want of fuel). It is 'going out' in the sense that it is the extinction of all desires or cravings and so a man in this state is freed from the cycle of samsara—he has reached the goal.

Yet although nirvana is the goal of all Buddhists one can say no more about it other than that it is the state in which a man is no more reincarnated. Perhaps the nearest to what can be called an explanation is contained in the words of the Buddha:

There is, disciples, a condition where there is neither earth nor water, nor fire nor air, nor the sphere of infinite consciousness, nor the sphere of the void, nor the sphere of neither perception nor non-perception . . . that condition, disciples, do I neither call a coming nor a going, nor a standing still nor a falling away . . . but that condition is without fixity . . . it is the end of woe.

In other words, nirvana can best be described in negatives—we can say what it is not rather than what it is.

THE THREE UNIVERSAL TRUTHS

Three other basic Buddhist beliefs are known as the Three Universal Truths.

1 *The idea of anicca* (literally, 'impermanence'). The Buddha was very careful to point out that nothing is the same at this moment as it was a moment ago. Even the 'everlasting hills' are gradually being worn away (as any geologist will confirm). Modern scientists will support this idea of the Buddha that all things are transitory and in a state of flux; biologists tell us that we are in a state of 'dynamic equilibrium' which means that a person is never the same chemical being for more than a couple of seconds at a time. We are physically changing every minute; from the moment we are born we begin to die.

Anicca is like an ever-rolling wheel with four segments as can be seen in the diagram. Nothing is permanent; all is in a state of flux. Life is in a state of flux; it is transitory, passing, fleeting. Whatever else one says of Buddhism, few would argue that this is not so. Because of the transitory nature of life the Buddha concluded that no rest within this world is possible because everything we have here—wealth, fame, power, even love and happiness—are all subject to change.

Anicca

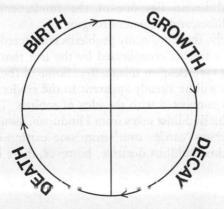

2 *Dukkha* (literally, 'suffering'). 'One thing I teach', said the Buddha, 'dukkha and the ending of dukkha.' The word 'suffering' is only one translation of the word 'dukkha' for it covers all that we understand by pain, ill, disease (physical or mental) including minor irritations such as discomfort or boredom and even awareness of meaninglessness. So to the Buddha dukkha is something we all encounter; no one can escape from it. The teaching of the Buddha was offered as a means of overcoming this problem of suffering.

The essence of early Buddhism can be summed up in the phrase 'seeing things as they really are' (*yathabhutam*). One does this through *prajna* (wisdom). When the Buddhist talks about wisdom he does not mean sagacity or prudence, rather he means a faculty by which one sees into the true nature of things. It is by 'seeing things as they really are' (particularly the true nature of dukkha) that one eventually attains to nirvana.

3 *Anatta* (literally, 'no-soul'). One cannot complete a survey of basic Buddhist ideas without a short summary of the difficult concept of *anatta*. Literally, the word means 'no-soul' and is the idea that man has not, as other major religions teach, a soul. In several religions a basic belief is that man has a soul or spirit, not to be identified with the body of the person, which carries on after death and which gives the person his identity. In the Buddhist doctrine of anatta we have the opposite belief—the idea that there is nothing more to man than we see and know of him. Man is made of five components or constituents (called *skandhas*):

i The body (*rupa*).

ii Feeling or sensation (*vedana*).

iii Ideas (*sanna*).

iv Mental processes and acts (*sankhara*).

v Awareness or consciousness (*vinnana*).

The soul is not to be found in any one of these nor in the sum of them. The idea of anatta is the exact opposite of that of *atman* in Hinduism and herein lies one of the fundamental differences between Buddhism and its parent religion.

Unfortunately, there are many problems connected with this idea and the issue is further complicated by the fact that the Buddha's teaching is not very clear on this matter. Some of the problems this doctrine raises will be already apparent to the reader, but the most obvious one is connected with the idea of rebirth. The idea of rebirth, which the Buddhist takes from Hinduism, assumes that some part of the person 'carries over' from one existence to the next. According to this Buddhist doctrine, however, there is no enduring reality, no part of the person which carries over and so the idea of rebirth is illogical if one thinks of karma as reproducing an individual who has existed before. It is not the individual who is carried over but rather the energy created by all individuals who have died; it is this energy which is reincarnated in those who are born after them.

It is only fair to point out that this is only the beginning of the problem for many Buddhists maintain that the Buddha did not teach anatta. As the Buddha's teaching here is not very clear, and as arguments centre round the interpretation of texts written in Pali, we cannot really hope to reach a satisfactory conclusion as to whether it is an essential Buddhist doctrine or not. Perhaps it is best to maintain what the Buddha would call 'a noble silence' on this matter.

TEACHING OF THE BUDDHA

The first sermon that the Buddha preached in the Deer Park is recorded in the Buddhist scriptures and contains the essence of Buddhist doctrine: The Four Noble Truths and The Noble Eightfold Path.

THE FOUR NOBLE TRUTHS

The Buddha said there were four truths which, when perceived, would open the way to a new life.

1 The first truth was that all life involves suffering (one, you will remember, of the Three Universal Truths).

2 The Buddha then proclaimed that men suffer only because of *tanha*. This word cannot really be translated but is roughly equivalent to our word 'desire', and refers to the craving or desire men have to live on, to cling to the cycle of rebirth, in spite of the suffering that existence involves. In other words, the fact that men feel a compelling desire to go on living will mean that they will suffer. This may seem an odd statement to us at first but if thought about it is obviously logical and correct and has further implications. This is the second Noble Truth.

3 If one accepts these first two statements then one must ask, 'What is to be done? How can man escape from the suffering of this world?' The most obvious answer is, in a sense, suicide, but the Buddha did not countenance suicide, for he saw it as a running away from the problem; to want to die was as bad as wanting to live; both involved *tanha* or desire. This is the third Noble Truth.

4   The fourth Noble Truth is a systematic way of escaping from the suffering of this world and entering nirvana. It is called the Noble Eightfold Path, proclaimed by the Buddha as the Middle Way, i.e. the middle course between undue asceticism (self-torture) and over-indulgence.

BUDDHIST BELIEF

NIRVANA

Bodhisattva or Arhat in search of Nirvana.

the eightfold path

Right Concentration.
Right Mindfulness
Right Endeavour
Right Livelihood
Right Action
Right Speech
Right Resolve
Right View

Stipulations about Yoga or Spiritual training

Stipulations about Moral training

Intellectual acceptance of path

thelfour noble truths

Eightfold Path
Cessation of Dukkha
Cause of Dukkha
Fact of Dukkha

the three universal truths

Anatta
Dukkha
Anicca

THE NOBLE EIGHTFOLD PATH

The Path comprises eight steps or principles which one must follow. Each is prefixed by a word which is translated as 'right' in English but which is nearer in meaning to the Latin *summum* or 'highest'.

There are three stages in the Path: the first two steps are the result of Enlightenment and prepare the pilgrim's mind for the way ahead. The next three steps give directions as to how such a state of mind should be applied—how a Buddhist should behave, the practical morality of the Buddhist. The last three steps deal with mind training (yoga) which produces a state of mind necessary for entering nirvana. The eight steps are:

1 *Right View*, i.e. a view which is consistent with the Buddha's view. Obviously, if one is to attain nirvana, one must believe in the teachings of the Buddha—the Three Universal Truths, the Four Noble Truths and the Noble Eightfold Path.

2 *Right Resolve*. Once one has decided that the teaching of the Buddha is correct one must resolve to do something about it, i.e. follow the Eightfold Path. If one does not then one is the most selfish and foolish of creatures, knowing the truth and not acting upon it.

3 *Right Speech*. Having resolved to follow the way of the Buddha it is necessary to act with compassion and consideration for other people. Therefore one must never utter lying, slanderous or harsh words.

4 *Right Action*. One must obey the Five Precepts and not kill, steal or lie, and abstain from sensuality and intoxicants.

5 *Right Means of Livelihood*. One must abstain from earning one's living by means which cause bloodshed or by sale of intoxicating liquors or by trafficking in women and slaves.

6 *Right Endeavour*. If one is leading one's life in a correct way then it is easier to develop the mind in its search for the truth of nirvana. It is necessary to use one's energies correctly with a view to ridding oneself of all evil and striving towards the goal of life.

7 *Right Mindfulness*. One must learn to control the mind in its contemplation.

8 *Right Concentration*. If one follows all the steps of the Path and has right concentration then one can develop the mind to heights beyond normal understanding. It is a state of mind in which waves of confusion aroused by thought are stilled. The training of the mind to be completely subject to one's will is known by the comprehensive term 'yoga'.

IS BUDDHISM ATHEISTIC?

A question which is debated endlessly by students of Buddhism is whether it is atheistic, i.e. whether the Buddha believed in a God or gods (atheism = there is no God).

Throughout the teaching of the Buddha there is no object of veneration or worship. There are no gods or Brahman, there are no sacrifices, there is no priesthood, no idea of sin, no petitionary prayer—only contemplation. Certainly if the Buddha did believe in gods he does not find them relevant to his teaching. Therefore, can a way of life which has no idea of a supernatural being or beings, no idea of salvation from sin, no priests or ritual, be called a 'religion'? Many would think not but the position is complicated by the fact that a later form of Buddhism, which we will examine in a separate section, introduces all these things into its dogma. However, if we are to be true to the Buddha's original teaching we must conclude that he found belief in God or gods unnecessary. This is not to say he did not believe that supernatural beings existed; he may have believed in them but thought that they would not or could not help man. Certainly the Buddha does not deny that supernatural beings could exist. As 'atheism' is the belief that there are no supernatural beings, one could not say that this applied to the early Buddhist teaching. Perhaps a better term would be 'agnosticism', i.e. the Buddha did not know whether or not a supreme being existed and in any case he considered the question unimportant.

Because of this agnostic trait in early Buddhism the religion has often been regarded as all the more assimilable in the West where in recent years men have become more and more reticent about presenting religious notions in categorical formulations. To some extent this is true and the teaching of the Buddha does tend to make sense to many who, in the secular, empirically motivated milieu of Western culture, search for a dimension beyond the purely material. However, a glance at a translation of any of the numerous Buddhist scriptures will reveal that Buddhism is not the purely rational religion it is often presented as being. The Buddhist writings contain just as much (if not more) myth and miracle as the sacred writings of other major religions. As mentioned previously, this is particularly true of the Birth Stories (Jatakas) of which there are no less than 547. This, however, is not a cause of concern to Buddhists for many feel that it is only consistent that the birth of the Lord Buddha should be accompanied by extraordinary events.

BUDDHISM AND HINDUISM

The relationship of Buddhism to Hinduism is a complicated one. The essential notions and the philosophical expression of Buddhism, wherever it is practised, betray the original relationship. In this sense Buddhism has disseminated Indian culture throughout the Far East and S.E. Asia. Mahayana Buddhism has similar gods in its mythology and the belief in karma and transmigration is to be found in both Buddhist schools. Generally, too, Buddhism is similar to Hinduism in that they have the same sort of world-denying ideals of conduct.

Yet although Buddhism originated in India in the same religious and spiritual atmosphere as Hinduism, it has now almost disappeared from that continent. There has been considerable conjecture as to why this is so. Some say that Buddhism was assimilated into the Hindu tradition (for we have seen in the earlier chapter on Hinduism. what a comprehensive and all-inclusive philosophical system it is). Others say that Buddhism suffered because of the opposition of the Brahmins (who saw the implication of the Buddha's teaching on ritual and caste as dangerous to their own authority). Although Hinduism is tolerant it is likely that Buddhist universalism went too far; it ignored features essential to the Hindu status quo. If this is so then it is hardly surprising that Buddhism does not flourish in India. Contributory factors to Buddhism's decline in India would certainly seem to be the unfavourable reaction of the people to a religion which was too austere for them.

During the sixth century A.D. the White Huns invaded North India, pillaging the Buddhist monasteries and generally creating havoc. But apart from physical damage there was also the resurgence of Hinduism in bhakti movements. The Buddha was adopted as the ninth avatara of Vishnu and this alone would no doubt constitute a serious threat to the continuance of Buddhism as a distinct religion. The popularity of the Gita and the later Krishna stories did much to commend Hinduism to the populace. Also, the Muslim conquest of India (about A.D. 700-1200) made life for the Buddhists intolerable. In A.D. 1193 Maghada, the last Buddhist stronghold, fell to the Muslims; this was the death-blow. The main areas of influence of Buddhism today are S.E. Asia, Tibet and China. In America a sect of Japanese Buddhism called Zen is gaining some prominence. Buddhism tends to survive best in strong nation-states, e.g. Ceylon, Burma and China in the T'ang dynasty. Buddhism survived in India for almost as long as the Christian religion has been in the West.

In the twentieth century, however, India has begun to show a new interest in Buddhism. Many of the Harijan people (i.e. 'children of God'—Gandhi's name for those outside the caste system) have turned whole-heartedly to Buddhism as an alternative to the ritualistic exclusiveness of the caste system. Even some caste Hindus accept Buddhism as more in line with the egalitarian ideals after which India is striving.

HINAYANA (THERAVADA) AND MAHAYANA BUDDHISM

There are two very different types of Buddhism called *Hinayana* and *Mahayana*. The word 'Hinayana' is usually taken to mean 'lesser vehicle' or 'lesser course' whereas 'Mahayana' means 'greater vehicle' or 'greater course'. 'Hinayana' is a depreciatory name used by Mahayanists to indicate that their own religion is the more comprehensive and large enough to carry all mankind to salvation. However, the Southern Buddhists call themselves *Theravada* Buddhists (the word 'Theravada' means 'Doctrine of the Elders') and at the assembly of the World Fellowship of Buddhists in 1950 it was unanimously decided that the word *Theravada* should be used as the proper appellative for Southern Buddhists.

Theravada and Mahayana are so different as to be almost regarded as separate religions. This is not so strange as it may seem at first glance for any examination of history will reveal that religions are always splitting up into sects. Christianity split into Catholicism and Protestantism and the two, although both are Christian, are very different. The Protestants then split into smaller groups— Anglicans, Methodists, Presbyterians, Congregationalists, Baptists and others. Islam split between the Sunni and the Shi'a and the latter split again into Seveners, Twelvers, Ahmadiyyas, and so on. So with Buddhism—it split into Theravada and Mahayana and the latter split again into smaller groups.

If we ask ourselves why religions split in this way we will probably find that they do so according to a certain pattern. They all tend to divide into liberal and conservative sections. The conservative section always claims to remain more faithful to the teaching of its founder or to the earliest tradition and is more reluctant to change (e.g. the Sunnis). In Buddhism the Theravadins claim that they alone remain true to the Buddha's original teaching but, as we shall see, the Mahayanists are more liberal and try to widen the appeal of their religion.

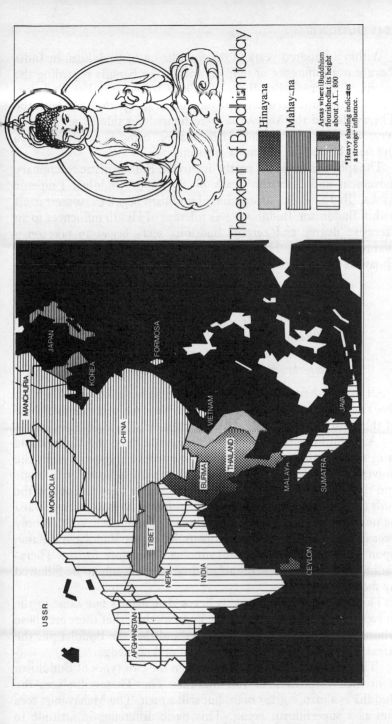

The extent of Buddhism today

Hinayāna

Mahayāna

Areas where Buddhism
flourished at its height
about A.D. 800

*Heavy shading indicates
a stronger influence.

USSR

AFGHANISTAN

NEPAL

INDIA

TIBET

MONGOLIA

MANCHURIA

JAPAN

KOREA

CHINA

BURMA

THAILAND

VIETNAM

FORMOSA

MALAYA

CEYLON

SUMATRA

JAVA

Within a hundred years of the foundation of Buddhism in India there was a difference of opinion within the Sangha regarding the means of attaining Buddhahood. The Chinese traveller Fa-hsien, who was in India between A.D. 399 and 414, reported that both the Theravada and the Mahayana were flourishing side by side. However, when his compatriot, Hsüan-tsang, came between A.D. 629 and 645 the decline was most apparent.

The split was no doubt partly due to the Brahmanistic reactionary movement and after the death of the pious Buddhist Emperor Asoka, 'Buddhism's Constantine', Hinduism began to reassert itself within Buddhism. Buddhism was tolerant of Hindu influences to an excessive degree and certain Buddhist sects began to take on a Brahmanistic tinge. However, the Mahayana does not regard the Hinayana as heretical:

> While Hinayana regards Mahayana as a corruption of the original Buddhism, or at the best a false and decadent branch, Mahayana regards Hinayana not as false or contrary to true Buddhism, but simply as incomplete, or the superficial doctrine which Sakyamuni taught to those who were incapable of comprehending the more profound truths of Mahayana.[1]

All that we have said about Buddhism so far is believed by both the Theravadins and the Mahayanists. Now we will examine some of the main differences.

1   A vital difference between the Theravadins and the Mahayanists is in the way they view man and his purpose and position in the universe. The Theravadin believes that man is completely alone and that there is no one to help him; his fellow men cannot and the gods (if they exist at all) will not. Therefore if he is to reach nirvana he must do it by his own efforts. The Theravadin believes that only *knowledge* of the Middle Way propounded by the Buddha and action upon it will help him to attain nirvana. Therefore for the Theravadin religion is, as it were, a full-time job and only to be followed by monks.

The Mahayanist, however, believes that man is not alone in the universe, that we can and must help each other, that there are those whose help can be enlisted by prayer and that the Buddha put the stress on *compassion* for others and not on knowledge.

2   The second great difference between the two types of Buddhism is in their estimation of the Buddha. The Theravadin sees the Buddha as a man, a great man, but still a man. The Mahayanist sees him as a superhuman being. This basic difference in attitude to

[1] W. M. McGovern. *Introduction to Mahayana Buddhism* (Kegan Paul, Trench, Trubner & Co., 1922), p. 123.

the Buddha means that each sect has a different outlook on life. The Theravadin believes that the Buddha was an example of a man who strove for salvation and attained it by his own efforts and passed on the knowledge of how to attain this salvation to his fellow men. No one will attain nirvana without intense self-effort and discipline. A man can only receive help from one person—himself.

The Mahayanist believes that the Buddha entered our sphere of existence to help us and can still help us even though he is in nirvana. If the Buddha was compassionate enough to postpone entry into nirvana so that he could tell his fellow men how to attain it, then that must be the great virtue in life—compassion. Therefore the Mahayanist has a religious structure (similar to a church) in which he can pray, give praise and thanks and seek the help of the Buddha. The Mahayanist believes in universal salvation, i.e. the idea that all men can be 'saved'.

These differing ideas are expressed in the types of 'ideal' man which each group wishes to produce. The Theravadin ideal is the *Arhat* (literally, 'worthy one'). The Arhat is worthy of praise because he strives alone and with single-minded zeal towards the goal of nirvana, letting nothing distract him. The ideal of the Mahayanist is the *Bodhisattva* (literally, 'Buddha-to-be') and he is the person who does not let his striving for nirvana interfere with his concern and help for other people.

In a later section we shall be examining some of the different branches of Mahayana Buddhism and we shall see how divergent these developments are from the original Theravada Buddhism.

FESTIVALS AND CUSTOMS OF THE THERAVADA

There is a certain emphasis on the human remains of the Buddha and veneration of relics is widespread. This is also the case with the remains of prominent Arhats. Attention to relics would appear to be a feature of religions with a historical founder (Christianity and Islam) whereas in Hinduism this kind of veneration tends to be somewhat remote, e.g. erecting a temple over a god's footprint as at Baya and Benares. (The Buddha, too, is said to have left his footprint at Sumanakuta in Ceylon and Saraburi in Thailand.)

The famous temple at Kandy in Ceylon boasts possession of one of the Buddha's teeth (Temple of the Sacred Tooth). During the *Perahera Festival* in August many relics, though not the Tooth, are

The Temple of the Sacred Tooth at Kandy

borne through the streets of Kandy—painted elephants, dancers, musicians and gay crowds make this a most spectacular occasion.

Wesak is the most important festival as it commemorates the birth, Enlightenment and entry into nirvana of the Buddha. The streets are filled with decorations and donations of food and money are made to the poor.

In Ceylon the *New Year* is brought in by splashing friends and neighbours with water. Floats depicting important events in the life of the Buddha are drawn through the streets and Buddha-images are washed. Presents are given to monks. In Thailand New Year's Day (Songkran Day) is celebrated by acts of kindness to fish and birds. As New Year falls in April, the hot season, ponds and canals often dry up and the fish are stranded in small pools. The people catch the stranded fish, keep them in jars until Songkran Day and then release them in the river. It is believed that merit is gained by releasing a life. Birds are sold in small wooden cages especially for releasing. (It is curious to note, however, that fish-fighting and cock-fighting are popular Thai pastimes.) As in Ceylon, water splashing is popular in Thailand. Young people organize water-fights and although the custom has been prohibited in Bangkok it is still enjoyed in the provinces.

Meditation in the wats (monasteries) is an individual activity and there are few external acts of piety. Meetings of the Sangha are held at times. When the laity attend places of meditation they tend to listen and contemplate rather than take a recognizably active part in what is going on. Sometimes a bhikkhu (monk) will read to them.

A BUDDHIST ORDINATION CEREMONY

One of the rules of Buddhism is that during the 'Lent Season', that is the three-month rainy season from the middle of the eighth lunar month (July) to the middle of the eleventh lunar month (October), bhikkhus should remain in their monasteries for meditation and study. Consequently, those who wish to enter the priesthood are obliged to do so at the end of June before the 'Lent' period begins.

It is the custom for men of twenty-one to enter a monastery during the 'Lent Season' to study their religion. A special course of instruction is prepared for them as part of the first year's course in the theological school. This instruction is intended to help them when they return to the lay state for not all young men wish to remain in the monastery. In Thailand, for example, the government grants leave of absence for three months to government officials of twenty-one years of age for ordination purposes.

It is the hope of every parent that each son should be ordained and because of this the custom is very popular among young men. When one is ordained as a monk one does not take irrevocable vows. In Thailand there are very few Buddhist men who have not spent several months at least in a monastery either as a novice (before the age of twenty) or as a monk.

In Thailand the rituals and customs preceding ordination are of considerable interest and are not often witnessed by visitors from the West. When the young man decides that he wishes to enter the priesthood he is known as 'Naag'. There is a folk tale which explains why this title is used. 'Naag' or 'Naga' in Sanskrit is the name for the mythological serpent. Legend has it that once a Naga meta-morphosed into a man and became ordained. However, when the serpent-monk was sleeping his magical powers left him and the fraud was soon discovered. When the Buddha heard about it he expelled the Naga from the Sangha for only humans can be ordained. The Naga was insolent enough to request a favour of the Buddha and asked that his name, Naga, be given as a nickname to all intending monks. The Buddha was gracious enough to grant the request. 'Naga' has taken the form 'Naag'.

Before he is permitted to enter the Sangha the Naag must settle all debts. If he cannot prove solvency then the elders will not accept him for a monk must be the kind of person who can live a life of disciplined poverty. The Naag visits relations and superiors and presents them with tapers, incense and flowers on a salver. Prostrating himself before them he asks for their blessing. 'May any acts of mine, whether of thought, word or deed, which have trespassed against you, be kindly forgiven as an act of cancellation.' Having received a blessing the Naag makes further visits to other appropriate people.

Friends and relations always join the young man's parents as sponsors for it is believed that those who encourage a young monk receive 'merit'. Often the Naag will be followed by a friend with a bell or gong. He strikes the gong and lets everyone know that his associate is about to enter the Sangha.

A great party is held in the parents' house on the night before the ordination. Friends bring presents in order to 'make merit'. There is much music and chanting. Sometimes the songs are light-hearted and describe the feelings of the Naag's girl-friend or wife.

The Naag will already have made arrangements with the abbot of a wat. He will have received some preliminary training in the monastery and will have learnt how to make responses in Pali to ordination questions which will be put to him in Pali. Many of the early Buddhist scriptures are written in this language which is more ancient than Sanskrit.[1] More often than not the Naag does not understand Pali and he might well become tongue-tied during the ordination ceremony.

Before the Naag can be admitted to the ceremony he must have his head, eyebrows and beard shaved. This is to show that he has forsaken personal interest and vanity. Also, on the day of the pre-ordination party, he dresses in a white robe to indicate purity of motive and, with someone holding a large umbrella over him, he and his friends walk from street to street or village to village as a kind of public declaration of his intention. This procession sometimes includes musicians and dancers. At dusk the group returns to the party.

On the morning of the ordination the Naag leaves home dressed in ornate clothes representing those worn by the wealthy prince Gotama before he forsook the comfortable life. This consists of a

---

[1] See the glossary of terms in the Appendix.

A Naag being paraded through the town by his friends before his initiation ceremony

cone-shaped hat and a thin net robe embroidered in gold. In an attitude of reverence he makes his way to the wat holding a wax candle, a joss stick and a flower between his palms. He then walks three times round the wat, takes off the princely robe and throws coins to the crowd (the Buddha's renunciation of wealth). His father takes him into the ordination hall where the monks and elders are waiting. When everyone is seated the Naag approaches the bhikkhus and sits on his heels before them holding the yellow robes (orange in Ceylon) in his hands. He then asks in Pali for his ordination. When the bhikkhus agree to this he withdraws to put on the three yellow garments and is usually given some assistance by someone experienced in arranging them.

He then asks the abbot to instruct him. The abbot says a few words about the monks' life and then asks the ordinand a number of questions: Does he suffer from any kind of skin infection or from tuberculosis? Is he epileptic? Is he of sound mind? A male? Solvent? Has he permission from his employer to enter the monastery? Is he twenty-one years old? If he answers to the abbot's satisfaction the assembly is so informed and, so long as no member of the Sangha raises an objection, the young man is admitted to the monkhood.

THE KATHIN CEREMONY

In Thailand and other Theravada countries it is customary for laymen to make a formal presentation of gifts to the monastery in their area. The gift offered is usually that of robes and in Thailand the ceremony is called *Presentation of Kathin Robes* or *Tod Kathin*. It is a means of expressing gratitude to monks for maintaining the Buddha's teaching.

The Buddha taught that the amassing of wealth or the desire for wealth caused frustration and suffering and prevented spiritual progress. He therefore taught his monks to live without money and to make do with personal necessities only, such as a razor and a needle. Buddhist monks rely entirely on the laity for their needs. The laity are only too pleased to provide for them as such provision is a means of gaining 'merit'.

Gifts other than food are of two kinds: personal necessities such as cloth for the monk's robes; and communal and household items such as soap, eating utensils, teapots. All gifts in the second category must be shared. At Tod Kathin those in both categories are offered to the monks.

When Kathin robes are presented the Sangha selects one particular monk to receive them. A great variety of other gifts is also presented and consists of items which will be used in the monastery during the coming year. The gifts are generally presented by the community although in Thailand the King is allowed to present his personal Kathin gifts at a royal monastery (Wat Luang). Buddhism is the State religion of Thailand and the monarch participates in many religious ceremonies. When he visits a monastery he treats the monks as his superiors by virtue of their high spiritual status.

Only one Kathin can be celebrated in each monastery during one year. When the ceremony is over a flag bearing the outline of a crocodile is hoisted for the remainder of the Kathin season to let the laity know that they should find some other monastery if they wish to make donations.

Why I am a Buddhist

Life for me is a strange and entrancing journey. Because I can never know what it is really like to be any other person, or indeed what it is like to be a tree or a fish or a flower, everything around me holds a mystery which can never be fathomed. Who knows what it is like to be you? Only you—and it is the only thing about which you have true knowledge. Everything else you can know about, but you can never be at the centre of any thing as you are at the centre of yourself. At my centre I am at one with a moving, changing, wonderfully coloured and featured world, a physical world to which my body-mind organism is a part of and belongs. In fact, my body and personality have emerged from the world like a wave from the sea and can in no way be separated from anything else in the physical universe.

Thus, at my centre, I am at the receiving end of everything that my senses give me. Because my centre is not vulnerable or changing like the world. It is not any of those marvellous, fragile, durable objects (including my own body) which make up the physical universe. Instead, my centre seems to me very truly the ground of being, the timeless living clarity which is my essential natureless nature.

But I did not always feel like this or even know that I could feel like it. When I was younger I was hardly aware of my centre at all. Just occasionally I would be intensely moved by something—a view of mountains or the sound of the sea or stillness among trees—and would feel a sense of greatness which was both to do with me and not to do with me. But mostly I thought of myself as an object among other objects, solid and 'real' and entirely separate from everything else. As a 'thing' I cared intensely what other 'things' thought of me and I always felt myself to be a pretty awful specimen. I was boxed up in a body of bones and flesh and hair, and happiness depended on this apparatus looking and sounding right to an alien world which, I thought, was always scrutinising and judging me. Sometimes my apparatus passed the tests quite well and then I thought I was happy, but at the back of that happiness was always the terrible uncertainty that the next time might not come off so nicely. Really it was as though I had placed myself outside, in the position of an observer looking at myself, and was living my whole life from out there.

But life lived in this fashion is basically unreal. In my case it was when this unreality became intolerable and I could not any longer live in this way, that the return journey from my periphery to my centre began. Not everybody has to make a very lengthy return journey, it depends how far away from the centre you have placed yourself, but I had been pretty far out and had a long way to go. People like me need signposts, at least at the beginning, and it was here that Buddhism came to my help in a way that no other religion seemed able to do. It began when I read a poem by a Chinese Zen master, Seng-Ts'an, called 'On Believing in Mind' which went like this:

> *The perfect way knows no difficulties*
> *Except that it refuses to make preferences;*
> *Only when freed from hate and love*
> *It reveals itself fully and without disguise;*
> *A tenth of an inch's difference,*
> *And heaven and earth are set apart.*
> *If you wish to see it before your own eyes*
> *Have no fixed thoughts either for or against it.*

> *To set up what you like against what you dislike—*
> *That is the disease of the mind:*
> *When the deep meaning (of the Way) is not understood,*
> *Peace of mind is disturbed to no purpose.*

> *(The Way) is perfect like unto vast space,*
> *With nothing wanting, nothing superfluous.*
> *It is indeed due to making choice*
> *That its Suchness is lost sight of.*

This seemed so wise and so close to my own conditon that I felt I must find out more about a religion which viewed life in these terms. So I read books about Buddhism and thought about it a lot and then I joined a group of Buddhists who practised meditation and talked freely about all the signposts to reality which I was beginning to discover. It did not seem odd to turn to Buddhism rather than the Christianity in which I had been brought up. Buddhism talked my language and therefore I felt easy as a Buddhist.

Buddhism has three main schools, or set of signposts, all pointing to the Centre (which is sometimes called the Void). Of the three I found that Zen spoke to me most clearly. All three have meditation as their main practice but whereas the oldest two (Theravada and Mahayana) emphasize a gradual understanding (and sometimes warn you that it may take several lifetimes!) Zen says: Find your centre right now. Wake up to who you are. Zen always stresses the immediate experience. Here and now. No judgments, no concept-making, no living in ideas—

but the full experience of what is, at this moment. Seeing the real truth of things is liberation. When the Buddha was dying, he said: 'See Truth as an island, see Truth as a refuge. Work out your own salvation with diligence.'

It is this foundation of reality, of not believing things because you have been told them but testing them for yourself, that makes Buddhism a living religion for me and not a dead one. It means that its signposts point in the right direction, and this is important to know when you are not sure where you are going. Books are a help, and other people's opinions too, but most of all Buddhism helped me to see who I really was, not as an intellectual idea but as a real experience. When you see who you are you find you are at one with the essence of all religion and all life.

Ann Lobstein

CHAPTER SIX

Zoroastrianism
THE RELIGION OF THE PARSIS

Zoroastrianism is the religion founded by the Persian prophet Zoroaster (or Zarathushtra, his Persian name). The vast majority of the adherents of this religion are called *Parsis* and the religion is also referred to as *Parsism*.

Although it is estimated that there are only 114,000 Zoroastrians the religion is still important, mainly for two reasons:

1 The Parsis are respected and influential members of the community in India (where most of them live) and are noted as being generous, wealthy and intelligent.

2 Zoroastrianism influenced the development and beliefs of Judaism and therefore, indirectly, of Christianity and Islam. The religion has a high moral tone (it is often referred to as 'the Good Religion' or 'the Good Life'). Its belief in a resurrection of the body, a life everlasting, the coming of a Saviour, and rewards for good behaviour and punishments for bad, are very similar to the three monotheistic faiths of Judaism, Christianity and Islam although it is a moot point as to exactly how far these three religions were influenced by Zoroastrianism.

LIFE AND TEACHING OF ZOROASTER

The Greeks have given us the name of Zoroaster as it seemed easier to pronounce than the Persian original, Zarathushtra, and it is by the name of Zoroaster that he is referred to in the West.

We know very little of the life of Zoroaster. It is even difficult to determine exactly when he lived but the traditional dates for his life are usually given as 660-583 B.C. He may have been a member of a priestly caste, but whether this was so or not we know his message to have been a simple one: he denounced idolatry and proclaimed belief in one God—Ahura Mazda. He appears to have had one convert only in ten years (a cousin) until he came to Bactria and converted the king there. There is a tradition that he was killed by a foreign ruler who stabbed him in the back near a fire altar. We know little of the religion Zoroaster sought to reform. As the Iranians and Indians originally were of one stock, some have suggested that the common elements of the Rig-Veda and the Avesta give us some indication of the religion at the time of Zoroaster. We are told by ancient historians that the Persians sacrificed to the Sun, Moon, Earth, Fire, Water and Winds and so probably the religion Zoroaster sought to reform was a worship of the forces of nature.

Zoroaster called for righteousness and adherence to Ahura Mazda, the 'Wise Lord' or 'God of Wisdom'. Zoroasters' teaching about Ahura Mazda raises a very vexing question as to whether Zoroastrianism is dualistic or monotheistic. Monotheism is, of course, the belief in one all-powerful God and dualism is the belief in two opposing, and equally balanced, forces of good and evil in the world. The problem lies in the fact that Zoroaster does believe in Angra Mainyu, the Spirit of Evil, and appears to give him equal status with Ahura Mazda. One passage in the Avesta refers to Ahura Mazda and Angra Mainyu as being 'two brothers in one womb'. Another passage says, 'Now the two primal Spirits who showed themselves as Twins are the Good and the Bad in thought, word and deed. The wise one will choose rightly between these two, the foolish will not.'

It does seem that this is a metaphysical dualism but many are careful to point out that Zoroaster did believe that ultimately Good (Ahura Mazda) would triumph over Evil. This being so, the belief could be classed as monotheistic as the two forces of Good and Evil are not equally balanced, because the Good eventually triumphs. In the Zoroastrian scriptures texts can be found in support of monotheism, dualism and even a form of polytheism, and since the scriptural position is by no means clear most of what is said about Zoroastrian doctrine is conjecture. The question is a vexed one and worthy of a much more detailed examination, but as this is only an introductory book we must leave our study of this problem.

It would seem that Zoroaster had hoped ultimately to convert all living men, even the worst robber and murderer. He did in his teaching offer temporal gifts in this life for good behaviour, but mostly Zoroaster sees the inequalities and injustices of this life being redressed in the next. Zoroaster's main message was that life was a 'spiritual combat' in which one had to decide either for or against Ahura Mazda.

There was no one to carry on Zoroaster's work (as there was in Palestine where the prophets carried on from Moses), so the religion he founded tended to degenerate over the years into superstition.

THE AVESTA

There are many diverse writings included in the Zoroastrian scriptures known as the *Avesta*, but the oldest are the *Gathas*, or Songs, from which most of our information about the life of Zoroaster comes. The Zoroastrian writings, like the Hebrew scriptures, cover a vast period of time and, like the Vedas, were circulated orally long before they were committed to writing. They are written in a dead language, an East Iranian dialect.

According to tradition the original copy of the Avesta was written in gold ink on ox-hides and kept at Istakhr in the royal library. It is said to have comprised some 12,000 hides. The story goes that Alexander the Great destroyed the complete book and only a third of it had been retained in the memories of the pious. All this, however, is legend and probably contains little truth.

There are three main divisions in the Avesta:

1 *Yasnas or hymns*. These are recited by the priest during the ceremonials and rituals. Included in the Yasnas are the *Gathas*, of which there are seventeen.

2 *The Vendidad*, the 'Leviticus' of the Avesta, dealing with purification rites and punishment of offenders.

3 *Yashts* or hymns of praise. This section contains prayers which can be used by the laity.

HISTORY OF THE PARSIS

The invasion of Alexander the Great and the rule of the Seleucids from 330-250 B.C. led to bitter persecution of the Zoroastrians. Under the Sasanian Empire (founded 226 B.C.) things improved, and Zoroastrianism began to flourish as the state religion until the invasion of the Muslims in A.D. 652, after which the Zoroastrians were crushed and oppressed. The Muslim conquest marks the end of Zoroastrianism as a vital religious force in its homeland for the vast majority of the population became Muslim.

Whilst the remaining Zoroastrians in Persia continued to be poor, depressed and illiterate, a band of exiles emigrated to India in the eighth century A.D. ; they were granted asylum by a ruler in Gujerat. There are only about 10,000 Zoroastrians in Iran, most of whom live in the isolated areas around Yazd and Kerman.

The history of the Zoroastrians is very similar to that of the Jews, which perhaps accounts in some measure for their similar beliefs. Both communities were oppressed and exiled for their beliefs and both believe that ultimately Good will overcome Evil. Only Judaism and Zoroastrianism of the really ancient religions believed that history had a purpose, only they saw time as a progression towards a final and glorious end. (Compare the Buddhist and Hindu idea of rebirth.) Christianity and Islam, of course, inherited this from Judaism.

THE PARSIS OF INDIA

The word *Parsi* means 'inhabitant of Persia' and is the name by which Zoroastrians are known in India. Most Zoroastrians now live there (about 90% of them) centred in and around Bombay. The Parsis are renowned in India for their industry and good faith. The ideal they live by is 'good thought, good words and good deeds', which means that Parsism is an intensely *active* religion. This is in marked contrast to Islam which is very fatalistic. A characteristic of the Parsis is hope for the future, and they endeavour never to succumb to evil but battle against it. The ethical results are to be seen in many Parsi leaders. The Parsis divide roughly into two classes —the Orthodox and the Reformers.

THE ORTHODOX PARSIS

Orthodox Parsism, following the teaching of the Vendidad, lays a strong emphasis on ritual or ceremonial and tradition. The ritual begins for the Parsi with the initiation ceremony between the ages of seven and fifteen. At the ceremony a shirt and girdle are put on and the creed and prayers are recited. Many of these prayers are repeated often during the religious life of the Parsi, but they are in a language unknown to most Parsis and hence are meaningless to the vast majority of them.

The ritual which most people immediately associate with the Parsis is that of tending the sacred fire, and this practice has given Parsi followers the nick-name of 'fire-worshippers'. However, this name is most unfair as the fire is merely a symbol of the sole God. Indeed, symbolism plays an important part in Parsi belief and worship and unfortunately in uneducated Parsism it is taken as more than symbolism.

There is a great deal of ritual associated with death, and the utmost care is taken in carrying out funeral rites. The ritual is centred round a building (found in any large Parsi community)

A boy being initiated into the Zoroastrian religion

called the *Tower of Silence*. Here the dead bodies are left to be devoured by vultures, as cremation and burial are forbidden because fire and the earth are considered sacred. Every Parsi community has two main buildings—the Tower of Silence for the dead and the *Fire Temple* for other ritual services and worship.

Passages of scripture concerned with the torments of hell figure prominently in Orthodox Parsi services, and are said to move the listeners deeply. Certainly the torments are depicted so powerfully that they must be a great deterrent against evil-doing.

THE REFORMERS

Not surprisingly, some modern Parsis find this emphasis on ritual and fear of hell rather galling. Many find the prospect of washing a corpse in gomez (bull's urine) rather irksome, even though, strictly speaking, it is a requirement of Orthodox Parsism. Also many modern Parsis are not content with prayers mechanically droned, and the stultified ritual of the Orthodox service. However, the problem remains that if the religion is removed of its tradition and ceremonial it almost ceases to be a religion and the Orthodox Parsis are often bitter in their attacks on those Parsis who would attempt to reduce the religion to an intellectual acceptance of the monotheistic and ethical emphasis of Zoroaster's teaching. The reforming Parsis counter by saying that true Zoroastrianism is to be found only in the Gathas, and that much of the rest of the Avesta is later tradition which tends to obscure the true message of Zoroaster.

This struggle between the 'progressives' and 'conservatives' can be found in many religions today—certainly in Christianity there is a similar struggle between the radical 'Death of God' theologians and the Evangelicals. In a way it is a sign of a vital religion in that it shows an attempt to readjust and meet the challenges of new situations.

THE FUTURE OF ZOROASTRIANISM

In spite of the attempts by some Parsis to meet the challenge of the modern situation, the future of Parsism does not really look good. Many Parsis are ceasing to practise their religion because of indifference or non-belief, and the number of Parsi adherents (small enough already) appears to be diminishing. Yet the small number of Parsi followers is not really a true indication of the influence Zoroastrianism has had on civilization. At its best it is a religion of high ideals and true spiritual insight and its contribution to man's religious understanding can never be measured in quantitative terms.

PARSI RELIGIOUS LIFE

Orthodox Parsis advocate daily attendance at temples. Failing this they should attend on at least four holy days each month. Before entering the temple the Parsi must take off his shoes, wash his hands and feet and pray for the conquest of Evil by Good. The priest gives him some ashes from the sacred fire after which the worshipper says privately some set Parsi prayers and makes personal petitions. He then leaves, taking great care not to turn his back on the sacred fire. The priest alone can enter the sanctuary where the fire is located and even then he has to wear a white cloth over his mouth so as not to contaminate the fire with his human breath. Otherwise there is no distinction between worshippers, and men and women have the same status. Parsism, however, is the only religion which does not allow spectators in its temples.

There are no statues or representational paintings whatsoever. Worship is a private affair and there is no public religious teaching. The priesthood is hereditary but not all members of priestly families follow the calling. Such men are distinguished from the ordinary lay-people by a white turban.

There are three kinds of fire-temple, the nature of the fire being different in each. The commonest kind is the *Atash Dadgah:* this is often an ordinary house which is utilized for worship. Where ten or more Parsi families are living a temple called the *Atash Adaran* is erected. The congregation bring the fire from their own homes and the priests consecrate it. Most important of all is the *Atash Behram.*

Parsi priests before the sacred fire

At present there are only ten of these, the reason being that the preparation of the fire is involved and extremely costly. The fire-altar consists of a large metal cauldron set in stone. It is erected in such a position that the flames can never be obscured by the brightness of the sun.

FESTIVALS

There are six seasonal festivals or *Gahambars*. These are celebrated with parties and ceremonial. There are various rituals associated with the time of year.

New Year is an important festival but some Parsis (the *Kadimis*) insist that it occurs in August while others (the *Shenshahis*) say that it is in September. Both sects celebrate the festival with great feasting and ceremony. A third group, the *Falsi*, base their calculations on the ancient Iranian solar calendar and celebrate the New Year on 21st March. All three groups regard this date as the Spring Festival also.

Farvardegan days are in memory of those who have died. They are holidays and devout Parsis use the time to visit the Tower of Silence where they leave bunches of flowers. Temple services are also held.

The days appointed for remembering the birth and death of Zoroaster are occasions of the greatest solemnity.

Why I am a Parsi

Zarathushtra enjoined his followers to lead the good life. He taught that there is an unceasing mortal struggle between Good and Evil. Everyone must consciously choose to fight for good as no human being is immune from this struggle; no man can opt out or sit on the fence. The struggle must be faced with absolute integrity, without expectation of reward.

The elements of the good life as crystallized in the ancient precept 'Good Thoughts, Good Words, Good Deeds' are Truth, Compassion and active Service of mankind, not for the rewards to be gained in the hereafter but for their own sake. 'Ashem Vohu' the prayer every practising Parsi offers on waking and several times a day may be freely translated as follows:

> *A righteous life is the supreme bliss. Blessed is he who leads the righteous life for its sake alone and not in the hope of earthly gains or heavenly rewards.*

Zarathushtra elevated Truth in all its connotations to the highest level of morality—the untiring striving for justice, the hatred of superstition, the love of knowledge. These are qualities which even today characterize the aspirations of the Parsis, who form a minute but extremely prominent community among the teeming millions of India.

Compassion towards all humanity, as proclaimed by Zarathushtra, has guided the actions of his followers throughout their glorious history. When Cyrus liberated the Jews of Babylon and built places of worship for them, he was practising a degree of tolerance which is in marked contrast to certain major religions of today, which lay claim to tolerance but have a long, blood-soaked history of pogroms, genocide and burnings at the stake.

Further, Zarathushtra bade his followers be active in the service of mankind. Not for the true believer the spiritual comfort of a monastic life, but unceasing concern, particularly for the halt and the lame. The believer is required to be industrious, generous and to husband resources. Zarathushtra was one of the first prophets to bless the man who made two blades of grass grow where only one grew before. And, in this combined spirit of service and generosity, the Parsis of today have been foremost in endowment of hospitals, schools, clinics, research institutes for the benefit of all communities in India.

Zarathushtra has profoundly influenced the philosophy and ethic of Judaism, Christianity and Islam. The ancient Persians taught the world (Greek historians notwithstanding) the concepts of justice and the search for truth. They were pioneers, long before the Romans, of the art of good administration with equal rights for all races and religions. They were great road builders and pioneered postal services within their vast domains which helped to bring diverse cultures together. Zarathushtra's tenets of cleanliness and personal hygiene have only gradually been accepted in the West within the last century. The ancient Iranians were vigorous, zestful and relished life at all levels.

The Parsis of today, a little over 100,000 in all (about the population of a small London borough), continue the glorious traditions of their ancestors. They are found in all corners of the world as business and professional people who jealously guard their integrity. They pioneered modern industry in India; the first cotton mill, steel factory, hydro-electric works, internal and international airlines were all Parsi enterprises.

The only three Indian (indeed, non-European) members of the British Parliament were Parsis. The first of these, Dr Dadabhai Naoroji was one of the earliest fighters for Indian independence.

They lead with relish and gusto their 'good life', educating their youth, succouring the weak, leading a meaningful life according to their light—fighting the good fight in the spirit of Zarathushtra's teachings: 'Good Thoughts, Good Words, Good Deeds'.

This is the faith, to preserve which the old pilgrims sought shelter in India nearly 13 centuries ago, having abandoned their homes, their land, their civilization and everything they held dear, having faced untold hardships, decades of wandering; and to which we, their descendants, so proudly and with such ardour adhere.

Mr Manek Vajifdar, B.A. (Phil.), M.A.A.

CHAPTER SEVEN

Sikhism

Sikhism is an Indian monotheistic religion in which ideas from two great religions, Hinduism and Islam, are brought together; it is a synthesis of these two faiths and yet remains unmistakably Indian. Many Sikhs feel that it is the only major religion of India which is purely Indian. Hinduism came with the Aryans from Central Asia, Islam from Arabia, Christianity from the Middle East and Zoroastrianism from Persia. Buddhism enjoys little following in the country of its origin. They also point out that Sikhism is perhaps the only religion which has not split into differing denominations.

The Sikh religion was founded towards the end of the fifteenth century A.D. by Nanak who is the first of the ten Gurus of the Sikhs. Sikhs limit the use of the word *guru* to these ten. (*Guru*, it will be recalled, means 'teacher'.) The word *Sikh* comes from the Sanskrit *shishya* which means *disciple*, and Sikhs are disciples of the ten gurus some of whose writings have been collected in a sacred book called the *Granth Sahib*. There are about eight million Sikhs most of whom are to be found in the border state of Punjab where, in the nineteenth century, they created a powerful state before the British took over the country. They constitute less than 2% of the Indian population yet their share in the country's life is by no means negligible. They are also to be found in other parts of the world and there are some flourishing Sikh communities in the major cities of Great Britain, e.g. London, Birmingham, Leeds, Glasgow.

We have already seen how Buddhism attempted to loosen the hold which Brahmanism and the caste system held on religion in India. Sikhism is such an attempt. It has borrowed some of its ideas and devotional hymns from those religious teachers who found fault with Hinduism, of whom there were several. In the twelfth century A.D. Jaidev taught that yoga was valueless when compared with true worship of God in thought, word and deed. Ramananda, in the fourteenth century A.D., denounced all kinds of caste restriction, and

Kabir condemned the use of images in temples and the Hindu fascination with ritual.

The Muslims began their invasion of N. India in the eighth century A.D. in accordance with their doctrine of 'Holy War' against 'pagans'. Unfortunately they were responsible for the destruction of many beautiful temples in the north. It is interesting to note that they conquered the same geographical area as the Indo-Europeans about two thousand years earlier. By the fifteenth century they had taken the whole of N. India and many Hindus had become Muslims, particularly those in the Punjab and Bengal. You will remember, however, that Hindus show a remarkable tolerance towards other religions and are quite prepared to borrow ideas which they consider to be of value. This attitude of the Hindus resulted in several movements which aimed at merging the best of Hinduism with the best of Islam—a kind of compromise. Sikhism is such a movement.

Kabir (1440-1518) was not a Sikh but his ideas came from similar sources to those of Guru Nanak and are not unlike his. Some of his writings are to be found in the Granth Sahib. He was born in a Muslim family of weavers at Benares and throughout his life collected many ideas from a variety of religions. According to Kabir, who must be rated as one of the most remarkable teachers in the religious history of India, there is truth in all religions but there is only one God. This one God is known by various names: he is Allah, he is Rama, he is Krishna. 'O God, whether Allah or Rama, I live by thy name', said Kabir.

Kabir became a disciple of the Hindu guru, Ramananda, who taught that truth was not to be found in the performance of formal rituals or in learning complicated philosophy but in simple trust and devotion to God. In other words, Ramananda was a product of the bhakti movement and bhakti is an important idea in Sikhism.

During the fourteenth and fifteenth centuries Hindus suffered persecution from the Muslims and Kabir felt that he could not be associated with those Muslims who were so short-sighted that they thought that only they knew the truth about God. Instead he taught a religion of love, a religion in which the Muslim and the Hindu could be one. He spoke in simple terms of the soul being united with God and this union with God was for all people; you did not have to belong to a particular caste or religion, and you did not have to perform rituals or endure bodily hardships to realize that you were at one with God. Personal devotion (bhakti) to God was all that was required.

Kabir was a great poet. He wrote many songs in simple Hindi which ordinary people could understand and they are still loved by both Muslims and Sikhs in N. India and Pakistan although, because of changes in the Hindi language which have taken place since Kabir's time, they are no longer so easy to understand. Today there are about a million disciples (Kabirpanthis) who base their ideas on his teaching and sing his hymns.

Although the Sikh scriptures comprise the work of many poets, like Kabir, Ramananda and Jaidev, as far as Sikhs are concerned it was Guru Nanak who initiated, in founding Sikhism, a distinct and independent religion. Sikhism is essentially his religion.

THE TEN GURUS

Nanak and his nine successors are called the Gurus of the Sikhs. The final and immortal Guru is the Granth Sahib. The founder of Sikhism, Guru Nanak, is said to have been reincarnated in all nine of the following Gurus and it is said that God revealed himself to them in a special way; the spiritual insight was handed on from Guru to Guru like a flame from candle to candle. They were all perfect men who inspired and made themselves at one with all kinds of people. They were not incarnations of God but led humble lives. Guru Nanak thought of himself as of little significance. They accepted suffering as the will of God and two of them became martyrs. It is the Guru who guides the development of the Sikh to perfection. The Sikh finds this perfection by being united with the Gurus in spirit, and especially with Nanak: he becomes one with them and feels them living within him, making available to him a

TIME CHART OF THE GURUS

1. Nanak	1469–1539	Japji. Monotheism. No asceticism.
2. Angad	1504–1552	Granth takes shape. Gurmukhi. Gurdwaras.
3. Amar Das	1479–1574	Eat together (caste). Division of country.
4. Ram Das	1534–1581	Golden Temple. Hereditary succession on Muslim lines.
5. Arjun Dev	1563–1606	Granth enlarged. Built many gurdwaras Tortured. Advised military force.
6. Har Govind	1595–1644	Sacred army. Meat. Victories over Muslims
7. Har Rai	1630–1661	
8. Har Kishen	1656–1664	Very young brother of Har Rai.
9. Teg Bahadur	1621–1675	Har Govind's second son.
10. Govind Singh	1666–1708	Khalsa. Singh. Five K's. Revision of Granth. Granth final immortal Guru.

source of divine power. The Sikhs look upon the Gurus with devotion (bhakti).

I NANAK (1469-1539)

Although Nanak probably never met Kabir it is evident that both teachers shared similar ideas. Whereas, however, Kabir was a Muslim influenced by Hinduism, Nanak was a Hindu influenced by Islam. It is interesting to note that Nanak, the founder of the Sikhs, was a contemporary of Martin Luther, the Christian Protestant reformer.

Guru Nanak was born at Talwanda Rai Bhoi (now called Nankana Sahib), to the south-west of Lahore. In caste he was a Kshatriya. As a youth Nanak was always interested in the teachings of the wandering Hindu hermits. It is said of Nanak that at the age of nine he refused to be invested with the sacred thread. He told the family priest that the wearing of the thread signified nothing for it did not of itself make a man pure in heart. As an adult he led a comparatively normal life in that he did, for a time, work for his living, was married and had children but his greatest interest was in religion. God was not to be found in the forests only; he was to be found in the home and at work. Nanak also showed interest in the political situation: 'kings are butchers, cruelty their knife. Dharma has taken wings and vanished.'

When he was thirty he became a teacher (guru) and stressed the importance of bringing the two great religions, Hinduism and Islam, together. In order to show that he put his teaching into practice he wore both the yellow robe of the Hindu holy man together with the turban and prayer beads of the Muslim. He visited both Mecca and Benares. Kabir had said, 'Benares is to the East, Mecca to the West: but explore your own heart, for there are both Rama and Allah.'

Nanak drew his inspiration from the bhakti movement and from the Muslim Sufis. Sufism is a movement within Islam which points out that although Allah is one and cannot be divided, he is yet to be felt as manifesting his greatness and his oneness in all his creation: 'wheresoever you turn, there is the face of God'. It might seem to you at first sight that this is not true Islam but this kind of thought is very popular in N. India. The Muslim emperor Akbar, for example, who ruled N. India during the early days of Sikhism was very impressed by the bhakti movement. What bhakti is in Hinduism, Sufism is in Islam. It was the blending of Sufism and bhakti which fostered the new religions of India. (Akbar was not a particularly devout Muslim and had actually married a Hindu princess.

He instituted *Din-i-Ilahi* (Divine Faith) which was an attempt to improve Hindu-Muslim relations. Succeeding Moghul emperors were not so tolerant.)

Basically it would be true to say that Nanak rejected many of the Hindu ideas with which he had grown up and accepted more from Islam. He was a strict monotheist and for him God was personal and loving, not like the impersonal Brahman of the Upanishads. He criticized caste and insisted that all men have the right to seek God; caste, he said, has absolutely nothing to do with religion. Neither is truth to be apprehended as a result of bodily austerities: 'Penance, fasting, austerity, almsgiving are inferior to truth; right action is superior to all', said Nanak. Mortification of the body is forbidden in Sikhism.

While bathing he is said to have had a vision of God holding out a cup of nectar (*amrita*) saying, 'Go and repeat my name and make others do so.' He then taught his disciples (Sikhs) to repeat the word *nam* which is Punjabi for name.

He kept the idea of samsara and karma but condemned the notion of avataras. Because he objected to idols he forbade his Sikhs to enter Hindu temples where, of course, you find images in abundance. He also condemned the practice of yoga as a means of salvation: belief in God as the 'Name' is quite sufficient—for him there was no Hindu, no Muslim.

Nanak, then, was the first Guru of the Sikhs for around him grew a keen religious following. Before his death in 1539 he made it clear that he did not wish the guruship to go to either of his sons but named Lehna as his successor. Lehna takes the name of Guru Angad.

2 ANGAD (1504-1552)

It was during Angad's guruship that the Granth Sahib began to take shape. (*Granth*=book. *Sahib*=holy.) It contained some of the poems of Kabir, of Guru Nanak together with some of Guru Angad's own ideas. So as to make it clear that these were no ordinary writings Angad is said to have invented a special Sikh alphabet called *Gurmukhi*, 'the guru's tongue', by modifying the Sharada alphabet. He also built temples called *gurdwaras* from which Nanak's teaching could be proclaimed.

Before he died in 1552 Guru Angad requested that the guruship should go to Amar Das.

3 AMAR DAS (1479-1574)

The third Guru, Amar Das, stressed Nanak's teaching on caste and made all his Sikhs eat together. You will remember that Hindus of different caste will not sit down for a meal together. He also divided the country up into twenty-two sections with missioners in charge of each. Amar Das died in 1574 after having indicated that the guruship was to go to his son-in-law Jetha, under the name of Ram Das.

4 RAM DAS (1534-1581)

The Muslim emperor Akbar who, in accordance with his idea of Dīn-i-Ilahi, wished to merge Indian religions into one (for political reasons), gave Bibi Bhani, the daughter of Amar Das and wife of Ram Das, a beautiful stretch of land. On this site Ram Das ordered a large tank to be dug, in the centre of which the famous Harimandir, or Golden Temple, was later to stand.

5 ARJUN DEV (1563-1606)

Guru Arjun's major contribution to Sikhism was his compilation of the Granth Sahib. He collected the writings of his predecessors together with those of some Hindu and Muslim sages whose teaching tallied with that of the Gurus. He also added his own hymns. Besides this he built many gurdwaras.

The Golden Temple at Amritsar

The Golden Temple was completed in 1579 and around it was built the city of Amritsar ('the pool of nectar'). The temple of Amritsar has become a kind of Mecca of Sikhism. Doors on all four sides of the temple indicate that it is open to everybody and its low position indicates submission to God. Mian Mir, a Muslim saint, laid the foundation stone.

Guru Arjun's Granth (1604) has been preserved with chemicals and is today kept in the large gurdwara known as the Sheesh Mahal (Palace of Glass) at Kartarpur.

Unlike the Muslim emperor Akbar, his successor, Jahangir, did not promote religious tolerance and the weight of state administration was tilted in favour of the Muslims. Arjun, for befriending Jahangir's rebel son, Prince Khusru, incurred the emperor's wrath. He was imprisoned because he refused to pay a fine which Jahangir demanded of him and was tortured to death at Lahore in May 1606. The Guru left his son, Har Govind, instructions that the rights of the Sikhs must be protected by military force.

6 HAR GOVIND (1595-1644)

Har Govind became Guru at the age of eleven and soon afterwards only narrowly escaped assassination. He later organized his Sikhs into an army—a kind of military theocracy. Jahangir had him imprisoned in Gwalior Fort but after some time he was released. Some think that he was released because he settled Arjun's fine. On his release he scored notable victories over the Muslims who were led by Shah Jehan but the Shah was more interested in demolishing Hindu temples than in destroying the Sikhs.

Guru Har Govind carried two swords: one indicated spiritual power (*Peeri*) and the other military power (*Meeri*). In his *Dabistan-i-Mazahib* Mohsin Fani, a contemporary of Har Govind, relates that 'the Guru had seven hundred horses in his stables: three hundred horsemen and sixty artillerymen were always in his service'.

7 HAR RAI (1630-1661)

Har Rai seems to have led a comparatively quiet life without becoming involved to any great extent in politics. It is said that his son Ram Rai changed a line of the Granth Sahib to please the emperor, Aurangzeb. After this Har Rai refused to see his son again. On the death of the Guru his five-year-old brother, Har Kishen, assumed the guruship.

8 HAR KISHEN (1656-1664)

Har Kishen died with smallpox at the age of eight. Before he died he uttered the words 'Baba Bakala' which meant that the next Guru would be found in the village of Bakala.

9 TEG BAHADUR (1621-1675)

Har Kishen's successor from Bakala turned out to be Teg Bahadur, Har Govind's second son. In 1675 he was executed by Aurangzeb because he had organized Hindu action against Islam and refused to accept the Muslim way of life. Teg Bahadur's son, Govind Rai, became Guru.

10 GOVIND RAI (1666-1708)

Govind Rai, the tenth and final Sikh Guru, made some very important contributions to the Sikh religion. He changed his name to Govind Singh. *Singh* means 'lion' and all Sikh men now bear this name.

This Guru was responsible for organizing his Sikhs into a highly efficient military body. At the Hindu New Year of 1699 he called a gathering of his followers at Annandpur, a town in the Himalayan foothills built by his father, Teg Bahadur. There he initiated five of them as members of a Sikh brotherhood called *Khalsa* ('Pure'). Although they were from different castes they all drank nectar (*amrita*) from the same bowl and all adopted the new name 'Singh'. They made a vow to keep what nowadays are called *the five K's* (*Kakars* = symbols):

i   *Kesh*—not to cut the hair on the head or face. This is meant to indicate living in harmony with the will of God. Shaving the hair is an interference with nature and, as such, suggests lack of submission to God.

ii   *Kangha*—to wear a comb to fasten the uncut hair beneath the turban.

iii   *Kachha*—to wear shorts. The loose dhoti of the common people of India was not practical. By adopting the shorts it was intended to symbolize the spiritual and mental break-away from traditional dress and thought. The shorts are often regarded as a symbol of chastity. The shorts are now usually hidden under long trousers.

iv   *Kara*—to wear a steel bracelet on the right wrist. The kara binds the Sikh with a strong, unbreakable link to his religion.

v   *Kirpan*—to carry a sword. The sword is the symbol of self-respect and freedom from oppression. Some Sikhs carry a miniature kirpan.

After initiating these five Sikhs, Guru Govind Rai was initiated by them and thus became Govind Singh. When the ceremony was over the Guru proclaimed: '*Wah Guru ji ka Khalsa, Wah Guru ji ki Fateh*', which means 'The Khalsa are the chosen of God, victory be to God.' This ceremony is called *Khanda-di-Pahul*—Baptism of the Sword.

About 80,000 Sikh men followed suit and joined the Khalsa. Some of them, however, called the *Sahajdharis*, or those who wished to take some time in making up their minds about the new form of Sikhism, remained clean-shaven and often would not wear a turban. This division between Khalsa and Sahajdharis still remains in Sikhism.

The line of religious succession ended with Govind Singh. Instead of electing a new guru he had the ingenious idea of making the Granth, which he had just edited, the final and immortal Guru of the Sikhs and this is how Sikhs think of it today. The Khalsa, too, is thought of as the embodiment of the Guru. The Guru gave his Sikhs these final instructions:

> *I have entrusted you to the immortal God. Ever remain under his protection and trust no one besides. Whenever there are five Sikhs assembled who abide by the Guru's teachings, know that I am in the midst of them. He who serves them shall win his reward—the fulfilment of his heart's desires. Read the history of your Gurus from the time of Guru Nanak. Henceforward, the Guru shall be the Khalsa and the Khalsa the Guru. I have infused my mental and bodily spirit into the Granth Sahib and the Khalsa.*[1]

Thus the Guru is impersonal in the Granth yet personal in the Khalsa in a corporate sense.

The last mortal Guru was attacked and died in 1708, at Nandad in Hyderabad. As a result of his institution of the Khalsa brotherhood the Sikhs obtained political independence in 1764.

SIKH DOCTRINES

Nanak believed that man could, by his own effort, attain the supreme good in this life if he followed in a spirit of sincerity and charity the best teaching available to him in his environment. Sikhs believe that truth may be approached by diverse paths; this

[1] *Bachittar Natak* of Guru Govind Singh trans. by M. A. Macauliffe, *The Sikh Religion*, vol. 5 (Oxford, 1909), p. 243.

is why Nanak did not insist upon or inculcate a particular creed which must be accepted by all. He thought of the different religions as different languages. He did not seek to create a new order of faith distinct from the religious milieu of the India of his day yet his teaching became the foundation upon which his nine successors built and upon which modern Sikhism still stands. Were it not for that element of organization which was incorporated into Sikhism with the formation of the Khalsa it is to be doubted whether the religion would have survived as a distinct faith with its own doctrines.

In Sikhism there is no notion of exclusive salvation, no idea of a chosen people. It has incorporated Islamic monotheism, the Buddhist stress on ethical conduct, the Jewish concern for the solidarity of the family and the social unit, and the Christian concept of neighbourly love and service—all this within an essentially Hindu frame of reference. In Sikhism women were rehabilitated, enjoying religious freedom and equality with men.

According to the Sikh religion no prophet is unique in the sense that he is the greatest of all or the final and authoritative revealer of God. All prophets receive their message from the same source and proclaim it to men in accordance with the needs of the time. Nanak taught that there are no avataras; all ten Gurus were mere men; God is not subject to incarnations.

The law of karma is operative but only inasmuch as it is subordinate to the will of God. God is sovereign over all that is. Sikhs use the term *hukam* or '*order*'—whatever happens is by God's hukam. God's hukam is that one must merge one's will with his will. Man has the divine essence within him (the possibility of perfection) and it is God's hukam that man should be merged into God and thereby end the cycle of karma and samsara. The sense of God's hukam produces humility and self-effacement as the Sikh realizes that all that comes to him is of God.

> *What thou doest is for my good,*
> *Nanak seeketh happiness at thy feet alone.*

Sikhs believe that man is totally responsible for his actions and he cannot escape punishment through the intercession of any saint or leader. A man's actions will bear testimony for or against him at the time of judgment. *Yamas*, the messengers of the Lord of Death, take the individual to the Lord of Justice (*Dharam Raj*) who keeps a perfect account. The scribes *Chitra* and *Gupta*, who have written out the account, are asked to come forward to present the balance sheet. If a man has done evil deeds he is born to a lower life; if he has done good deeds he is born again as a human. The man who has reached perfection will achieve perfect bliss in God. There is no heaven or hell; they are conditions of mind only.

THE GRANTH AND THE GURDWARA

The centre and the inspiration of the Sikh religion is the Guru Granth Sahib. At the beginning of the Granth are a number of aphorisms composed by Nanak called the *Japji*. The Japji consists of thirty-eight stanzas and it is the only poem in the Granth which is said: all the others are sung. Most Sikhs recite the beginning of the Japji (the Mool Mantra) in their morning prayers. This mantra is a kind of basic creed of Sikhism:

> *There is but one God whose name is true, the Creator, devoid of fear and enmity, immortal, unborn, self-existent; by the favour of the Guru* (repeat his name).

> *The True One was in the beginning; the True One was in the primal age.*

> *The True One is now also, O Nanak; the True One also shall be.*

After the Japji comes the *Asa-di-Var*. A *var* (or ode) is a popular Punjabi literary device and in this var Nanak exults God and the *Name*. He outlines the way by which the ordinary man may become the perfect servant of God. This var is sung early in the morning in every gurdwara. Next come the *Rahiras* or hymns by various gurus. The most popular is the *Sukhmani* ('touchstone of happiness') of Guru Arjun; it advocates *simaran*—becoming one with God in a spirit of surrender, devotion, humility and adoration. The Granth also contains Kabir's poems, which are works of great beauty, together with the writings of thirty-six other Muslim and Hindu saints. Had it not been for Guru Arjun's compilation of the Granth many of the works of the bhakti saints would no doubt have been forgotten. It is not an exaggeration to say that the Granth contains some of the finest religious literature man has yet produced. Many of Kabir's poems, for example, compare very favourably with the Hebrew Psalms.

The hymns, which are written in Punjabi and punjabinized Hindi, are set to classical Indian chants. The songs express the idea of the union of the soul of man with God through humility, morality and participation in the world so that one might help others and not become inward-looking. This last point is where the Sikh differs, in his religious practice, from the Hindu. But this is not to suggest that Hindus are not concerned for the well-being of others.

A visit to a gurdwara will reveal the respect with which the Granth is treated. At the Golden Temple special rituals are observed in the morning and at night. Before the ceremony begins the holy book is carried into the main hall of the temple, having been awakened with song; at the end of the last service it is carried back in procession and put to sleep with appropriate songs. At Amritsar the holy book is carried in a chest called a *palki* and to carry the Granth is a great privilege. The scriptures are sung from morning till night at the Golden Temple and it is customary for Sikhs to arrange to have the Granth read on their behalf there at times of sorrow and rejoicing.

In an ordinary gurdwara the Granth is not moved about and is always to be found in the main body of the building. It is set on a cushion under a canopy and covered with a silk cloth. The attendant

An attendant waves the chauri at a reading from the Granth

waves a whisk over the Granth. The whisk, or *chauri*, is a symbol of sovereignty for the Granth is a royal book. The chauri is usually made of peacock's feathers but the material used is of no significance.

On entering the gurdwara the Sikh walks straight up to the Granth, kneels down and then bows before it. He may then walk round the book in a clockwise direction. Offerings are placed on a cloth spread out before it. Towards the end of the service, after the final prayer has been said, an attendant presents each member of the congregation with a small quantity of pudding (*Kara Prasad*) made from butter, sugar, flour and water. It is cooked during the service and crossed with a kirpan before it is distributed. The pudding is placed in the hand and then consumed; it is a fellowship meal. The meal shows clearly that Sikhs are not bound by the caste system; they can all eat together. The sword symbolizes self-respect and freedom from oppression.

Before entering the main body of the gurdwara you must remove your shoes (as, of course, you would before entering the main body of a mosque) and hand them in to an attendant. There are no seats and everyone sits on carpets facing the Granth. (An exception is the gurdwara at Toronto where the congregation sit on chairs.) The men sit on the right side of the Granth and the women on the left. There are, of course, no images to distract them.

Serving food to the hungry and to visitors has always been an essential function of a Sikh gurdwara. A gurdwara without a *langar* (community kitchen) is inconceivable. In its inception Sikhism was a protest against the inequalities of caste and again the langar is a symbol of Sikh teaching on this topic. Those who profess other faiths are as freely allowed to partake of and help in the running of the kitchen as the followers of the Sikh faith themselves. No distinctions whatsoever are made—between man and man, between Sikh and non-Sikh, between high caste and low caste—in seating or serving food in the Guru's kitchen.

Most Sikhs possess a copy of the Granth. The hymns are easy to find as each copy of the Granth has the same paging as Guru Arjun's copy at Kartarpur. There are 1430 pages. Some Sikhs keep a special Granth room in the home.

SIKH FESTIVALS

In their homeland Sikhs observe most of the festivals celebrated by Hindus in Northern India. They sprinkle coloured water at Holi and light the lamps at Divali. The religious part of the ceremonial naturally takes place in a gurdwara and not in a Hindu temple. Sikhs also keep their own special festivals and of these six are particularly important: the birthdays of Guru Nanak and Guru Govind Singh; the martyrdoms of Guru Arjun (the compiler of the Granth) and Guru Teg Bahadur and the two sons of Govind; the day of the founding of the Khalsa and Hola Mohalla (celebrated at Annandpur after Holi).

On these holy occasions the Granth is usually taken through the streets in procession. It is placed on a large cushion of flowers set high on a carriage. On either side two Sikh men carry the Guru's ensign (Nishan Sahib) and five men, representing Guru Govind's first initiates, go before the Granth with swords at the ready. The men walk at the front of the procession and the women at the rear. Music is played and swordsmen demonstrate their skill. The processions are usually followed by parties in the community kitchen of each gurdwara.

SIKH CEREMONIES

A Sikh child is named by opening the Granth Sahib at random; a name has to be found which begins with the first letter of the first word of the passage read from the holy book.

Pahul (baptism) takes place when boys and girls attain puberty. The ritual is the same as that performed by the tenth Guru at the first Pahul in 1699. A place has to be set aside for the ceremony. It can be held in a house or in a gurdwara. Only the persons who are to be baptised and six others who officiate participate in the ceremony. A mixture of sugar and water (*amrita*) is stirred with a double-edged sword while a number of sacred writings, including the Japji, are recited. The new Sikhs are given five handfuls of amrita after which they all repeat loudly after the leader, *Wahiguru* (Wonderful Lord). A little amrita is also put on the hair and eyes.

The Sikh marriage ceremony is called *Anand Karaj* and was legalized in 1909 by the institution of the Anand Marriage Act. It differs from the Hindu ceremony in minor detail only.

Like the Hindus, Sikhs cremate their dead. The period of mourning varies from four to ten days depending on the age of the deceased. During this period of mourning it is the custom to move all the furniture out of the house and to sleep on the floor.

All Sikh men have the word *Singh* as part of their surname. The corresponding name for women is *Kaur*. A convert to the Sikh faith will adopt the appropriate name at the Pahul ceremony.

A RELIGIOUS MOVEMENT BECOMES
AN INDEPENDENT NATION

Sikhism, then, is a monotheistic faith which is simply and clearly expressed in the Punjabi language. The one God is not worshipped by means of images but by prayer, the good life and the repeating of the name (*Nam*) so that after various incarnations the soul is at length at one with God. All rituals are meaningless and Sikh worship in the gurdwaras is very simple. As in Islam, there is no priesthood and adults of either sex can lead the ceremonies. Asceticism is not encouraged. The caste system does not interfere with daily life although Sikhs still marry within caste. Sikhs are allowed to eat meat. Anything which is injurious to health, e.g. smoking, drinking, drugs, is forbidden. The Sikhs fought alongside the British troops during both World Wars. Many distinguished themselves in action in France, Africa and the Middle East.

When India became independent of Britain in 1947 there followed the partition of the country into India and Pakistan—a religious partition. This meant that the western part of the Punjab became Pakistani territory; in other words, the Sikh community was cut in two. About $2\frac{1}{2}$ million Sikhs had to leave Pakistan and cross into India where they forced out the Muslims. The Sikhs suffered great hardship during the years immediately following Partition and the refugees received virtually nothing by way of compensation. As a result the Sikhs demanded a self-governing Sikh state and in 1966 the Congress Party agreed to create in Punjab a separate Punjabi-speaking state in which the Sikhs would number about 55% of the total population. We must remember, however, that the Sikhs are not a race apart. Sikhism is a religion.

There are some who think that Sikhism will eventually be re-absorbed into Hinduism for many Hindu sects tend, after a time, to drift back into the mainstream. They are unlikely to be absorbed into Islam for hatred of Muslims is a kind of tradition among them but Hinduism is an exceedingly attractive religion and, as we have seen, can incorporate a great variety of religious beliefs within itself. However, Sikhism is still a missionary religion. Wherever you find a community of Sikhs, there too you will find a gurdwara and perhaps Sikhism will have a better chance of survival away from the influence of Hinduism than it will in its homeland.

Why I am a Sikh

Sikhism is a world religion not in the sense that it commands the allegiance of a large number of people but in the sense that the Sikh people are scattered almost all over the world and can be recognized easily by their turbans and beards. Its doctrines and ideals are eminently suited to the requirements of seekers of truth irrespective of their colour and country or sex and status. Sikhism is perhaps the latest significant faith produced by the evolution of the religious thoughts of mankind. As a Sikh I feel that it is relevant and that it produces in its followers that pragmatism for which we are noted. My religion, I believe, excludes all that is unnecessary for man's direct communion with God. We feel that complicated dogmas and ritualism are only barriers to the realization of the spiritual goal of man. In Sikhism blind faith and all superstitious practices are displaced by right beliefs and right actions. No priest is needed, no intercession by anyone is required to reach the ultimate goal. Individual merits in virtuous deeds, truthful conduct and service to humanity alone are helpful.

Sikhism, like other great religions, teaches monotheism, the Fatherhood of God and the brotherhood of man and the equality of man and woman. The Christian concept of neighbourly love and service, the Jewish concern for family and household, the Buddhist stress on ethical conduct and purity of thoughts all go into the making of the religious fabric of Sikhism.

The religion of Nanak is free from the stultifying effects of asceticism and austerities, the choking smell of tobacco and the baneful influence of liquors and drugs on the bodies and minds of his disciples. Sikhism's insistence on social justice, the dignity of labour and freedom of conscience places it at once in line with the democratic idealism of a modern state.

Mr Piara Singh Sambhi
Formerly President
The Sikh Temple
Leeds

PART THREE

The Far East

The Far East

CHAPTER EIGHT

Confucianism

EARLY LIFE OF CONFUCIUS

The most noteworthy of all famous Chinese thinkers is Kung Fu-tse, or Confucius, as Jesuit missionaries to China in 1700 called him. 'Master Kung' was born in 551 B.C. at Tsou in the principality of Lu which is now in the Shantung province in northern China, and died in 479 B.C. Many legends about his birth and life were circulated. It was said that Kung was born of a noble family and that at his birth dragons and spirits hovered about him. But of himself Master Kung said, 'When I was young I was without social prestige and lived in humble circumstances.' He was in fact poor and his father had died before he was born. (Muhammad, it will be remembered, was also an orphan.) His home life was not without its problems for of eleven children Kung was the only son without some kind of physical handicap.

Although his family had few material possessions Kung received a good education which found time for such pastimes as archery and music. His home background gave him much in common with poor people and he became a most sympathetic teacher. As a boy he did clerical work, learning from various teachers. At the age of nineteen he married. At twenty-one he started a school and so improved his financial condition. He was one of the most astute men of his day but was not widely read because books were comparatively scarce. They were made from strips of bamboo bound together with twine. It was not until a thousand years after Kung's time that the Chinese invented printing.

In his teaching the Sage made strict demands upon his pupils and would not consider those who were not eager to learn: 'If I present one corner of a subject to my pupil I expect him to know the other three'. Lessons were never repeated for the benefit of those who allowed their minds to wander.

EARLY CHINESE RELIGION

Religion in China before the time of Kung was an advanced animism which centred its attention on nature worship and ancestor worship. Sacrifices would have been offered to the great powers in nature, such as thunder, wind and rain. These powers of the sky were associated with Heaven (*Tien*). Popular Confucianism adopted this worship of Tien as its most important doctrine. The emperor was said to stand in a special relationship to Heaven. Below Heaven stands Earth, *Tu*, with which were associated spirits of the mountains, rivers, crops, and these earth-spirits were worshipped because they obviously controlled the prosperity and order of the State.

The emperor made a yearly sacrifice at the white marble altar of Tien in Peking at the winter solstice (around Christmas). Since Tien governed all things it was most fitting that the human governor of men should pay tribute to that which is the regulating principle of all.

ANCESTORS

Below Heaven and Earth come the numberless spirits of ancestors which pervade the universe. To the Chinese these spirits are very real and many sacrifices are offered to them. 'One must sacrifice to the spirits', said Kung, 'as though they were present at the sacrifice.'

In the past the tombs of rulers and rich men were elaborate buildings and housed many of the valuable items which had belonged to the tomb's inhabitant during his lifetime. It seems clear that in ancient Chinese religion when the husband died it was customary for the widow and steward to be buried alive with him. This took place as recently as A.D. 1398. Even later than this, the suicide of widows to accompany their husbands became a recognized practice, sometimes even performed in public.

Kung condemned the use of living victims. Later it became more usual to burn imitation possessions outside the tomb at burial. Those who cannot

A temple statue of Confucius

afford a large tomb set aside a room at the back of the house for homage. When a body is buried a small stone tablet is taken to the grave and the name and date of birth and of death are inscribed upon it. After the burial the stone tablet is taken back to the house and placed on a shelf in the room along with tablets bearing the particulars of other members of the family who have died. Every so often a simple offering is placed before the tablet for the tablet itself is meant to have some attraction for the spirit whose name it bears. The living respect and honour the dead who, in return, watch over and guard the living.

CONFUCIUS' TEACHING

The Sage thought that he would be best suited to an administrative post but unfortunately no ruler offered him a job which would give him the scope to put his ideas into practice. Instead he devoted himself to his pupils. This was second best as he firmly believed that 'Heaven' required him to carry out social reform. But he thought that if he concentrated on young people and influenced them he would in fact be able to influence the whole of China in future generations. The young were willing to be taught since they had not been hardened by the old ideas. His school became famous and he was hailed as Master Kung—the teacher. He taught his pupils good discipline, hard work and conscientiousness. This seed, he thought, would some day flower in the form of a new China of justice and peace. Many of Master Kung's pupils obtained really important positions in the country. He had taught them honesty and reliability and their employers knew that they could be trusted to do a good job and that they were not merely interested in the money they earned. Had it not been for the influence of his pupils, many of whom were more prominent than their teacher, Master Kung would not have been made a member of the Council of the State of Lu.

Kung suffered the fate of many great artists and poets in that whereas during his lifetime his work was for the most part ignored, his teaching was widely accepted after his death. The Duke of Lu had a temple built for the Master's grave and emperors came and paid tribute to him there and later sacrifices were made to him all over China. The temples were controlled by teacher-mandarins and there was no priesthood. Education consisted of studying Master Kung's writings and pupils had to sit examinations.

We cannot say for sure what Kung actually wrote for some of the works ascribed to him are clearly those of his disciples. However, it may safely be said that Confucian teaching is based on the Five Relationships:

1 Between ruler and subject.
2 Between father and son.
3 Between husband and wife.
4 Between older brother and younger brother.
5 Between older friend and younger friend.

Kung here gets to the root cause of wars and divisions within a country. How can a country, a large machine, composed of many individuals run smoothly if some of its cogs are not functioning correctly? If, on the other hand, peace and harmony exist between these five groups of people then there will be peace and harmony in the State as a whole. It will be noticed that the starting point in Master Kung's thinking is the family. The family is a miniature version of the State. If all is well with the family all will be well with the State as a whole.

Rulers must show kindness to their subjects and in return subjects must respond with loyalty. The father must love his son and the son must humbly obey him. The husband must treat his wife with great respect and in return she must be faithful and obedient. Elders must show consideration to all and younger people must treat them with the reverence due to old age.

What Kung is saying is that the political life of the country depends directly on the attitude of one person to another. 'What I do not wish others to do to me, that also I wish not to do to them', said the Master.

THE STATE RELIGION OF CHINA

Master Kung never claimed to be the author of any original ideas and certainly had no notion of starting a new religion, for to him such a departure from the established customs would have been sacrilegious: 'I am a transmitter and not a maker, believing and loving the ancients.' Nevertheless, his ideas have had a lasting effect on the Chinese.

The Chinese prefer to call Confucianism a School or Teaching. It is not a religion, they say. In fact there is no Chinese word corresponding to our word 'religion'. The three religions of China— Confucianism, Taoism and Buddhism—are described as 'three teachings'. They are not thought of as three distinct religions but as three schools of thought which do not necessarily contradict one another. The Chinese make use of all three teachings.

There is, in fact, very little religious teaching in the works of the Sage. He acknowledged the existence of Tien and of spirits to whom sacrifices should be made in as much as the well-being of the State depends on them to some extent. Otherwise Kung is entirely concerned with the present situation and with devising rules for governing his country.

By 195 B.C., however, an emperor offered sacrifices at Kung's tomb. Confucian teaching had become the basic education for all those embarking on a career in politics. And from that date all emperors continued to honour the Sage. Shrines were built in many parts of the Chinese empire where homage was paid to Master Kung, not as a god but as a great sage, an ideal man. At length, to express their admiration for him, Master Kung was spoken of as ranking with Tien and Tu. We cannot help wondering, however, whether Kung would have approved of this.

Twice a year the emperor visited the Confucian shrine in Peking and chanted:

> *Great art thou, O thou of perfect wisdom. Full is thy virtue, thy doctrine complete. Mortals have never known thine equal. All things honour thee. Thine ordinances and laws have come down to us in glory. Filled with awe we clash our cymbals and strike our bells.*

Since there is no longer a Chinese empire, Confucianism is not the State religion, but Kung's teaching is still remembered by the free Chinese and other followers.

The tomb of Confucius at Chufou

Why I am a Confucian

As a Confucian, I am often reproached with having no 'religion' in the true sense of the word, but at best only a 'morality'. I disagree with this extreme statement on the grounds that though our way of life is not founded on divine revelation, we nonetheless regard our life in this world and the lives of our fellow men with the piety that is proper to all great religions. However, it must be admitted that to be a Confucian is a very different matter from being, say, a Christian or a Muslim. We have no binding rituals comparable to baptism, no organized prayers, no priesthood, and no worldwide network of religious institutions. Instead, we respect other religions, and it is not impossible for a follower of Confucius to practise a second religion, such as Buddhism.

The reason for this relative freedom is, in my opinion, what constitutes the greatest virtue of Confucianism—the view that the things a man does in this life are more important than what he believes in. Almost all other religions demand that their followers should have unquestioning faith in their Gods and revelations; right action and doing good in this world come second to them. With us the priorities are reversed. A student of the teachings of Confucius must devote himself in the first place to attaining the correct attitude to life; that he should believe in a God is encouraged, but not necessarily required of him.

The strength of Confucianism is that it is firmly based on Reason. We avoid speculating about things we will never be able to know for certain, such as whether we are to be judged, and rewarded or punished after death. This reluctance to discuss the supernatural is summed up in a remark made by Confucius to his students: 'While you do not understand life, how can you know about death?' For it should be our central concern to preserve the right kind of relationship with other people. And are not people more important than ideas? I believe that while we cannot hope to understand God, we can and should try to understand ourselves and our fellow human beings.

Confucians are opposed to all forms of radicalism and rebellion. This is because of the respect we feel, especially for our superiors. We believe that we owe absolute obedience to our parents and to our rulers. I think it is easy to appreciate why this should be so: we need the protection our family gives us, and therefore we must treat parents and relatives in a way that merits their affection; similarly we need our political leaders and governments, and therefore we must obey their laws.

Unlike Christianity, which holds man to be corrupt, our philosophy regards man as essentially good. I think this is a very positive outlook on life, because it encourages us to cultivate our good qualities, instead of brooding over our sins. Every Confucian considers it his chief aim to attain a sense of justice, combined with kindness, propriety, and education. These are values that every man will find within himself, and once he has perfected them he will be able to live in harmony with the rest of the world.

Tsai Wen-Tse

CHAPTER NINE

Taoism

Taoism is to be found in China alongside Confucianism and Mahayana Buddhism. It still has a considerable following in China and in a sense is the opposite of Confucianism. Confucianism is practical, austere, demanding self-discipline, down-to-earth, with a clearly defined code of behaviour. Taoism is obscure, philosophical and difficult for the average person to understand and tends to be a religion for mystics and people of a high sensitivity and intelligence.

Taoism (pronounced 'Dow-izm') is derived from the word *Tao* which is very difficult to translate; it can mean 'way', 'course', 'method', 'the Way the Universe Works', or even 'the Absolutely Real', 'the Ultimate Reality' (cf. Brahman in Hinduism). Taoism is thought to have been founded by Lao Tzu, about whom very little is known.

LAO TZU AND THE TAO TE CHING

Lao Tzu is thought to have been born about 604 B.C. and lived 100 years. Literally the name Lao Tzu means 'Old Boy' or 'Old Philosopher' which is obviously a term of endearment given by later disciples and is not his real name (although if he did live to be 100 he certainly qualifies for the title!). There is a legend that he met Confucius and rebuked him for being proud and haughty. Confucius is said to have been impressed by his austere manner, although he did refer to Lao Tzu as a 'dragon'. Lao Tzu appears to have been a keeper of archives but found the corrupt government too much and withdrew from public life. He appears to have been a character who did not desire fame or fortune but rather the opposite; he wished to remain unknown and unhailed. He had no disciples in his lifetime. Legend says he wandered towards Tibet and on the way he met a mandarin who persuaded him to write down his teaching, which he did and this became known as the *Tao Te*

Ching, the Holy Book of the Taoist. Lao Tzu then disappears, purportedly into a cloud.

The *Tao Te Ching* has been translated as 'The Way and its Power' although we have seen that the word *Tao* is capable of many translations, which we can categorize as follows:

1 Ultimate Reality or the Absolutely Real.
2 The Way the Universe Works, the driving force of all nature, the principle of life.
3 The way man should live to fit into the pattern of the Universe and become one with it and in becoming one with the Universe man enters a state of bliss (akin to Nirvana in Buddhism).

The word *Te* means 'power' or 'virtue' and it is the power of virtue that the Taoist strives after. It manifests itself in two main forms in Taoism—Popular Taoism and Philosophical Taoism.

POPULAR TAOISM

At its best Taoism is a philosophical system which appeals to few but the intelligent and mystically-minded people. Popular Taoism, however, is of necessity simpler and more superstitious so it appeals to the common people. Popular Taoism is a system which claims to harness the power ('Te') of Tao through magic and ritual. The main power popular Taoism seeks is over death and so it has become a religion largely concerned with the quest for immortality, and has all the ritual that goes with a preoccupation with death—incantations, spells, charms, necromancy, spiritualism, sorcery. Popular Taoism has its priests and places of worship (although this appears far removed from the spirit of the Tao Te Ching). The priests are mainly concerned with cures for sickness and disease, and with exorcism. The Tao Te Ching itself is said to have magic powers and Taoist priests employ magic rites with noisy ceremonies in an attempt to drive out 'evil spirits' from habitations or people.

Popular Taoism has borrowed many of its ideas from Mahayana Buddhism (such as the transmigration of the soul) and has become as a result polytheistic. The traditional gods of China, plus many others, became part of the Taoist belief, and these were presented in old folk-lore tales and fantastic legends, which made them appear very real to the common people. In popular worship there are eight Genii (spirits of earth and heaven, good and evil), which are very important, but most important are three gods (cf. the Trinity of Christianity and the three Buddhas of Mahayana Buddhism), of which Lao Tzu is reckoned as one.

Women praying for babies, represented by dolls, in a Taoist temple

PHILOSOPHICAL TAOISM

Philosophical Taoism is entirely different in that it has no ritual and no hierarchical system of temples or priests. It tends to appeal only to the mystic. Its basic belief is that by cultivating an attitude of mind which involves perfect harmony and stillness one becomes a better receptacle for receiving Tao, the basic power of the universe. To reach a state where one can receive Tao one must empty oneself of all desires, emotions and impurities of thought and action. Taoism is often said to be a religion of 'do-nothingness' but this tends to give the wrong impression. Chuang-Tzu illustrates in a story:

> *Suppose a boat is crossing a river, and an empty boat is about to collide with it. Even an irritable man would not lose his temper. But supposing there was someone in the second boat. Then the occupant of the first would shout to him to keep clear. And if the other did not hear the first time, nor even when called to three times, bad language would inevitably follow. In the first case there was no anger, in the second there was; because in the first case the boat was empty, and in the second it was occupied. And so it is with man. If he could only roam empty through life, who would be able to injure him?*

In other words the Taoist is passive, trying to become selfless, empty, and it is only in this state that he can achieve harmony with Tao.

In order to reach this state the Taoist practises meditation not unlike the Mahayana and Zen Buddhists, involving controlling of the body and stilling of the mind. When the realization of Tao comes the Taoist is at once supremely active and supremely relaxed. The Taoist does everything easily, without effort, yet competently because he is at one with Tao and his Self, his inner being, is in perfect harmony.

There is a difference here to many religions and certainly to Confucianism; one does not attempt to behave in a certain way because right action will come as a result of being in harmony with Tao. The true qualities of the Taoist are competence without effort, influence without coercion, fame without glory-seeking.

The true Taoist does not wish to draw attention to himself, yet his influence is decisive. The Tao Te Ching says perceptively:

> *The leader is best*
> *When people barely know that he exists.*

Taoists are in fact against all forms of ambition, competition or self-assertiveness because they consider ambitious, arrogant people to be the root of much trouble in the world. They express this conviction in an odd way by pointing out that the value of a window or a door lies in the part that is empty.

The Taoist does not fear death because he does not see life and death as absolute opposites; to him all the world is in harmony—light-dark, big-small, black-white—they are not opposite but complementary. Even good and evil are not opposed, and categorical distinctions between the two are false.

.This is best illustrated by a story the Taoists tell of a farmer whose horse ran off. When the neighbours said how sorry they were that he had lost his only horse, he commented, 'Who knows what is good and what is bad?'

Next day his horse returned bringing with it many other wild horses. When his neighbours said how glad they were he commented, 'Who knows what is good and what is bad?'

Next day his son broke a leg trying to break in one of the wild horses. When the neighbours said how sorry they were, he merely commented again, 'Who knows what is good and what is bad?'

Sure enough, next day soldiers came to commandeer his son for the army, but could not because he was injured.

Although all this may seem very strange to the Westerner we must beware of dismissing it as nonsense. Taoism in a way has prepared us very well for our study of Mahayana Buddhism and particularly of Zen. It is true to say that Taoism today is not so popular as a result of the Chinese Communist purges, but there are signs that in spite of this the people of China are turning to it again. Certainly Taoism is a religion which is so entrenched in the Chinese character that it will be very difficult to remove.

CONFUCIANISM/TAOISM: TEMPLES AND FESTIVALS

TEMPLES

The most celebrated Chinese temples are those of the Ming dynasty at Peking. Since 1911 they have been opened to the public as buildings of historic interest. The famous Temple of Heaven where the emperors made sacrifice is now the kind of place where parents take their children for a day out; the grounds, with their five thousand cypress trees, are ideal for picnics. Many other Confucian temples are now schools or meeting halls.

In the more remote areas some beautiful Taoist temples are still to be seen. However, since 1911, those in built-up areas have been systematically destroyed. Taoists tend to shelter under the umbrella of Buddhism.

FESTIVALS OF 'FREE' CHINA

New Year. In preparation for the New Year festival temples, houses and statues are tidied up; this symbolizes the driving off of the forces of evil. All the deities go to the palace of the Jade Emperor, a kind of divine administrator, to account for their activities. In every home the kitchen god is presented with a variety of delicacies. A miniature image of this god is set on a bamboo stool with a horse cut out of paper and a summary of the family's progress over the past year. As the father of the house says some prayers these replicas and the summary are set on fire and by means of the smoke the kitchen god ascends to the residence of the Jade Emperor to inform him as to the state of the family. While they are still burning, some sticks from the bamboo stool are taken and placed in the hearth to start the fire for the New Year.

On the night before the festival (New Year's Eve) the family will stick red paper round the doors to prevent good luck from escaping through the cracks. Texts are pinned to the doors together with pictures of door deities. The father offers gifts to his ancestors in the room set apart where the stone tablets are kept. Fire crackers are lit to drive off evil spirits.

The Festival of Lanterns is held on the fifteenth day of the New Year. Huge paper dragons are paraded round the town and set alight in the hope of providing rain for the crops.

The Festival of Hungry Souls is held at full moon during the seventh month. Joss sticks are burnt and replica clothes and money are set alight for the convenience of ancestors. When it is dark boats made of paper or thin cardboard bearing images of the gods are floated on rivers and, after prayers have been said, are set alight. They float away and sink. It is believed that these boats will be of use to the ancestors in their travels.

For many, however, these festivals are of secular rather than of religious significance.

CHAPTER TEN

Shinto

The Japanese have a peculiar form of chivalry called *bushido*, in which the virtues of loyalty, valour and self-control are paramount. Reverence for ancestors is also an essential part of this creed. The ethical qualities of bushido are honesty, chastity and temperance. All these are qualities of the well-known *samurai* (warrior).

This feature of the Japanese character explains to some extent the peculiar features of their religion, Shinto. Shinto means 'way of the gods' and strictly is not really a religion but a code of ceremonial behaviour. Although there are many gods, some of the features Westerners associate with religion, e.g. belief in life after death, are absent in Shinto. Like Hinduism, Shinto has no founder and is very much a part of Japanese culture.

An integral part of the ceremonial of Shinto are the services held twice a year in Japanese temples for the cleansing of the people. The temples of the Japanese are not used for congregational worship but solely as the 'home' of a god. There are no idols in Japanese temples as they abhor idol-worship.

As with the Chinese, ancestor veneration is a potent force.

THE IDEA OF KAMI

The uneducated Japanese worships countless gods of nature—spirits known as *Kami*. Kami really means anything strange or awful, or an object of veneration and respect, but is loosely taken to mean 'gods'. It is not worship of 'ghost' spirits, but rather the life manifested in every living phenomenon.

Shinto cosmology is very crude, taking rise in a primitive nature mythology. There are many myths and many gods, but the most important is the Amaterasu myth. Two gods—'The Male who Invites' and 'The Female who Invites'—were the parents of the earth and sea and the islands of Japan. Of all their offspring Amaterasu (the Sun Goddess) was most important, and she gave the rule of Japan to her grandson. This grandson married the goddess of mount Fuji, and one of their grandchildren became the first Emperor—Jimmu Tenno. Japanese tradition declares that the Mikados, descendants of the first Emperor, should rule the kingdom for ever. Veneration of the Emperor was only stopped by the public declaration of the Emperor on 1st January, 1946 that he was not divine.

The heavenly Kami are certainly not pillars of morality to be emulated. In fact their conduct in the myths is quite reprehensible for they are always quarrelling, fighting, making love and living debauched lives. Their superiority to man lies in their possession of magical powers, but they still have the passions and desires and all the failings of humans. Service to the gods is devoid of any ethical significance.

Indeed, there are no moral laws or demands in Shinto. There is no idea of sin. The absence of belief in immortality means that there is no teaching of rewards and punishments in another life. Shinto is, in fact, essentially materialistic.

Of the many gods worshipped in Shinto the most important after the Sun Goddess is Uke-mochi, the 'Food-possessor', the spirit of food and drink. Inari, the Rice-god, has shrines in many villages and is very important.

A river festival with lanterns floating as an act of worship to the god of water

THE DEVELOPMENT OF SHINTO

No date can be given for the beginning of Shinto. It is the old, indigenous religion of Japan before Buddhism and has no founder. The ancient religion seems to be linked with that of China, as there is a resemblance between the two in the worship of spirits, the sun and the veneration of ancestors.

However, the great change in the religious practices of the Japanese came with Buddhism. Today Buddhism has more adherents than Shinto in Japan. In the next chapter on Mahayana Buddhism we shall see how it developed in Japan.

In the eighth century A.D. Buddhism became very influential and attracted the more thoughtful Japanese. Shinto degenerated into divination and sorcery for nearly a thousand years.

However, a revival of Shinto began about A.D. 1700. Several important and influential thinkers championed the cause of Shinto and it revived as a patriotic, political and religious movement. Shinto thrived on the agitation against foreign interference (especially from Russia and America) which Japan experienced in the nineteenth century, and catchy slogans ('Adore the throne and expel the barbarians') became the cry. In 1867 the Emperor was re-established as ruler, and there followed sweeping changes. In 1871 Shinto was made the official State religion. All Shinto priests were appointed by the government and were given the status of government officials. In 1940 all citizens were required to observe Shinto ceremonies, although it must be noted that State Shinto was then said not to be a religion but a national obligation prior to religious allegiance. Shinto was compulsorily taught in schools up to 1946. In 1946, however, it was abolished as the Emperor made his public statement:

> The ties between Us and Our people have always stood upon mutual trust and affection. They do not depend on mere legends and myths. They are not predicated on the false assumption that the Emperor is divine and that the Japanese people are superior to other races and are fated to rule the world.

After such a declaration one would have thought that Shinto would have slowly declined and disappeared. Yet no religion so embedded in the culture of the people can disappear so quickly and, indeed, it seems as if Shinto is showing signs of revival. Perhaps this is because it is essentially a materialistic creed which allies well with the rapid industrial expansion of Japan and the national aspirations of the Japanese to make theirs a rich economic country.

SECT SHINTO

No survey of Shinto is complete without reference to Sect Shinto as opposed to State Shinto (see above). The folk piety of the masses, uninterested in complicated concepts and theories of religion, manifested itself in a popular type of Shinto which became distinguished from the suprareligious national cult established in 1871. Divination, spirit possession, protection from misfortune and disease, and magical formulae are all part of what has become known as Sect Shinto as distinguished from the official State Shinto. Because Sect Shinto was not under State control it was able to develop more freely to meet the needs of the people.

Sect Shinto is divided into 13 main denominations known as 'churches'. The denominations are usually grouped thus:

1 *Pure Shinto*—emphasizing loyalty to the throne and veneration of ancestors.
2 *Confucian Sects*—an amalgam of Shinto and Confucianism.
3 *Mountain Sects*—those who believe their deities live in sacred mountains.
4 *Purification Sects*—so called because of their emphasis on purity, both ritual and physical.
5 *Faith-healing Sects*—which are perhaps the most interesting.

Two of these faith-healing sects are particularly important:

i The first was founded by Bunjiro who uttered revelations to the effect that there was only one God. He repudiated superstitious practices and encouraged extempore prayer. He also taught universal brotherhood and love for all men. This sect has about 3 million followers. Its similarity to Christianity (emphasis on love and monotheism) makes it a serious rival but the next main faith-healing sect is an even more serious rival.

ii The second sect was founded by a woman, Maekawa Miki, whose teaching is similar to that of Mary Baker Eddy (Christian Science). She taught that sickness and evil are spiritual and advised purification rituals to rid oneself of them. This sect has 4 million adherents and is growing.

These main groupings, which often have little in common, have subdivided into further splinter groups and the whole makes a very confusing picture for any student of Japanese religion.

SHINKO—SHUKYO: THE NEW RELIGIONS

Since the defeat of Japan in the Second World War and the statement of the Emperor in 1946 in which he relinquished his 'divinity' there has been an explosion of religious activity. In 1945 there were 43 Japanese denominations registered with the Ministry of Education. By 1951 the total was 720: 258 Shinto, 260 Buddhist, 46 Christian, 156 unclassified. This number was perhaps rather misleading due to the method of classification. By 1961 the total was estimated at 170.

No doubt Japan's defeat engendered in her people a state of great uncertainty and anxiety with the consequent psychological need for something beyond the purely material—religion, the rock on which man steadies his nerves. This kind of situation was ideal for the advent of new religious sects which hold out problem-solving creeds and group identity. The growth of the Japanese sects can be put down in large measure to the rapid industrial expansion. (Marx saw religion as an expression of the feeling of insignificance found among socially and economically depressed workers. That the divisions within the Christian Church in recent times has been brought about, to a greater or lesser degree, by economic factors is manifestly apparent.) Many Japanese workers feel that the old Japanese religion does not supply the answer, does not offer security and identity. Christianity does not seem relevant to them because:

> the total membership in the numerous Christian sects totals only about seven hundred thousand persons, less than the membership of any one of a number of the new Japanese sects that have arisen to prominence since the end of World War II.[1]

The strongest sect is the *Soka Gakkai* (Value-making academic-society) with its strong eschatological emphasis (as in some Western sects, e.g. Jehovah's Witnesses, who anticipate the imminent re-structuring of society following the elimination of all those who do not concede their doctrine) and political aspirations; they are a significant group in parliament after the Liberals and Socialists. Converts are made by means of highly organized propaganda techniques which involve a kind of mental beating into submission. The teaching of many of these sects, however, is found to be intellectually unacceptable by educated Japanese.

---

[1] Edward Norbeck, *Changing Japan* (Holt, Rinehart & Winston, 1965), p. 18.

SHINTO RELIGIOUS LIFE

The ground occupied by the simple wooden shrines of *State Shinto* is said to be sacred. At the shrines one finds groves of trees giving the structure a serene and still ethos. The shrine itself is called a *honden*. Generally speaking, the honden is a small building erected in any convenient place. Larger shrines are situated on elevated ground or in woods. In the centre of the honden is a symbol of the god; usually this is a mirror but in some cases other symbols are used. The symbol is not an object of worship. Sakaki branches adorn the room together with pots in which are placed gifts for the god.

The honden can only be used by priests, the laity remaining in a larger room (the *haiden*) for 'congregational worship'. Here sacred plays are often acted. In every shrine there is a bamboo pole called a *gohei*. At the top of the pole is a split into which cloth is inserted in such a manner that it hangs down in strips. This is a sign that the building is sacred. The *shime-nawa*, a length of rope to which pieces of paper are attached, surrounds and sets apart all sacred objects and helps to ward off evil spirits. The same device is used to keep evil spirits away from the home. All the ritual is performed by priests who cultivate the art of quiet and elegant movement. The attention of the god is attracted by clapping the hands once or twice.

The most famous shrine is that of Amaterasu at Isé to which all Japanese are supposed to make at least one pilgrimage.

The shrines of *Sect Shinto* are similar to those of the State religion but tend to have larger 'congregations'. In *State Shinto* the laymen do not actively participate in the ceremonies and the members only visit a shrine when they feel the need. There are no 'services' as such and sometimes the shrines are not open to the public.

When a layman visits a shrine he stands outside and rings a bell to let the god know that his services are required. The worshipper donates some coins (these are for religious use only) and claps his hands. He will then say brief prayers which are Buddhist in character as there are no specifically Shinto prayers. Indeed, the Shinto 'scriptures' were not compiled until about the eighth century A.D. (for, apparently, written script was not known in Japan before the fifth century A.D.) and therefore have not escaped the influence of Buddhism which was introduced into Japan from China. The word 'scripture' is not really applicable to the Shinto writings for they are regarded as ordinary literary works and are not revelatory in character. The most important writings are the *Kojiki* (Reports on Ancient Matters) and the *Nihongi* (Chronicles of Japan). However, in practice, Shinto is more or less as it was before the advent of Buddhism.

The most likely occasion for a layman to visit a shrine is in time of personal crisis. At many shrines sacred objects are on sale which are said to put evil spirits to flight and avert catastrophe.

In many Japanese homes and places of work there is a *kami-dana* ('god-shelf'), which is a miniature shrine containing symbols of the gods, fixed to the wall. The *shime-nawa* is suspended above it. Texts, talismans, ancestral tablets and other aids to veneration are arranged on its shelves. Jugs of beer and sakaki leaves are given to the gods. On important occasions prayers are said before the shrine.

FESTIVALS

NEW YEAR

Preparation for the New Year festival is made by ridding the house of evil spirits, taking down the old kami-dana and erecting a new one and prayers for good fortune in the year ahead. All debts must be cleared, the house is thoroughly cleaned and plenty of rice, a ceremonial dish, is prepared so that no cooking need be done during the first three days of the New Year. The house is then decorated with plants and white paper images to indicate purity. It is customary to visit friends and make the journey to the shrine at Isé. Six weeks later evil spirits are cast out from all shrines and holy places.

OTHER FESTIVALS

Most Shinto gods have festivals in their honour at different times of the year and the sects commemorate the anniversaries of their founders. Shinto shares many festivals with Buddhism and is to some extent influenced by the Confucianism of China. For example, there is a Shinto *Festival of the Dead* which is virtually identical to the Confucian Festival of Hungry Souls.

A Shintoist Statement of Faith

To obtain a profession of faith from a Shintoist on the same lines as the other 'professions' would have been rather complicated. The following is an extract from Sokyo Ono's book *Shinto, The Kami Way*.[1] Ono is a well-known representative of the Shinto world. He is a professor at the Kokugakuin University and a lecturer for the Association of Shinto Shrines. This extract is a simple, unpedantic statement of what Shinto means to the writer, and also to many fellow-believers who would, however, have difficulty in expressing it so well.

Man is a child of Kami, he also is inherently good. Yet there is no clear line of distinction between himself and the kami. In one sense men are kami, in another they will become kami. Man owes his life, which is sacred, to the kami and to his ancestors. He is loved and protected by them. He is endowed with the life and spirit of the kami, but at the same time he receives his life from his parents, grandparents, and ancestors through countless ages. Man is dependent for his continued existence on both nature and society. He is a social being. He cannot live in isolation.

Man owes gratitude to the kami and his ancestors for his life, and for their all-encompassing love. He also owes much to his present family, his community, and the nation. His life is full of blessings and so he must accept his obligations to society and contribute to the vital development of all things entrusted to him.

Man possesses a personality, which is distinct in each individual. To this personality given by the kami there is added the tradition of the family and the contributions of many individuals and the society in which he lives. These together constitute his characteristics.

There is no place for egotism in Shinto. Egotism runs counter to the spirit of worship. Worship makes the interest of the community and public welfare paramount. This does not mean that the rights of the individual and the family are ignored. On the contrary, against the background of religious rites, the nature of the individual and the authority of the family are fully supported by society. The spirit of the people guarantees this.

Man is born with a purpose, a mission, in life. On the one hand, he has the responsibility of realizing the hopes and ideals of his ancestors. On the other hand, he has the inescapable duty of treating his descen-

[1] Sokyo Ono, *Shinto, The Kami Way* (Bridgeway Press, 1962), pp. 103-4.

dants with even greater love and care, so that they too may realize the hopes and ideals of the ancestral spirits. Ancestors and descendants are lineally one. Reverence for ancestors must never be neglected. It is the only way in which man's life can be lived which will fulfil the reason for his coming into this world.

In order that man may be his best, he is theoretically regarded as kami. He is blessed with words of praise, with the power of words (kotodama), which can bring about a transformation in his character. In practice, however, men are not as a rule called kami until after death, when they achieve a new dimension.

CHAPTER ELEVEN

Mahayana Buddhism

We saw in the earlier section on Buddhism how there were two branches of this religion, Hinayana (Theravada) and Mahayana. The latter, it will be remembered, had as its ideal the Bodhisattva who postponed his entry into nirvana to help others. This noble aim of world salvation was developed into the idea that there were beings who had been on earth in a legendary past and now appear as saviours. So there grew a belief in many of these saviours. We will now see how Mahayana Buddhism has manifested itself in different forms in the countries of Tibet, China and Japan.

MAHAYANA BUDDHISM IN TIBET

Mahayana Buddhism was not established in Tibet until comparatively recent times perhaps because it had to contend with a polytheistic type of nature religion (*Bon*) already found in Tibet. There are two main Mahayana Buddhist sects—the 'Yellow Hats' and the 'Red Hats'. Of the 'Yellow Hats' one in four is said to eventually become a monk. The 'Red Hats' work in closer contact with the people. The Dalai Lama is the religious and spiritual leader and is said to be a Bodhisattva.

Buddhism in Tibet appears to be in a state of decline. Many temples are in disrepair and the Dalai Lama himself is in exile in Northern India where he fled from the Communists in 1959.

MAHAYANA BUDDHISM IN CHINA

It is said that Buddhism came to China in the first century A.D. but possibly it arrived before then. The story is that the Chinese Emperor Ming Ti, about A.D. 60, had a dream in which he saw a golden figure hovering above the Temple and he was told it was the shining Buddha of India. He then sent messengers to India to find out more about this 'god'. Two Buddhist monks were brought

The Dalai Lama on a visit to India, with Mr Nehru and his daughter Mrs Gandhi

back, bringing relics and scriptures, and they founded the 'first Chinese Buddhist Temple in A.D. 67. (Some scholars consider that Buddhism was not established in China until the third century A.D.)

However, Buddhism did not have an easy passage in China, because in many ways it conflicted with the established religions of Taoism and Confucianism. The Chinese found the ideas of monasticism and rebirth particularly repugnant. Gradually, however, Buddhism was adopted by the Chinese as they re-interpreted a few Buddhist notions (e.g. nirvana in terms of the Taoist 'non-action'). As stated before, a Chinese person can be a follower of one of the 'Three Ways' or a follower of all three at once.

There are three main sects of Chinese Buddhism:

1 The *Pure Land* Sect is the most important and widespread. Founded by a Taoist convert, the Taoist hope of a Pure Land or Paradise is taken as the goal of bliss and Amitabha Buddha is thought of as the merciful Father of this region. Salvation can be attained through belief in Amitabha[1], and the laity often utter the 'Lord's Prayer' of Buddhism: 'I flee to Thee Amitabha, glory be to

[1] Chinese name O-Mi-T'o-Fu.

Kuan-yin

Amitabha.' Kuan-yin, 'The One Who Hears the Cry', is another who is worshipped, particularly by women. Another very popular Bodhisattva is Maitreya, the 'Buddha-who-is-to-come'; he is fat and jolly, the personification of goodwill.

2 The *Ch'an* sect was brought to China in A.D. 520 by Bodhidharma. Oddly, there is no trace of this sect in India where it is supposed to have originated. Briefly, Bodhidharma's doctrine was that there was no doctrine. Ch'an tends to despise texts and scriptures. In many ways it is a synthesis of Taoism and Buddhism. It is better known by its Japanese name of Zen and we shall examine it more thoroughly in the next section under 'Mahayana Buddhism in Japan'.

3 The *Tien Tai* sect is based on the *Saddharma-Pundarika Sutra*[1] and has a considerable following.

It can be seen that Mahayana Buddhism in China is a complex picture of overlapping sects and religions. The Chinese have a capacity for assimilating and re-casting religions to conform to their own character and temperament.

[1] One of the chief scriptures of Mahayana Buddhism.

MAHAYANA BUDDHISM IN JAPAN

Buddhism came to Japan from China through Korea, traditionally in A.D. 552. Buddhism was in a sense the transmitter of Chinese and Indian culture to Japan. We have seen in the section on Shinto how Buddhism became very prominent in Japan until 1867 when the Shinto reaction relegated it to a minor place and how, since the war, there has been a revival of Buddhism in Japan. There are now said to be twelve Buddhist sects in Japan, but only the important ones will be mentioned here.

1 The *Tendai* and *Shingon* sects are very comprehensive in the sense that they tolerate many forms of Buddhism; their all-embracing character emphasizes *unity* at the expense of distinctiveness.

2 The *Jodo* sect is the Japanese equivalent of the Chinese Pure Land sect, with its stress on universal salvation and worship of Amida (Amitabha).

3 The *Nichiren* sect, founded in the thirteenth century, is a reaction against the Jodo sect, denouncing worship of Amida and calling men back to worship the one true eternal Buddha, Sakyamuni.

4 *Zen Buddhism* is perhaps the most interesting form of Buddhism in the world today, so we will look at it in a little more detail.

ZEN BUDDHISM

This has a large following among intellectuals and its influence on Western thinkers has been considerable (Aldous Huxley, Heidegger). Zen came to Japan from China where it is known as Ch'an. It is said to have its origin in the Buddha's 'flower sermon', where the Buddha did not resort to words but held aloft a golden lotus; only one disciple, Mahakasyapa, got the point and this insight has been transmitted from teacher to pupil throughout the ages. The perpetuation of Zen rests on the transmission of a specific state of awareness directly from mind to mind like a flame passed from candle to candle. Zen states that its doctrine can only be felt—any attempt to express it in speech or writing is bound to fail.

It has been said that entering the world of Zen is like stepping through Alice's looking glass—it is a world where everything seems quite mad. It is a world of puzzling dialogues, obscure conundrums and blatant contradictions.

Enlightenment or *satori* is the main theme of Zen. Unfortunately no one can know what satori is unless he has attained it, and if he has attained it he cannot tell others what it is because it is an

The raked sand of a Japanese garden provides a place of contemplation for a Zen monk

awareness. Satori is obtained by gradual training which culminates in sudden illumination. The training consists in solving problems or *Koan*, e.g. 'What was the appearance of your face before you were born?' or 'We have all heard the sound of two hands clapping, what is the sound of one hand clapping?' or 'How many elephants in a blade of grass?'

A Zen trainee cannot dismiss these as nonsense; he cannot protest that an elephant cannot get into a blade of grass, for such a remark shows that he has not even begun to get the point. The idea is to baffle and exhaust reason, and when its inadequacies are fully exposed then intuitive knowledge will break through. The Zen novice submits his views on the Koan to his teacher, who knows instantly whether he has the point; if he has not he will be told in no uncertain manner to go away and think again. The attempt is to blast the novice out of the comfortable verbal retreat into which he has settled. Words can be a barrier to experience; one can say the correct things about a painting without the slightest aesthetic feeling for it.

The training of monks is not left to chance—there are strict rules. Monasteries usually consist of seven buildings, including the main meditation hall where one practises *Zazen*, i.e. sitting cross-legged, meditating, controlling the breathing. Lectures, given in a lecture hall, are usually paraphrases of a well-known book, and not an argument or discourse.

Zen may be eccentric, but it cannot easily be dismissed as 'just another religion'. Certainly all are agreed that those Zen adherents who do attain satori have a depth and quality of being which makes the ordinary man feel very inadequate. Perhaps Zen is a timely reminder that our complex modern society has an infinite capacity for manipulating abstractions but has failed in the basic quest for the depth of being.

MAHAYANA RELIGIOUS LIFE

In Asia the Buddha Amitabha receives greatest veneration. In Japan he is known as Amida and in China he is called O-Mi-T'o-Fu. Pure Land doctrine asserts that faith in him assures the worshipper of rebirth in Amitabha's paradise and his name is repeated numerous times in order to guarantee such a rebirth. The Bodhisattva Avalokitesvara guides the worshipper to Amitabha's paradise. In Tibet the Dalai Lama is said to be the incarnation of Avalokitesvara. The prayer associated with this important Bodhisattva is *Om mani padme hum* ('Hail to the Jewel in the Lotus') and Tibetan Buddhists repeat this prayer throughout the day. Prayers in Tibet are offered on prayer-wheels. These are cylinders which contain

A hand prayer wheel showing the prayer roll and its silk bag

A Buddhist priest at a prayer wheel

written prayers. Each time they revolve the prayer is made effective. Prayer-wheels vary greatly in size; most Tibetan Buddhists own a hand-wheel but in temples the wheels are as tall as a man. These are revolved by the wind or sometimes by heat from candles. Some are attached to chimney pots. Tiny bells are attached to the wheels and the tinkling sound reminds the Buddhist that merit is being built up on his behalf. On the wheels is the prayer '*Om mani padme hum*'. The rituals of Tibetan monasteries are at least as colourful and ornate as those of Roman Catholicism. Many Buddhists use rosaries as aids to devotion; monks carry rosaries made up of a hundred and eight beads, each half standing for the fifty-four steps involved in the process of becoming a Bodhisattva. A large bead in the middle represents the Buddha. The laity own smaller rosaries.

In China Avalokitesvara is known as the female Kuan-yin and in Japan as the male Kwannon. There are numerous Buddhas and Bodhisattvas which are invoked in Tibet, China and Japan but space does not allow us to deal with them.

Although in China religion is not encouraged, Buddhism has received a certain protection under Communism and most of the best temples have been preserved. Monks are still allowed to perform their sacred duties but the trend seems to be towards a lay-Buddhism

A mass ordination of Chinese Buddhist priests at which shaven heads are pierced with burning joss sticks

rather than the monastic life. This tendency has been carried over from the Pure Land of China to the Jodo of Japan. As far as Zen is concerned, however, monasteries are vital as places of seclusion.

In all Mahayana countries there has been the tendency to associate the existing deities with Buddhas and Bodhisattvas and this largely accounts for the overlapping of religious cultures in China, for example. Like the Shintoists, Buddhists in Japan have a small shelf (*butsudan*) in the home bearing a chinoiserie of the Buddha Amida in front of which are an oil lamp and flowers. In China many people keep a shelf in honour of the Buddha Amitabha. Japanese worship is often congregational, the liturgy being of great beauty.

Belief and worship in Mahayana Buddhism is rich and diversified and presents a somewhat confusing picture to the Western observer; but no doubt Christianity can appear equally confusing.

> *... no matter how many peripheral differences one finds in Buddhism, there does exist a basic unity of teaching founded on the Four Noble Truths about human suffering and the Eightfold Path of Deliverance that brings an end to suffering, chiefly through conquest of the ego. Buddhism is able to contain within itself the same wide range of viewpoint and practice as Christianity, which has managed to hold inside its loose compass such contrasting institutions, philosophies, sects and people as the Vatican, the Quakers, the Inquisition, Holy Rollers, image worshipping Italian and French peasants, the 'heresies' of Meister Eckhart and Teilhard de Chardin, the miracles of St. Theresa, the 'communism' of Simone Weil, the intellectual thrust of Tillich, the 'old-fashioned' fundamentalism of Billy Graham—just to select at random a sampling of Christian paradoxes. At the heart of the manifold efflorescences of Buddhism there remains a calm centre; an intuitive yet rational, compassionate yet uncompromising focus of psychological teaching concerning man as 'the creator of his own world'.*[1]

FESTIVALS OF THE MAHAYANA

The main festivals of Mahayana Buddhism are the anniversaries of important Buddhas and Bodhisattvas together with decisive events in the life of Gotama. The birth and death of the founders of the various sects are also celebrated.

[1] Nancy Wilson Ross, *Hinduism, Buddhism, Zen* (Faber, 1966), p. 133.

During the Japanese *Higan* festival which occurs twice a year, prayers are offered on behalf of the dead. At the *Bon* festival (*Festival of Lanterns*) it is believed that the departed return to their earthly homes for help from their relatives. There are a number of festivals which are celebrated at full moon. The birth, Enlightenment and entry into nirvana of the Buddha are usually celebrated in May. Many Mahayana Buddhist festivals are influenced by pre-Buddhist religions.

BUDDHISM AND THE WEST

There has been a Buddhist Society in England for fifty years and the members, some of them eminent scholars, have produced and published some important Buddhist texts. The founder and president of the Society, Christmas Humphreys, has written a number of informative books. In America there are over a hundred Buddhist Societies.

CHAPTER TWELVE

Religion in China Today

Precisely what chance any religion has of survival under Communist rule is not yet certain. Since the republican revolution of 1911 the old State rites have disappeared and ancestor worship has dwindled. Communism accuses Confucianism of spreading superstition and the Confucian national holiday was abolished in 1949. It is interesting to note, however, that in 1962 Master Kung was honoured, even under the Chinese political system, by the official restoration of his tomb. Kung's teaching was religious in respect of its ethical content only and veneration of the Sage was really a typically Chinese expression of indebtedness to a significant figure of the past. Kung was a political philosopher rather than a prophet. The religious, or quasi-religious elements in his teaching were based on what already existed. He was evidently non-committal on all matters of religion and his religious terminology was in strict conformity with the traditions which he wished to perpetuate. Classical Confucianism admits of no God at all. Moral law is that impersonal something behind the universe. And perhaps ancestor veneration is not necessarily a religious activity. Is Confucianism more of a religion than Communism?

To Communists Kung, the traditionalist, represents all that impedes progress and social change. Confucianism kept China conservative for two and a half thousand years. 'I hated Confucius from the age of eight', declared Chairman Mao, yet at the same time he feels that the Chinese are to some extent indebted to the Sage. It is against this background of extreme political conservatism that Mao adopted Trotsky's idea of a 'continuous revolution'. For Mao the political situation must always be kept 'on the boil' and the Revolution must progress until it has overcome the world. (Herein lies the ideological rift between China and Russia: Stalin abandoned the idea of perpetual revolution.) Confucian ethical teaching is also out of favour. It is described as 'reactionary', 'feudalistic'. The modern intellectual is brought up as a Marxist.

Mao is idolized by the Chinese people; in his own lifetime he has become a legend and is regarded by peasants as omniscient and omnipotent. His writings are regarded as 'scripture' and quoted whenever possible. The mass-gatherings in Peking and all the slogan-chanting and emotive outbursts that go with these political meetings bear some resemblance to the phenomena of religious enthusiasm. In Malaya, Formosa and Hong Kong (areas untouched by Communism) religious customs are still observed.

At the popular level, pre-Communist Confucianism represented a strongly animistic attitude with emphasis on divination and magic. In the minds of the populace the Sage's teaching had become clogged with much which he would have rejected and some point out that with the coming of Communism there has been not a turning away from but a returning to true Confucianism. In a sense Communism has had a purgative effect on Chinese culture. Ancestor veneration continues to some extent but under the People's Republic the great families have been reduced to biological units, i.e. parents and children, and the Marxism/Leninism taught in schools can hardly encourage the perpetuation of ancestral rites. Some Chinese insist that what is encouraged today is an evolved Confucianism which, until recent times, had been neglected.

But if Confucianism cannot be described as an essentially religious phenomenon then Taoism can make such a claim. Taoism is the old individualistic religion of China which took on an organized form with the advent of Buddhism in that country. Taoists tended to organize themselves into esoteric societies of a quasi-political nature. The 'Boxer Rising' and the 'Pervading-Unity Tao' are examples of recent movements and when the Communists achieved power it was movements such as these that they felt obliged to suppress. It looks as if Taoism might well withstand the eroding influence of Communism for it is an integral part of Chinese life and, along with Buddhism, will provide a kind of safety-valve.

Although several Buddhist temples have been converted for secular use, Buddhism is still tolerated as a popular religion in China; it is estimated that it has 50 million conscientious devotees and many more occasional supporters. However, the Sangha is vital to the future of Buddhism and it is sad to reflect that Buddhist monasteries in China are little more than living museums.

It must be remembered that for many living in Asia today political issues must appear far more important than religion. For this reason a number of well-known Buddhists have stated that Buddhism and Communism are not incompatible. We cannot here analyse

A Buddhist priest burns himself to death in protest against the Viet Nam government

the similarities and differences between the two philosophies but it would appear that the attitude of some Chinese Buddhists is expediential only. (But this is not to say that there are no similarities between Mahayana Buddhism and dialectical materialism.) The immediate future of Buddhism in China is not good but the Buddhist-Communist dialogue may possibly create the kind of intellectual climate in which a feasible synthesis might be arrived at. In recent times there has been a greater willingness on the part of Buddhists from different countries to exchange ideas; this should help to weld together the various Buddhist traditions and make for greater solidarity in the face of opposition. Perhaps the intellectual stimulus, both from outside and from within Buddhism, will bring about a Buddhist renaissance in China and the Communist countries. As Edward Conze wrote in an article on 'Buddhism' in *Asia Handbook* (Penguin, 1966), p. 387: 'A religion which has tamed the descendents of Genghis Khan need not necessarily fail with the successors of Mao Tse-tung.'

Communism and Religion

WHAT IS COMMUNISM?

The purpose of this chapter is to examine Communism to see whether it is true to say that it is in any way a religious movement. There are some people who maintain that the great changes which have occurred in the Western world since 1850 (primarily as a result of the Industrial Revolution) have led to a new type of society, a new type of thinking, and a new type of philosophical world-view. This changed society, it is claimed, has produced new needs which cannot be catered for by conventional religious systems, but which can be satisfied within the movement of Communism. In view of the large Communist following in the world today, it is worth considering whether it is in fact a new type of (or perhaps a different expression of) religion. The latter part of this chapter will be devoted to that question. First, however, it is necessary to try to define as succinctly as possible what Communism is.

Communism is difficult to define precisely. Yet although the exact nature of Communism is somewhat elusive, it is possible to delineate certain defining characteristics. The proponents of Communism claim that it is a pragmatic philosophy relating man to society; it is an economic political theory concerned with social existence and organization. (It has been called 'an economic philosophy of the suffering classes'.) Primarily, it is an attack on the economic and ethical bases of capitalistic society, a rejection of the competitive and social organization normally found in the more advanced industrial and technological countries. In its demand for collective ownership, it is an ethical criticism of such economic systems. Its effectiveness lies in the fact that it is an organized political force. A brief examination of its history and development may help to clarify some of these characteristics.

THE ORIGINS OF COMMUNISM

It is perhaps difficult for us nowadays to realize how the psychic and mental make-up of modern man was changed by the Second Industrial Revolution (about 1870 to 1910). Not only did this era mark the emergence of a large stratum of society which could be called the working class, it changed the whole pace, structure and outlook of modern society. Philosophy was radically changed by the rise of *Positivism*, the philosophy of the scientific outlook. Basically, it was not only a belief in science, but more a belief in the scientific method. There are two presuppositions to such an assumption: first, that the world consists of a reality which can be manipulated by scientific techniques; second, the belief in the idea of progress. One can readily see that this kind of outlook might clash with a certain type of 'other-worldly' religion which tended to place the emphasis on a paradise in heaven rather than on earth. What happened as a result of this positivistic thinking was a shift in emphasis from the control of man and nature by God, to man being able to control nature and hence his own destiny. It is in this kind of atmosphere that socialism later flourished.

Communism springs out of the wider movement of socialism. This term was adopted by the followers of Robert Owen in 1841. Marx and Engels characterized the early attempts at socialism as *Utopian Socialism*, as opposed to *Scientific Socialism*, which is based on the materialist concept of history—the notion that economic and political factors will inevitably determine the collapse of the capitalistic system and initiate the institution of socialism.

Perhaps the earliest attempts at socialism can be identified with the work of St. Simon and Charles Fourier in France. St. Simon (1760-1825), although he believed in unequal rewards, may be considered one of the precursors of socialism in that he insisted that it was the duty of the State to plan and organize the use of the means of production. St. Simon also made a distinction between the producers and the owners of the means of production. This can be considered prototypical of the theory of classes.

Fourier was a younger contemporary of St. Simon. He disagreed with St. Simon's over-centralization and the idea of a large technocratic machine. Fourier was one of the first to advocate a unit of social organization (of about 1500 people) in which the members were equal in status and income. However, they still retained property rights—people were capitalists as well as workers. It was also an entirely voluntary system.

The followers of Robert Owen in England denounced competition as leading to exploitation. They advocated communal living. The Owenite movement influenced the more vigorously anti-establishment movement of Chartism, which is often referred to as an incipient socialist movement. It was intended to be politically rather than economically defined, on the basis of the belief that by gaining universal suffrage and triennial parliaments power would automatically pass to the working class.

After 1848 there emerged in England a movement known as *Christian Socialism*. Many Christian consciences were appalled by the social conditions of the time and some eminent Christians set about establishing small working associations to improve things. The movement collapsed in England but developed on the Continent, particularly in France and Germany. An important movement was Lassalle's Universal German Working Men's Association, which fused in 1874-5 with the rival Social Democratic Party. It is at this point that we see a significant change of emphasis within the socialist movement—the advocating of political agitation and action to achieve the desired social reforms. In France, Blanqui and Louis Blanc were active political agitators, the latter being the originator of the formula, 'From each according to his ability, to each according to his needs'.

KARL MARX

It was in this atmosphere of political and social ferment in Europe that Karl Marx formulated his ideas. When at the University of Berlin he was influenced by Hegelian philosophy—the idea that the world is a dynamic and spiritually progressive process, revealing itself in a reasonable order. (Hegel did not speak of the God of traditional religion but of a 'World Spirit'.) History was marked by stages, each stage being explicable only in its cultural and social context. Marx was also influenced by the philosopher Feuerbach, who criticized existing religion as being a projection of human needs and ideals. However, Marx did not follow Feuerbach in his call for a new religion of humanity based on the ideal of love, but rather turned his attention to the overthrow of political institutions. Marx also affirmed that man's nature was governed not only by social but by historical factors. Hence Marx's doctrine of *historical materialism*, the idea that the economic structure of society determines the life and social coherence of that society.

It is somewhat difficult to describe the thought of Karl Marx briefly, for he is a cumbersome and complex writer. Particularly difficult to grasp is his notion of *ideology*. However, this is important to his theory, and this aspect of Marx's thought has been misrepresented, so it warrants some examination. Normally the word ideology is used to embrace any coherent set of political beliefs. For Marx, however, ideology represents a set of transient truths applied to the present under the pretext that they are universal truths. In other words, for Marx ideology signified a *false consciousness* of economic and social realities. Every ideology embraces a set of beliefs; these beliefs motivate the behaviour of that ideology's adherents. Every social class adhering to an ideology does so because it meets a specific (but transitory) set of economic arrangements. It is the division of man from man in the division of labour which has led to the existence of ideology. Marx therefore looked for the day when there would be no ideology (political or religious).

Karl Marx

As can be seen, Marx's thought is not easy to comprehend. However, what is obvious is that Marx was deeply concerned with the social organization of man, and he saw this as being governed by historical and economic factors, leading to the existence of ideologies and political theories which had no contact with the basic economic facts of life. Marx strongly believed in the dignity of man; he must strive to master his own fate. He should not allow himself to be cowed by any religious dogmas or tyrannies of the State or political institutions. Marx's socialism inherently presupposed equal rights and powers by citizens to determine the administration and content of government. Marx's conception of socialism was a rational and planned collectivized economic society, in which all social and moral difficulties would disappear.

From this basic theory emerges Marx's concept of the 'class struggle'. For Marx a class is an economic group. He contended that private ownership of the means of production inevitably leads to conflict. This expresses itself in politics. In particular, the State is the apparatus of coercion to keep the *status quo* and prevent the inevitable open conflict. In the classless society there will be no need for the State. Marx's expectations were not really so different from those of the Utopian Socialists who looked for a day when there would be no war, no crime, no resentment; everyone would seek the good of all.

Marx believed that man in present society is *alienated*. For, in the first place, man envisages himself as being in the grip of impersonal powers and forces, but in fact these are his own forms of social life, the fruits of his own action, which are falsely objectified and endowed with independent existence. Again, man sees himself as a free agent in areas of life where social and economic norms are dictating the rôle he plays out.

Marx makes a distinction between life as a means to labour and labour as a means to life. In the alienated society, labour becomes a mere means to physical existence. Labour is alienated from the labourer; it is not part of his life, rather he sees it as the sacrifice of his life. Only in the free society will men live in order to work, when they see it as an aid to their own self-development.

Marx's special contribution to the socialist dogma is perhaps in his idea of how socialism is to be brought about. Starting from the premiss that men make their own history, Marx goes on to say that the socialist era can be initiated by political action. Once the working class gains political awareness and resolution, the change will inevitably follow. The economics of the capitalistic society are such

As the Capitalist machine moves on, more and more of the common ownership of land and wealth is consumed. If the masses cannot earn enough in slumps, they part with their wealth to live. After each slump, more of this wealth has been transferred to the rich, leaving the masses—the proletariat—worse off.

that the gap between the rich and the poor becomes wider and wider. Inherent in the capitalistic economic system are slumps and depressions, which affect the working class more than any other. There will be an inevitable conflict between the oppressed and the oppressors.

SOCIAL DEMOCRACY

Socialism went its different ways in different countries. In Germany the Social Democratic Party became a parliamentary party. In Russia, however, political conditions prevented the formation of a socialist parliamentary party. Hence all the opposition to the ruling régime tended to be revolutionary. The seeds of what is popularly known as Communism were sown.

A very different type of socialist strategy was worked out by the Fabian Society (founded 1884) in England. Its policy was evolutionary socialism, i.e. working towards the socialist state through the normal political channels. It is said to have taken its name from the Roman general Fabius, known as 'the Delayer' because of his deliberate and long range strategy. This socialist group influenced the development of the Labour Party.

It is worth noting that not all the early influential socialist thinkers thought that violence and revolution were essential in ushering in socialism. For example, an influential socialist thinker in Germany called Bernstein asserted that the gradual movement towards socialism was everything, the ultimate goal of socialism nothing. The really important aspect of the socialist movement was the enriching of the lives of the workers by increasing their participation in politics and industry. Socialism was a way of life to be experienced here and now, and not to be relegated to some longed-for utopian day in the distant future.

THE RUSSIAN REVOLUTION

Communism as we know it was thrust upon the world in the cataclysmic event of the Russian revolution. As we have seen, socialism up to the revolution was a diverse, complex and loosely defined belief. The revolution of 1917 was the catalyst needed to set the more radical socialist movement in motion.

We have not space here to go into the complex historical background of which what has become known as Communism was born. Suffice it to say that at the outbreak of the revolution in 1917 there were four socialist parties:
1 *The Socialist Revolutionaries*—they appealed mainly to the peasants and were the largest socialist party at the outbreak of the revolution; 2 *The Social Democrats*—they appealed mainly to the urban workers; 3 *The Bolsheviks*, and 4 *The Mensheviks*— originally one party, they split in 1903. Whereas the Mensheviks wanted to model themselves on the socialist parties of Western Europe and work with the *bourgeoisie* for the revolution, the Bolsheviks wanted a strong, centralized and disciplined party to aim directly at power.

That out of the chaos of the revolution of 1917 the Bolsheviks emerged as the most potent and effective political party was due to the work of Lenin. Lenin deviated from the thought of Marx in that he saw the Communist state as being initiated by a small, organized and disciplined revolutionary party. The revolution needed the human agency to bring it about; it would not happen as a natural historical process as Marx thought. Lenin was a political and revolutionary genius who directed and guided the revolution to a successful conclusion. Believing that the capitalistic system would not automatically break down, he sought power and seized it.

Many of the Communist Party doctrines are derived from Lenin. 'Freedom of criticism' was for Lenin a self-contradictory notion— it had to be subordinated to the truth, and this truth was given by the Party which worked it out on the basis of its scientific philosophy. Majority support was not necessary; the Party *first* seizes power and *then* seeks to win the support of the majority. However, Lenin did believe that some day the majority would be politically aware enough for the state, the Party and the police to 'wither away'.

Much has been said about the Communist butcheries in the revolution and afterwards. It is interesting that Leon Trotsky gives the most able defence of Communist terrorism. He says that that which is morally permissible is that which leads to the highest moral ends of man. Terrorism for the Communist cause is morally justifiable because it is the only and necessary means to achieve the ends of socialism. As the ends of socialism are the highest moral ends of man, violence for the sake of Communism is justifiable.

Perhaps Stalin's greatest contribution to Communist thought is his well-known doctrine of 'Socialism in One Country'. When the Bolsheviks seized power in Russia they expected similar revolutions to take place in the Western world. When this did not happen, Stalin developed the notion of 'Socialism in One Country' by which he meant that the primary target of Communist workers should be to build up socialism in Russia (although still remaining in sympathetic contact with Communist workers in other countries). Thus Stalin built up a strong U.S.S.R. to protect it from invasion from capitalistic countries and in doing so he played down the idea of international revolution.

In his quest for a strong U.S.S.R. Stalin ruthlessly crushed all opposition with a series of 'purges' in which people were persecuted even after they had ceased to be a political threat, apparently for wrong (political) belief (whether held at the time or previously). Under Stalin Russia became one of the major political powers of the world and the focal point of the Communist movement.

MORE RECENT DEVELOPMENTS

There have emerged new left wing factions which give socialist thought a different look. Perhaps the most interesting are those which seek to combine psychological theories with political ones. Many take their theory from Sigmund Freud's famous book *Totem and Taboo*. Briefly, in this book Freud suggests that civilized repressed sexuality is derived from a timeless tyrannical Father who, at the dawn of time, denied his sons sexual access to his wife or daughters. In the ensuing conflict the Father was murdered and the guilt of the sons is expressed in the sexual customs and taboos of civilized society.

The *Freudian Left*, as they are known, derive their theory from a combination of two streams of thought: Freudian and Marxist. Contemporary thinkers such as *Marcuse* try to correlate the repression of pre-genital sexuality with the needs of the capitalist order. More simply, the contention is that the capitalistic system requires that the *libido* be concentrated in the genitals so that the rest of the body might be transformed into an instrument of labour. The influence of this kind of thinking can be seen in the so-called 'student power movement'. It has been argued that the student revolution in France in 1968 derived some of its impetus from this kind of theory. Certainly its influence can be observed in *Weatherman*, a group of left wing radicals very active in America. These developments illustrate how socialist thought is progressing along different lines.

IS COMMUNISM A RELIGION?

Our real task in this chapter is to attempt to answer the question, 'Is Communism a type of religion?' To answer this, one must first attempt to define what religion is, and this will be a useful postscript to our study of world religions. Usually, the word is used very loosely. People talk of 'cricket being his religion'. In such a statement the speaker is identifying religion as a great devotion to something. But religion is more than this. If one were asked to define religion one would usually think of it as entailing some belief in a supernatural being (or beings). These beings are usually worshipped or venerated because they are transcendental or powerful. Yet we have noted one religion (Theravada Buddhism) which does not have such a belief. Even more than this is involved in being religious, for primarily it is a state of mind which motivates action and belief. And religions usually have a ritual and emotional element. Accordingly, religion has been defined as:

> *A state of mind, comprising belief in the reality of a supernatural being or beings, endued with transcendent power and worth, together with the complex emotive attitudes of worship intrinsically appropriate thereto.*[1]

The real problem when defining religion is to find a definition which is not too broad and yet not too restrictive. Certainly the above definition would appear to be comprehensive, and yet it does not include, for example, Theravada Buddhism (or Communism).

[1] C. A. Campbell, *On Selfhood and Godhood* (Allen & Unwin, 1957), p. 248.

Paul Tillich, in his book *Dynamics of Faith*, defines religion as being grasped by an 'Ultimate Concern'. What Tillich means is that all other concerns are preliminary to the main concern which supplies the answer to the question, 'What is the meaning of my life?' Thus the primary concern is a religious one in that it becomes the motivating concern of one's life; it makes an absolute demand on one's adherence and also has an ultimate promise of fulfilment. If we follow this definition we can distinguish three different types of religion:

1   *Theistic religions*, where the object of ultimate concern is a transcendental being, e.g. Islam, Christianity and Judaism.

2   *Non-theistic religions*, where the object of ultimate concern is an all-pervading power or 'higher principle', e.g. certain types of Hinduism and Buddhism.

3   *Secular or Quasi-religions*, where the object of ultimate concern gives the movement a character which is unintentionally like other religions. What such a movement formulates and articulates resembles recognizable religion, e.g. Communism.

Can Communism really be called a 'quasi-religion'? In what way does it resemble other religions?

A superficial glance will reveal similarities. For example, the famous Communist symbol of the hammer and sickle serves a similar function to the star of David or the cross; it is consciously employed as a symbol to inspire loyalty and devotion. Again, *myth* is employed by the Communists. Russian art-forms are permeated with the myth of the revolution. The myth of the revolution, like all myths, provides a framework of meaning from which a pattern of action may emerge. (Cf. the myth of the wheel of karma which provides for the Hindu a meaningful religious system from which develops a body of moral rules.)

There is a very definite *ritual* element in Communism as seen in China. The mass gatherings in Peking, in which the participants rhythmically chant slogans with arms outstretched clutching *The Thoughts of Chairman Mao*, are agents of intoxication and conversion. It is noteworthy, too, that the Chinese Red Guard, by the uniform way they dress and their emphasis on obedience and discipline, suggest a comparison with some religious orders.

Communism has its 'Holy Books' (*The Communist Manifesto, Das Kapital, Thoughts of Chairman Mao*); its prophets (Marx, Lenin, Mao); and its revelatory event (the Russian revolution).

Perhaps the similarities between Communism and religion can best be understood in terms of the difference between a *belief* and a *commitment.* I can believe that the earth is flat, but I am hardly committed to that belief in the sense that it is the central, motivating force in my life. Plainly it is not. But a religious belief is a commitment in that it motivates the adherent's action; the belief is seen as a way of life. And, significantly, Communist believers are inspired by an ultimate devotion to what they contend is a way of life.

Again, it is illuminating to realize that there is a difference between religion as a *minority* creed and religion as a *majority* creed. When religion is a minority creed it tries to convert, to change the socio-cultural milieu. But when it becomes the established religion, the religion of the majority, it uses the socio-cultural milieu to change the people. It uses social means, such as education, to inculcate its beliefs. This is true of Christianity and Judaism and of Communism.

As a commitment, religious belief is necessarily exclusive (i.e. it contends that it alone is the true way of life). As such it tends to be intolerant of, and even persecutes those who hold contrary beliefs. This phenomenon is evident in the Spanish Inquisition and Muslim Holy War. But it can be strongly maintained that the purges of Stalin fall into the same category, for people were persecuted for what they believed, not necessarily because they were a political threat.

On a deeper level than this, however, the Communist concept of history is very similar to that of the religions of Islam and Christianity. For example, Christianity sees man as originally living in a blissful non-alienated state (cf. the Garden of Eden). Due to the inherent evil will of man this blissful state was lost (the Fall doctrine). However, restoration to the previous state has been made possible through the revelatory event of Christ and ultimately the Kingdom of God will be established.

Communism also believes that there was an original state of non-strife, non-alienation of man from man, before the rise of classes. This state was lost when man's greed drove him to compete with his neighbour and hence gave rise to the oppressors and the oppressed. The Russian revolution, however, revealed that this state of affairs could be changed, and the revolution gives hope that ultimately a Utopia can be established where man is no longer set off against man in competing units.

There would thus seem to be good grounds for calling Communism a quasi-religion. Although it may not be a religion in the true sense, since it fulfils the functions of a religion it cannot be ignored in any survey of them.

Why I am a Communist

I assume that my task in these few lines is not to say what I believe as a Communist, but why I believe it.

Primarily, I am a Communist because for me it is the only creed which provides a complete and final answer to the problem of both social and racial injustice. As a young man in the 1930's I found my faith in democracy utterly shattered by the failure of Britain and France to stand up to Fascism. In a sense my conversion to Communism was through despair. I despaired of Western values. I was more than contemptuous of democratic liberties, for they are liberties of the bourgeois. The idea of progress under expanding capitalism to the abolition of power politics and injustice is obviously false. 'Boom' and 'slump' are inherent in capitalism and social injustice and power politics are a natural concomitant.

In my work for the Communist Party I find fulfilment as a person. It often demands sacrifices but this is amply compensated for by the pleasure of working with my comrades for the liberation and development of the under-privileged. To be a Communist is to affirm life. It affirms respect for others; it affirms the true joy of working with others towards a common goal; it affirms the importance of our existence here and now.

My initial decision to be a Communist was not an entirely rational one; it was, I suppose, an act of faith. This is not to say that I think that reason cannot defend what I believe—just the opposite. It seems to me that Marx was a very great philosopher who stands at the pinnacle of Western thought. But in the final analysis I would admit that my first steps towards Communism were a 'gut reaction'. In retrospect, I can best describe why I became a Communist by means of a pun—in the face of revolting injustice, one has to revolt.

Anon.

APPENDIX

The Main Tenets of Buddhism, Hinduism and
 Christianity

Sanskrit and Pali Terms Used

Relationships Between the Religions

THE MAIN TENETS OF BUDDHISM, HINDUISM AND CHRISTIANITY

	THERAVADA BUDDHISM	MAHAYANA BUDDHISM	HINDUISM	CHRISTIANITY
VIEW OF MAN	Each man is an individual who is alone in the world. 'Salvation by Works'.*	An individual is nothing without others. 'Salvation by Grace.'*	Man is individual atman (soul) but atman is Brahman (Ultimate Reality). 'Salvation by Works'. (+Karma-less existence = Moksha).	Man is nothing by himself. Stress on 'involvement with others'. 'Salvation by Grace.'
KEY VIRTUE	Knowledge or wisdom.	Compassion.	Knowledge.	Love.
UNIVERSALITY OF RELIGION	A religion primarily for monks.	A religion for all.	A religion for all but some have special privileges.	A religion for all.
IDEAL	Arhat.	Bodhisattva	The Guru.	The Christ.
VIEW OF FOUNDER	The Buddha a man.	The Buddha a supra-mundane being.	No founder.	Jesus is God.

*For an elucidation of these ideas see James 2:14-26.

SANSKRIT AND PALI TERMS USED

Where only one term is given the corresponding expression in the other language is either
n-existent or unimportant. Pronounce: 'u' as in 'put': 'ya' etc. as in 'Yahweh': 'hi' as in 'hit'.

nskrit:	Pali:	Pronunciation:	Meaning:
IIMSA	AHIMSA	ahin(g)saa	non-injury, non-violence
IATMAN	ANATTA	anaatman; unuttaa	without ATMAN
RHAT	ARAHAT	arhut; arahut	'Worthy one': one who has attained NIRVANA
RYA	ARIYA	arya; ariya	noble, Aryan
MAN	ATTA	aatmun; utta	self, Self; breath, spirit
IAKTI		b'hucty	devotion, loving-adoration
IIKSU	BHIKKU	b'hikshoo; b'hikkoo	beggar, monk
)DHI	BODHI	bode-hi	enlightenment
)DHI-SATTVA	BODHI-SATTA	bodehi-suttva; sutta	Buddha-to-be
RAHMA	BRAHMA	brahmaa	Brahma, the Creator (personal: masc. word)
RAHMAN	BRAHMA	brahmun; brahma	'sacred power', Brahman
JDDHA	BUDDHA	bood'ha	Enlightened One
IARMA	DHARMA	d'harma; d'humma	Law, truth, doctrine
JHKHA	DUKKHA	dooh'kha	suffering, painfulness
JNA		goona	attribute, quality
JRU		guroo	teacher
VARA		eeshvara	'Lord': Brahman in its personal aspect
ARMA	KAMMA	karma; kumma	'Deed': law determining rebirth and status in rebirth
ANTRA		muntra	sacred saying, incantation
AYA		maayaa	illusion
OKSHA		moke-sha	release, liberation
RVANA	NIBBANA	nirvaana; nibbaana	'Waning away', extinction
JRUSHA	PURISA	pooroosha; poorisa	person, soul, man
AMSARA	SAMSARA	sung-saara	round (of rebirth), cycle of existence
	SANGHA	sung'ha	community, order (of monks)
AT	SAT	sut	'Being', 'truth'
ANDHA	KHANDHA	skund'ha; k'hund'ha	'Bulk', substance; 5 constituents of a living being: rupa: the body; vedana: sensation; sanna: ideas; sankhara: mental processes; vinnana: consciousness
PAS		tuppus	'Heat', austere practice, austerity
SHNA	TANHA	turshnaa; tun-haa	craving, thirst, hot desire
DA	VEDA	vay-da	'Knowledge', sacred scripture
DANTA		vaydaanta	exposition of Vedic teaching
)GA	YOGA	yaw-ga	'Yoking' — spiritual and physical training. System of orthodox teaching

n many books on Hinduism and Buddhism the Sanskrit and Pali terms are used inter-
angeably. The above list should therefore prove useful as an aid to further reading.

RELATIONSHIPS BETWEEN THE RELIGIONS

RELIGION	IDEA OF DIVINE	FOUNDER	COUNTRY OF ORIGIN	SCRIPTURES
HINDUISM	MONOTHEISTIC POLYTHEISTIC	NONE	INDIA	VEDAS; UPANISHADS; EPICS
BUDDHISM	NIRVANA	GOTAMA BUDDHA	INDIA	IMPORTANT ONES: MAJJHIMA NIKAYA; ASTASAHASRIKA PRAJNAPARAMITA; SADDHARMA PUNDARIKA SUTRA
JUDAISM	MONOTHEISTIC	MOSES	PALESTINE	OLD TESTAMENT; TALMUD
CHRISTIANITY	MONOTHEISTIC	JESUS	PALESTINE	THE BIBLE
ISLAM	MONOTHEISTIC	MUHAMMAD	ARABIA	THE QUR'AN
CONFUCIANISM	QUASI-AGNOSTIC	KUNG FU-TSE	CHINA	ANALECTS OF CONFUCIUS
ZOROASTRIANISM	MONOTHEISTIC DUALISTIC	ZOROASTER	PERSIA	AVESTA
SHINTO	THEOGONIC	NONE	JAPAN	KOJIKI; NIGHONGI
TAOISM	NOT DEFINED	LAO TZU	CHINA	TAO TE CHING
COMMUNISM	ATHEISTIC	MARX	ENGLAND	COMMUNIST MANIFESTO; DAS KAPITAL; THOUGHTS OF CHAIRMAN MAO;

Monotheism = belief in one god.
Polytheism = belief in many gods.
Atheism = disbelief in the existence of God.
Agnosticism = belief that knowledge of the existence of any-
thing beyond material phenomena is not

Dualism = belief in two equally balanced opposing
forces (Good v. Evil).
Theogonism = mythological belief in the genealogy or birth
of the deities.

BIBLIOGRAPHY

General

ADAMS, C. J. (ed.) *A Reader's Guide to Religion* (Collier-Macmillan, 1965)
BOUQUET, A. C. *Christian Faith and Non-Christian Religions* (Nisbet, 1958)
BOUQUET, A. C. *Comparative Religion* (Pelican, 1958)
BOUQUET, A. C. *Sacred Books of the World* (Penguin, 1967)
BRANDON, S. G. F. (ed.) *A Dictionary of Comparative Religion* (Weidenfeld & Nicolson, 1970).
DENNEY, A. *World Faiths and Modern Problems* (Hamish Hamilton, 1969)
ELIADE, M. *From Primitives to Zen* (Collins, 1967)
ELIADE, M. *The Quest: History and Meaning in Religion* (Chicago Univ. Press, 1969)
FINEGAN, J. *The Archaeology of World Religions* (Princeton Univ. Press & O.U.P., 1966)
HILLIARD, F. H. *How Men Worship* (Routledge, 1965)
HINNELLS, J. R. (ed.) *Comparative Religion in Education* (Oriel Press, 1970)
JAMES, E. O. *History of Religions* (Hodder, 1965)
LING, T. O. *A History of Religion East and West* (Macmillan, 1969)
NOSS, J. B. *Man's Religions* (Collier-Macmillan, 1969)
OTTO, R. *The Idea of the Holy*, trans. by J. W. Harvey (O.U.P., 1968)
PARRINDER, E. G. *Comparative Religion* (Allen & Unwin, 1962)
PARRINDER, E. G. *Worship in the World's Religions* (Faber, 1961)
PARRINDER, E. G. *Upanishads, Gita and Bible* (Faber, 1962)
PARRINDER, E. G. *The World's Living Religions* (Pan, 1969)
POTTER, C. F. *Great Religious Leaders* (Simon & Schuster, 1958)
SMART, N. *The Religious Experience of Mankind* (Scribners, 1969)
SMART, N. *Reasons and Faiths* (Routledge, 1958)
SMART, N. *World Religions: a Dialogue* (Penguin, 1966)
WACH, J. *The Comparative Study of Religions* (Columbia Univ. Press, 1961)
WACH, J. *Types of Religious Experience: Christian and non-Christian* (Routledge, 1951)
ZAEHNER, R. C. (ed.) *A Concise Encylopaedia of Living Faiths* (Hutchinson, 1964)

Rudimentary Religion

DURKHEIM, E. *Elementary Forms of the Religious Life: A Study in Religious Sociology*, trans. by J. W. Swain (Allen & Unwin, 1957)
ELIADE, M. *Shamanism* (Routledge, 1964)
ELKIN, A. P. *The Australian Aborigines* (Angus & Robertson, 1964)
FORDE, D. (ed.) *African Worlds* (O.U.P., 1963)
JAMES, E. O. *Prehistoric Religion* (Thames & Hudson, 1957)
KENYATTA, J. *Facing Mt. Kenya* (Secker & Warburg, 1969)
LEVI-STRAUSS, C. *Totemism* (Penguin, 1969)
MEAD, M. *Growing up in New Guinea* (Penguin)

MEAD, M. and CALAS, N. (eds.) *Primitive Heritage* (Gollancz, 1954)
PARRINDER, E. G. *Religion in Africa* (Pall Mall Press, 1970)
PARRINDER, E. G. *African Mythology* (Hamlyn, 1968)
PARRINDER, E. G. *Witchcraft: European and African* (Faber, 1968)
PARRINDER, E. G. *African Traditional Religion* (S.P.C.K., 1962)
PRITCHARD, E. E. EVANS- *Nuer Religion* (O.U.P., 1956)
PRITCHARD, E. E. EVANS- *Theories of Primitive Religion* (O.U.P., 1967)
SMITH, E. W. (ed.) *African Ideas of God* (Edinburgh House Press, 1960) Revised by E. G. Parrinder
WISSLER, C. *Indians of the United States* (Bailey, 1956)

Judaism

BAECK, L. *The Essence of Judaism* (Bailey, 1948)
BLAU, J. L. *Modern Varieties of Judaism* (Columbia Univ. Press, 1966)
BRIGHT, J. *A History of Israel* (S.C.M.P., 1960)
CASPER, B. M. *The Introduction to Jewish Bible Commentary*, World Jewish Congress (Yoseloff, 1960)
COHEN, A. *Everyman's Talmud* (Dent, 1949)
CRONBACH, A. *Reform Movements in Judaism* (Twayne, 1963)
EICHRODT, W. *Theology of the Old Testament*, 2 vols. (S.C.M.P., 1961, 1967)
EPSTEIN, I. *The Faith of Judaism* (Soncino, 1954)
EPSTEIN, I. *Judaism* (Penguin, 1968)
FISHMAN, I. *Introduction to Judaism* (Vallentine Mitchell, 1964)
FREEDMAN, M. (ed.) *A Minority in Britain* (Vallentine Mitchell, 1955)
GASTER, T. H. *Festivals of the Jewish Year* (Apollo, 1961)
HERTZ, J. H. (ed.) *The Authorized Daily Prayer Book* (Shapiro Vallentine, 1949)
JACOBS, L. *Principles of the Jewish Faith* (Vallentine Mitchell, 1964)
MUNK, E. *The World of Prayer*, 2 vols. (Feldheim, U.S.A.)
NOTH, M. *The History of Israel*, trans. by P. R. Ackroyd (Black, 1960)
ROTH, C. *A Short History of the Jewish People* (East & West Library, 1970)
SACHER, H. *Israel: The Establishment of a State* (Weidenfeld & Nicolson, 1952)
SCHONFIELD, H. *Popular Dictionary of Judaism* (Arco, 1962)
SILVER, A. H. *Where Judaism Differed* (Collier-Macmillan, 1956)
SIMON, M. *Jewish Religious Conflicts* (Hutchinson, 1950)
WERBLOWSKY & WIGADER *Encyclopaedia of the Jewish Religion* (Phoenix, 1967)

Christianity

BRANDON, S. G. F. *The Fall of Jerusalem and the Christian Church* (S.P.C.K., 1957)
BULLOUGH, S. *Roman Catholicism* (Penguin, 1963)
BULTMANN, R. *Primitive Christianity*, trans. by R. H. Fuller (Fontana, 1960)
CORBISHLEY, T. *Roman Catholicism* (Hutchinson, 1950)

CROSS, F. L. (ed.)   *Oxford Dictionary of the Christian Church* (O.U.P., 1957)
DIX, G.   *The Shape of the Liturgy* (Black, 1963)
DODD, C. H.   *The Apostolic Preaching and its Developments* (Hodder, 1936)
JAMES, E. O.   *A History of Christianity in England* (Hutchinson, 1949)
KELLY, J. N. D.   *Early Christian Doctrines* (Black, 1958)
MANSON, T. W.   *The Sayings of Jesus* (S.C.M.P., 1964)
MANSON, T. W.   *The Teaching of Jesus* (Cambridge, 1935)
MICKLEM, N. (ed.)   *Christian Worship* (O.U.P., 1954)
NOCK, A. D.   *St. Paul* (O.U.P., 1946)
SWEET, W. W.   *The Story of Religion in America* (Harper & Row, 1950)
UNDERHILL, E.   *Worship* (Nisbet, 1936)
WAND, J. W. C.   *A History of the Modern Church* (Methuen, 1952)
ZERNOV, N.   *Eastern Christendom* (Weidenfeld & Nicolson, 1961)

Islam

ARBERRY, A. J.   *Aspects of Islamic Civilisation* (Allen & Unwin, 1964)
ARBERRY, A. J.   *The Koran Interpreted* (Allen & Unwin, 1955)
ARBERRY, A. J.   *Sufism* (Allen & Unwin, 1950)
ARNOLD, T. W.   *The Teaching of Islam* (Luzac, 1956)
'AZZAM 'ABD-AL-RAHMAN'   *The Eternal Message of Muhammad* (Mentor, 1965)
CALVERLEY, E. E.   *Worship in Islam* (Luzac, 1957)
CRAGG, K.   *The Call of the Minaret* (O.U.P., 1956)
CRAGG, K.   *The House of Islam* (Prentice Hall, 1969)
CRAGG, K.   *Sandals at the Mosque* (S.C.M.P., 1959)
CRAGG, K.   *Counsels in Contemporary Islam* (Edinburgh Univ. Press, 1965)
GIBB, H. A. R.   *Mohammedanism* (O.U.P., 1953)
GRUBE, E. J.   *The World of Islam* (Hamlyn, 1967)
GRUNEBAUM, G. E. VON   *Muhammadan Festivals* (New York, 1951)
GUILLAUME, A.   *Islam* (Penguin, 1969)
HOTTINGER, A.   *The Arabs* (Thames & Hudson, 1963)
IKRAM, S. M.   *Muslim Civilization in India* (Columbia Univ. Press, 1964)
JEFFERY, A.   *The Qur'an as Scripture* (New York, 1952)
KATSH, A. I.   *Judaism and the Koran* (Barnes, 1962)
LEVY, R.   *The Social Structure of Islam* (Cambridge, 1957)
PADWICK, G. E.   *Muslim Devotions* (S.P.C.K., 1961)
PARRINDER, E. G.   *Jesus in the Qur'an* (Faber, 1965)
QURESHI, I. H.   *The Muslim Community of the Indo-Pakistan Sub Continent,*
    610-1947 (The Hague, 1962)
RAHMAN, F.   *Islam* (Weidenfeld & Nicolson, 1967)
SMITH, W. G.   *Islam in Modern History* (Princeton Univ. Press, 1957)
SWEETMAN, J. W.   *Islam and Christian Theology* (Lutterworth, 1947)
TRITTON, A. S.   *Muslim Theology* (Luzac, 1947)
TRITTON, A. S.   *Islam* (Hutchinson, 1951)
WATT, W. M.   *Free Will and Predestination in Early Islam* (Luzac, 1948)
WATT, W. M.   *What is Islam?* (Longmans, 1968)
WATT, W. M.   *Muhammad, Prophet and Statesman* (O.U.P., 1961)
WENSINCK, A. J.   *The Muslim Creed* (Cass, 1965)

Hinduism

APPASAMY, A. J. *Temple Bells* (S.C.M.P., 1930)
ASHE, G. *Gandhi; a Study in Revolution* (Heinemann, 1968)
BASHAM, A. L. *The Wonder that was India* (Sidgwick & Jackson, 1954)
BHANDARKAR, R. G. *Vaishnavism, Shaivism, and Minor Religious Sects* (Strassburg, 1913)
BHATTACHARYA, H. (ed.) *The Cultural Heritage of India*, Vol. IV: *The Religions*, Calcutta: The Ramakrishna Mission (Institute of Culture, Luzac, 1956)
BHAVE, V. *Talks on the Gita* (Allen & Unwin, 1960)
BOUQUET, A. C. *Hinduism* (Hutchinson, 1966)
DUTT, R. C. *The Ramayana and the Mahabharata* (Dent, 1969)
ELIADE, M. *Yoga: Immortality and Freedom* (Routledge, 1958)
IONS, V. *Indian Mythology* (Hamlyn, 1967)
KONOW, S. and TUXEN, P. *Religions of India* (Bailey, 1949)
MACNICOL, N. (ed.) *Hindu Scriptures* (Dent, 1938)
MORGAN, K. W. (ed.) *The Religion of the Hindus* (New York: Ronald Press, 1953)
O'MALLEY, L. S. S. *Popular Hinduism* (Cambridge, 1935)
PANIKKAR, K. M. *Hindu Society at Crossroads* (Asia Pub. House, 1961)
PARRINDER, E. G. *The Significance of the Bhagavad Gita for Christian Theology* (Dr Williams Trust, 1968)
PAYNE, E. A. *The Saktas* (O.U.P., 1933)
PIGGOTT, S. *Prehistoric India to 1000 B.C.* (Cassell, 1962)
PUSALKER, A. D. *Studies in Epics and Puranas of India* (Probsthain, 1955)
RADHAKRISHNAN, S. *The Principal Upanishads* (Allen & Unwin, 1953)
SARMA, D. S. *Studies in the Renaissance of Hinduism in the Nineteenth and Twentieth Centuries* (Benares Hindu University, 1944)
SASTRI, K. A. N. (ed.) *Development of Religion in South India* (Luzac, 1963)
SEN, K. M. *Hinduism* (Penguin, 1961)
SINGER, M. (ed.) *Krishna: Myths, Rites and Attitudes* (Chicago Univ. Press, 1969)
SLATER, G. *The Dravidian Element in Indian Culture* (Benn, 1924)
SMART, N. *The Yogi and the Devotee* (Allen & Unwin, 1968)
THOMAS, P. *Hindu Religion, Customs and Manners* (Luzac, 1956)
WALKER, B. *Hindu World: An Encyclopaedic Survey of Hinduism* (Allen & Unwin, 1968)
WHEELER, M. *Civilizations of the Indus Valley and Beyond* (Thames & Hudson, 1966)
WOOD, E. *Yoga* (Penguin, 1970)
ZAEHNER, R. C. (ed.) *The Bhagavad Gita* (O.U.P., 1969)
ZAEHNER, R. C. *Hinduism* (O.U.P., 1962)
ZAEHNER, R. C. (ed.) *Hindu Scriptures* (Dent, 1966)

Buddhism

ASVAGHOSHA *The Awakening of Faith*, trans. by T. Richard (Skilton, 1961)
BERVAL, R. DE (ed.) *Présence du Bouddhisme* (Saigon, 1959)

BLOFELD, J.   *The Jewel in the Lotus* (Sidgwick & Jackson, 1948)
CH'EN, K. K. S.   *Buddhism in China* (Princeton Univ. Press, 1964)
CONZE, E.   *Buddhism: its Essence and Development* (Faber, 1963)
CONZE, E.   *Buddhist Thought in India* (Allen & Unwin, 1962)
CONZE, E.   *Buddhist Scriptures* (Penguin, 1959)
COOMARASWAMY, A. K.   *Buddha and the Gospel of Buddhism* (Harper & Row, 1966)
DAVIDS, T. W. R.   *Buddhist India* (Luzac, 1959)
DUMOULIN, H.   *A History of Zen Buddhism* (Faber, 1963)
DUTT, S.   *The Buddha and the Five After-Centuries* (Luzac, 1957)
DUTT, S.   *Buddhist Monks and Monasteries of India* (Allen & Unwin, 1963)
ELIOT, C.   *Japanese Buddhism* (Routledge, 1935)
GARD, R. A.   *Buddhism* (Braziller, 1961)
GLASSENAP, H. VON   *Buddhism—A Non-Theistic Religion* (Allen & Unwin, 1970)
HUMPHREYS, C.   *A Popular Dictionary of Buddhism* (Arco, 1962)
HUMPHREYS, C.   *Buddhism* (Penguin, 1962)
HUMPHREYS, C.   *The Buddhist Way of Life* (Allen & Unwin, 1969)
HUMPHREYS, C.   *Concentration and Meditation* (V. Stuart, 1968)
JAYASURIYA, W. F.   *The Psychology and Philosophy of Buddhism* (Luzac, 1963)
LING, T. O.   *Buddha, Marx and God* (Macmillan, 1966)
LING, T. O.   *Buddhism and the Mythology of Evil* (Allen & Unwin, 1962)
MURTI, T. R. V.   *The Central Philosophy of Buddhism* (Allen & Unwin, 1961)
PE MAUNG TIN   *Buddhist Devotion and Meditation* (S.P.C.K., 1964)
PIYADASSI, THERA   *The Buddha's Ancient Path* (Rider, 1964)
SANGHARAKSHITA, B.   *The Three Jewels: An Introduction to Buddhism* (Rider, 1968)
SUZUKI, B. L.   *Mahayana Buddhism* (Allen & Unwin, 1959)
SUZUKI, D. T.   *The Essence of Buddhism* (Luzac, 1957)
SUZUKI, D. T.   *Studies in Zen* (Rider, 1955)
SUZUKI, D. T.   *Zen and Japanese Culture* (Routledge, 1959)
WELCH, H.   *The Practice of Chinese Buddhism* (O.U.P., 1967)
WELLS, K. E.   *Thai Buddhism* (Bangkok, 1960)
WENTZ, E. EVANS-   *Tibetan Yoga and Secret Doctrines* (O.U.P., 1958)
WRIGHT, A. F.   *Buddhism in Chinese History* (Stanford Univ. Press & O.U.P., 1959)

Zoroastrianism (Parsism)

GERSHEVITCH, I.   *The Avestan Hymn to Mithra* (Cambridge, 1959)
GUILLEMIN, J. D-.   *The Hymns of Zarathustra* (Murray, 1952)
GUILLEMIN, J. D-.   *Symbols and Values in Zoroastrianism* (Harper & Row, 1966)
HENNING, W. B.   *Zoroaster: Politician or Witchdoctor?* (O.U.P., 1951)
HINNELLS, J. R.   *Persian Mythology* (Hamlyn, 1971)
MASANI, R.   *The Religion of the Good Life* (Allen & Unwin, 1938)
MODI, J. J.   *The Religious Ceremonies and Customs of the Parsees* (Luzac, 1937)
ZAEHNER, R. C.   *The Dawn and Twilight of Zoroastrianism* (Weidenfeld & Nicolson, 1961)

Sikhism

ARCHER, J. C.   *The Sikhs* (Princeton Univ. Press, 1946)
ARORA, G. S.   *The New Frontiersmen* (Bombay, 1967)
GANDA SINGH   *A Brief Account of the Sikh People* (G. S. Press, Madras, 1959)
GURMIT SINGH   *A Critique of Sikhism* (Faqir Singh, Amritsar, 1967)
HARBANS SINGH   *The Heritage of the Sikhs* (Asia Publishing House, 1964)
JOGENDRA SINGH   *Sikh Ceremonies* (Bombay, 1941)
KEAY, F. E.   *Kabir and his Followers* (Calcutta, 1931)
KHUSHWANT SINGH   *A History of the Sikhs*, 2 vols. (O.U.P., 1967)
KHUSHWANT SINGH   *The Sikhs Today* (Orient Longmans, 1959)
KHUSHWANT SINGH   *The Sikhs* (Allen & Unwin, 1953)
MACAULIFFE, H.   *The Sikh Religion* (Luzac, 1958)
MCLEOD, W. H.   *Guru Nanak and the Sikh Religion* (O.U.P., 1968)
MCLEOD, W. H.   *The Sikhs of the Punjab* (Auckland; Graphic Educational Publications, 1968)
MANSUKHANI, G.   *Introduction to Sikhism* (India Book House, 1968)
MANSUKHANI, G   *The Quintessence of Sikhism* (Amritsar: Shiromani Gurdwara Parbandhak Committee, 1965)
TEJA SINGH   *Sikhism: Its Ideals and Institutions* (Orient Longmans, 1968)
TRILOCHAM SINGH et al.   *Selections from the Sacred Writings of the Sikhs* (Allen & Unwin for UNESCO, 1960)

Chinese and Japanese Religion

ANESAKI, M.   *History of Japanese Religion* (Routledge, 1963)
ANESAKI, M.   *Religious Life of the Japanese People* (Luzac, 1938)
ASTON, W. G.   *Nihongi*, trans. 2nd ed. (Allen & Unwin, 1956)
ASTON, W. G.   *Shinto, the Way of the Gods* (Longman, 1905)
BLACKER, C.   'New Religious Cults of Japan', in *Hibbert Journal*, lx, July, 1962.
CHAN, W. T.   *Religious Trends in Modern China* (New York, 1953)
CHIANG YEE   *A Chinese Childhood* (Methuen, 1946)
CREEL, H. G.   *Chinese Thought from Confucius to Mao Tse-Tung* (Eyre & Spottiswoode, 1954)
CREEMERS, W. H. M.   *Shrine Shinto after World War II* (E. J. Brill, 1968)
DE BARY, W. T. et al.   *Sources of Chinese Tradition* (Columbia Univ. Press, 1964)
EARHART, H. B.   *Japanese Religion: Unity and Diversity* (Prentice Hall, 1968)
FITZGERALD, C. P.   *The Chinese View of their Place in the World* (O.U.P., 1969)
HERBERT, J.   *Shinto: The Fountainhead of Japan* (Allen & Unwin, 1967)
HOLTON, D. C.   *Modern Japan and Shinto Nationalism* (Paragon, 1963)
HOLTON, D. C.   *The National Faith of Japan* (Paragon, 1965)
HORI, I.   *Folk Religion in Japan* (Chicago Univ. Press, 1968)
HSU, F. L. K.   *Under the Ancestors' Shadow* (Routledge, 1949)
KITAGAWA, J. M.   *Religion in Japanese History* (Columbia Univ. Press, 1966)
LIU WU-CHI   *A Short History of Confucian Philosophy* (Delta Books, 1964)
MASPERO, H.   *Le Taoïsme* (Paris, 1950)
MASPERO, H.   *Les Religions Chinoises* (Paris, 1950)

NORBECK, E.   *Changing Japan* (Holt, Rinehart & Winston, 1965)
OFFNER, C. B. and VAN STRAELEN, H.   *Modern Japanese Religions* (E. J. Brill, 1963)
ONO, S.   *Shinto, The Kami Way*, (Bridgeway Press, 1962)
RENOU, L.   *Religion in a Chinese Garment* (London, 1951)
RINGGENDORF, J. (ed.)   *Studies in Japanese Culture* (Tokyo, 1963)
SHRYOCK, J. K.   *The Origin and Development of the State Cult of Confucius* (Paragon, 1966)
SMITH, D. H.   *Chinese Religions* (Weidenfeld & Nicolson, 1968)
THOMPSON, L. G.   *Chinese Religion: An Introduction* (Prentice Hall, 1969)
TSUNODA, RYUSAKA et al.   *Sources of Japanese Tradition* (Columbia Univ. Press, 1964)
WALEY, A. D.   *The Way and its Power* (Allen & Unwin, 1934)
WALEY, A. D.   *Three Ways of Thought in Ancient China* (Allen & Unwin, 1939)
WEBER, M.   *The Religion of China* (Collier-Macmillan, 1968)
WHEELER, P.   *The Sacred Scriptures of the Japanese* (Allen & Unwin, 1953)
WILHELM, R.   *A Short History of Chinese Civilization* (Harrap, 1929)
YANG, C. K.   *Religion in Chinese Society* (California Univ. Press, 1967)

Communism

AVINERI, S.   *The Social and Political Thought of Karl Marx* (Cambridge, 1968)
DE GEORGE, R. T.   *The New Marxism* (Pegasus, 1968)
DEUTSCHER, I.   *Stalin: A Political Biography* (O.U.P., 1950)
FREUD, S.   *Totem and Taboo* (Routledge, 1950)
GARAUDY, R.   *Karl Marx and His Doctrines* (International Publishers, 1965)
HOOK, S.   *Marx and the Marxists* (Van Nostrand, 1955)
HOROWITZ, I. L.   *Radicalism and the Revolt against Reason* (Humanities Press, 1961)
KOESTLER, A.   *The Yogi and the Commissar* (Cape, 1945)
LENIN, V. I.   *Collected Works*, 42 vols. (Moscow: Foreign Languages Publishing House, 1960)
LENIN, V. I.   *The State* (Moscow: Foreign Languages Publishing House, 1954)
LENIN, V. I.   *The Teachings of Karl Marx* (International Publishers, 1964)
MANUEL, F. E.   *The Prophets of Paris* (Harper & Row, 1962)
MAO TSE-TUNG   *Selected Works*, 5 vols. (International Publishers, 1954)
MARCUSE, H.   *Eros and Civilization* (Allen Lane, 1969)
MARCUSE, H.   *One Dimensional Man* (Routledge, 1964)
MARCUSE, H.   *Reason and Revolution* (Routledge, 1968)
MARX, K.   *Capital, A Critique of Political Economy* (New York: The Modern Library, 1936)
MARX, K.   *The Economic and Philosophic Manuscripts of 1844* (International Publishers, 1964)
MARX, K. and ENGELS, F.   *The Communist Manifesto* (Russell & Russell, 1963)
STALIN, J.   *Dialectic and Historical Materialism* (International Publishers, 1940)
STALIN, J.   *The National Question and Leninism* (Moscow: Foreign Languages Publishing House, 1950)

INDEX